lonely planet

THE PACIFIC NORTHWEST

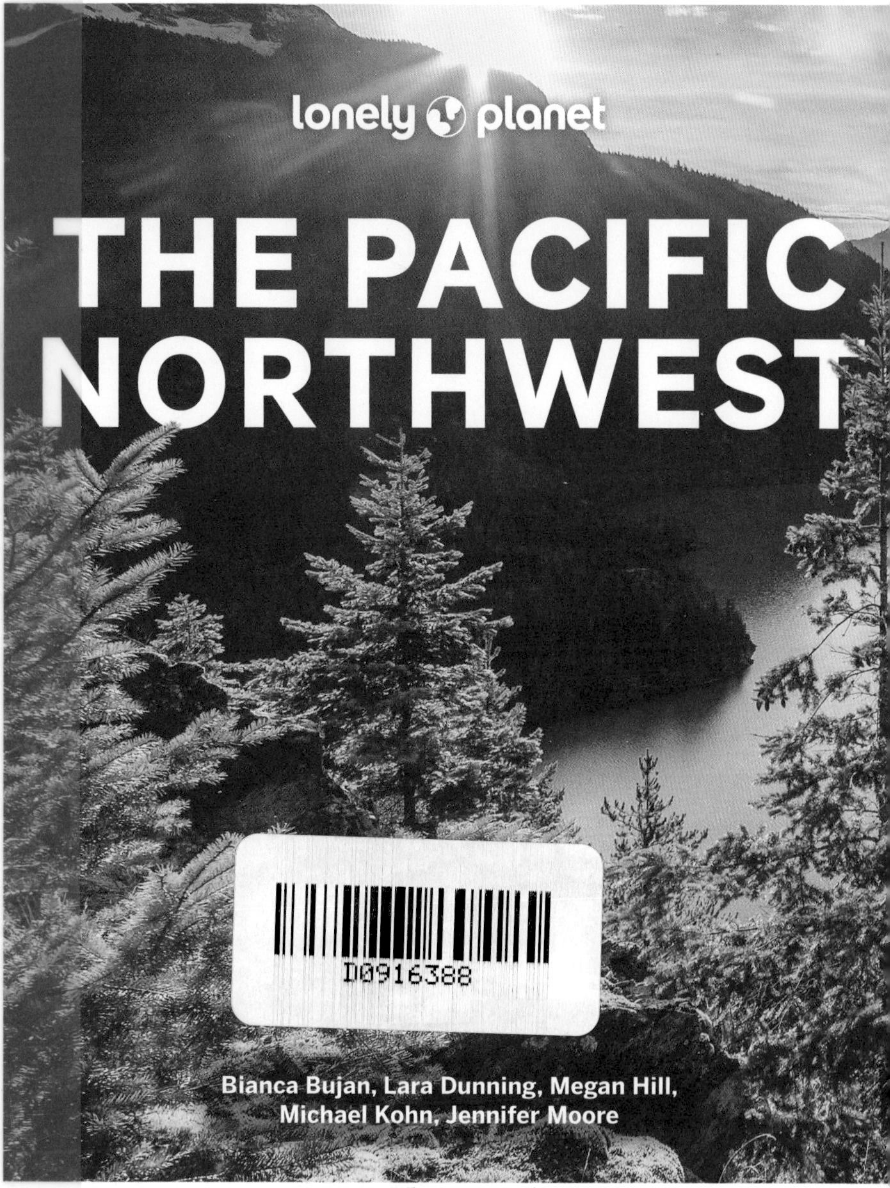

Bianca Bujan, Lara Dunning, Megan Hill,
Michael Kohn, Jennifer Moore

Meet our writers

Bianca Bujan

@bitsofbee @BiancaBujan

Born and raised in Vancouver, BC, Bianca has written for various high-profile publications and was featured in *Forbes* as a top Black travel writer to follow. Her insider tip for Vancouver travel is to join the Flights to Flights Ale & Air tour through Sechelt (p218) – 'it offers the perfect balance of sips and sights'.

Lara Dunning

@dreambigtravelsmall

Lara loves feasting on farm-to-table cuisine and sipping her way through Washington Wine Country (p114). Captivated by small towns, she dedicates her time off to exploring lesser-known destinations and always finds time for a scenic hike (p109).

Megan Hill

m.a._hill

Megan loves the urban-nature interface (p62) in Seattle, and the fact that it's possible to find hidden market gems (p48) in the morning, spend the afternoon on a sailboat or paddling a kayak (p60), then finish the day at a top-notch restaurant with cocktails and local, raw oysters at sunset (p66).

Michael Kohn

@michaelkohnsf

Michael lives in Bend, OR, where he works for the local daily paper, the *Bend Bulletin*. As well as family ski days at Mt Bachelor (p201) and hikes in the Deschutes National Forest, he loves beach visits, wildlife watching and camping along the coast near the Oregon Dunes (p180).

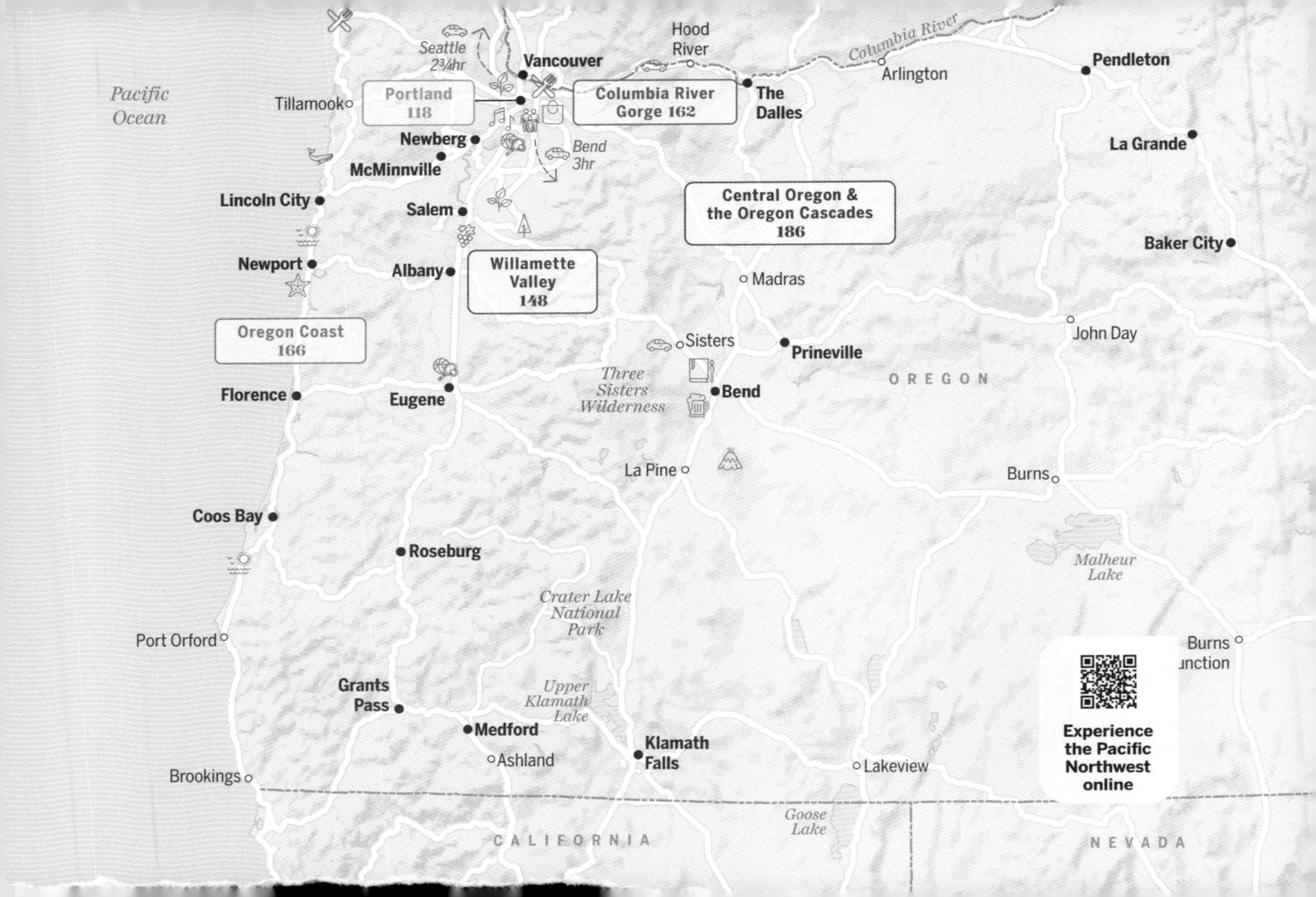
Pacific Ocean
Tillamook
Seattle 2¾hr
Vancouver
Portland 118
Newberg
McMinnville
Bend 3hr
Hood River
Columbia River
Columbia River Gorge 162
The Dalles
Arlington
Pendleton
La Grande
Baker City
Lincoln City
Salem
Central Oregon & the Oregon Cascades 186
Newport
Albany
Willamette Valley 148
Madras
Oregon Coast 166
Sisters
Prineville
John Day
OREGON
Three Sisters Wilderness
Florence
Eugene
Bend
La Pine
Burns
Coos Bay
Roseburg
Malheur Lake
Crater Lake National Park
Port Orford
Burns Junction
Grants Pass
Upper Klamath Lake
Medford
Klamath Falls
Ashland
Brookings
Lakeview
Experience the Pacific Northwest online
Goose Lake
CALIFORNIA
NEVADA

Discover the region's origins on an immersive, Indigenous-led tour. Savor freshly caught fish and creamy craft brews. Get up-close with black foxes, gray whales and bald eagles. Surf cold-water swells, ski powdery slopes and hike forest trails. Explore nature's playground on a family adventure. Navigate through a maze of meaningful metropolitan murals. Pick up a coast-inspired keepsake. Hit the road to explore historic lighthouses, volcanic peaks and wine regions. Then soak serenely in the woods.

This is the Pacific Northwest.

TURN THE PAGE AND START PLANNING YOUR NEXT BEST TRIP →

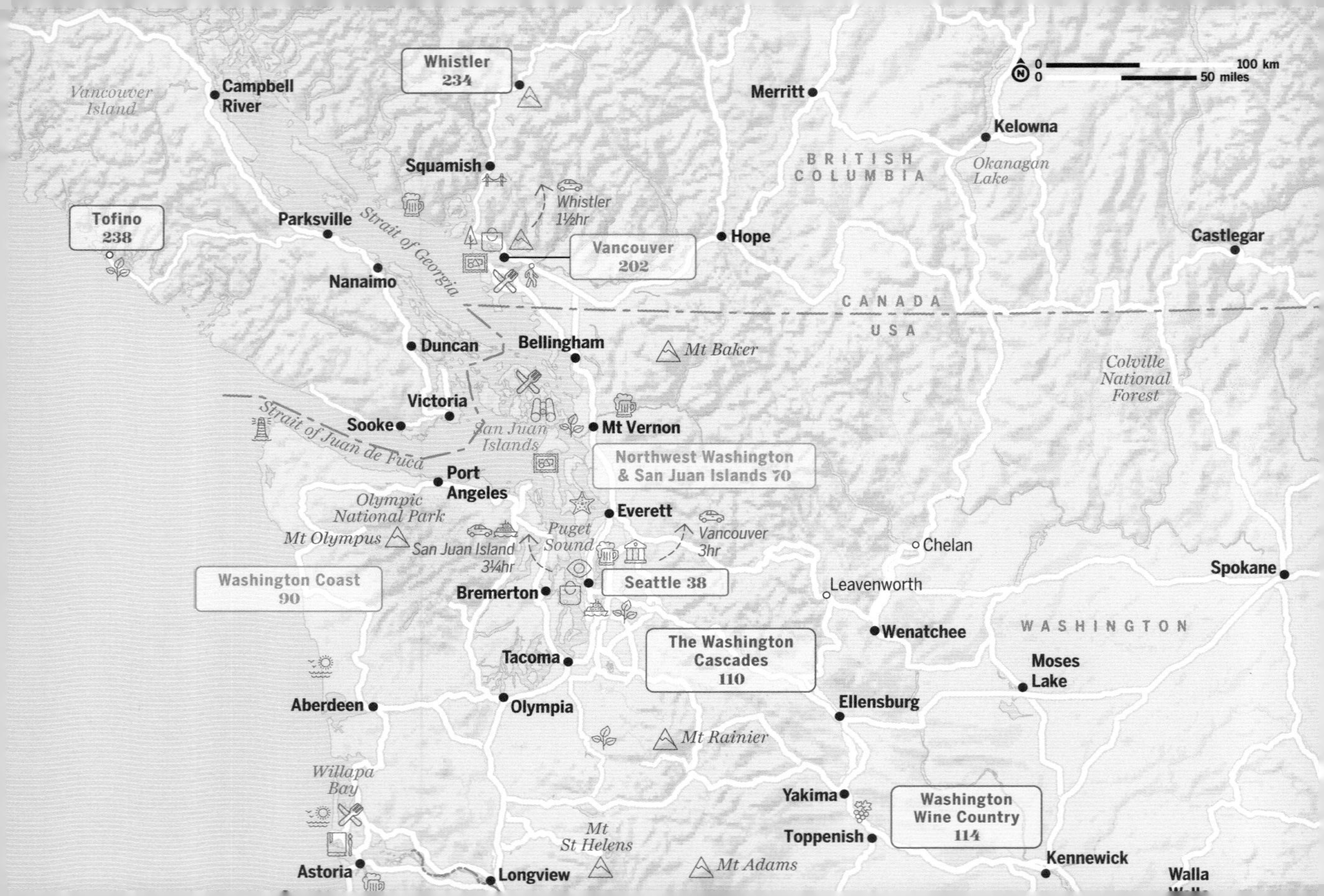

0
100 km
0
50 miles
Whistler
234
Tofino
238
Vancouver
202
Whistler
1½hr
Vancouver
3hr
San Juan Island
3¼hr
Northwest Washington
& San Juan Islands 70
Seattle 38
Washington Coast
90
The Washington
Cascades
110
Washington
Wine Country
114
Vancouver
Island
Campbell
River
Squamish
Parksville
Nanaimo
Strait of Georgia
Merritt
Kelowna
Okanagan
Lake
BRITISH
COLUMBIA
Hope
Castlegar
CANADA
USA
Duncan
Bellingham
Mt Baker
Colville
National
Forest
Victoria
Sooke
Strait of Juan de Fuca
San Juan
Islands
Mt Vernon
Port
Angeles
Olympic
National Park
Mt Olympus
Everett
Puget
Sound
Chelan
Spokane
Leavenworth
Bremerton
Wenatchee
WASHINGTON
Moses
Lake
Tacoma
Aberdeen
Olympia
Ellensburg
Mt Rainier
Willapa
Bay
Yakima
Toppenish
Mt
St Helens
Mt Adams
Astoria
Longview
Kennewick
Walla

Ecola State Park (p175), Oregon

Jennifer Moore

jenniferkaymo.com

Originally from Alaska, Jenni has been an Oregonian since 1993, residing in Portland for the last 10 years. On any given day she can be found enjoying live music (p128), feasting on brunch (p126), or retreating to nature areas like Kelley Point Park (p125) with her two dogs.

Contents

Science World (p230), Vancouver

COAST SALISH

Coast Salish indigenous peoples are connected linguistically, but comprise many distinct communities, each with its own separate dialect and tradition. Over a dozen Coast Salish languages are found throughout the region.

CULTURAL CONNECTIONS

For millennia, humans have inhabited the Pacific Northwest. The region is home to hundreds of diverse communities of indigenous peoples with unique and rich histories and deep-seated roots. Their continued contributions are honored and celebrated in distinct ways throughout the region, and through shared experiences, we can develop a deeper understanding of the cultural contributions – past and present – of the people who first called this land home.

Left Totem pole, Stanley Park (p228), Vancouver **Right** Petroglyph, Horsethief Lake State Park (p164) **Below** Traditional method of cooking salmon

→ HISTORIC SITES

From artwork and artifacts shared at regional museums, galleries and cultural centers, to guided tours through sacred lands and architectural sites, dive into the diverse history of each city.

▶ For a re-examination of American history, see p100

ALAN MAJCHROWICZ/GETTY IMAGES ©

IMMERSIVE EXPERIENCES

To best connect with regional culture, go on an Indigenous-led tour (p212). Through shared stories, songs and adventures, you can be fully immersed in the beauty of the culture and language.

RIGHT: DAVELOGAN/GETTY IMAGES ©
LEFT: STEVE STEDMAN/SHUTTERSTOCK ©

↑ INDIGENOUS CUISINE

In the Pacific Northwest, Indigenous communities are primarily hunter-gatherers, with cuisine comprised of salmon and other fish, berries, mushrooms, and meats such as deer, duck and rabbit (p213).

Best Indigenous Experiences

▶ **Discover the origins of Vancouver on an Indigenous-led Talking Totems tour** (p213)

▶ **See artifacts from the Indigenous Plateau at Museum at Warm Springs, Oregon** (p197)

▶ **Learn about Chinookan culture at Columbia Pacific Heritage Museum** (p106)

▶ **Spot petroglyphs and pictographs at Horsethief Lake State Park** (p164)

▶ **See the first tribal longhouse built in 150 years in Seattle** (p57)

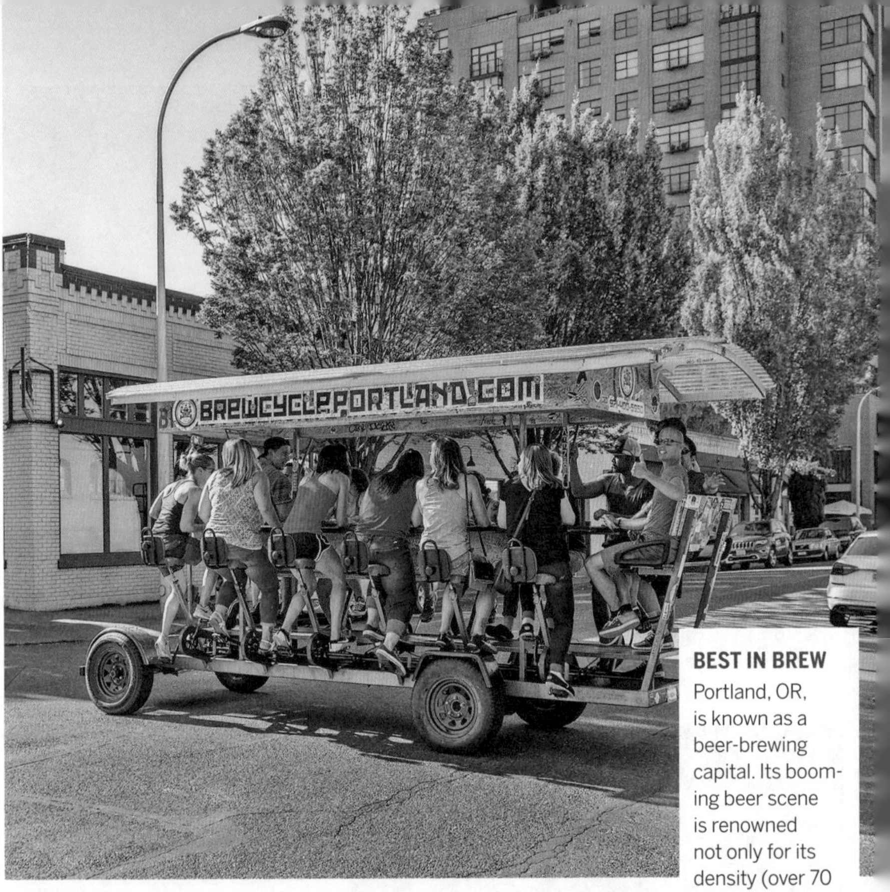
BREWCYCLEPORTLAND.COM

BEST IN BREW

Portland, OR, is known as a beer-brewing capital. Its booming beer scene is renowned not only for its density (over 70 breweries), but for its diversity. Tours (p131) are available by foot, bike or bus.

COASTAL PINTS **& PLATES**

From homegrown hops to freshly caught fish, the natural landscape of the Pacific Northwest lends itself to the freshest ingredients from land and sea. Salmon is king here, with five varieties that come fresh off the boat and are then seared, smoked or cured to perfection. Combined with international influences and local culinary and craft-brew artisans, the food-and-drink scene in the region is known around the world.

→ CRAFT BREWS

The Pacific Northwest is home to one of the most productive hop-growing regions in the world, resulting in an abundance of craft breweries sprouting up throughout.

▶ To embark on a famous Oregon ale trail, see p190

ROGUE

Left BrewCycle tour (p131), Portland
Right Craft beer bottles, Portland
Below Dungeness crabs in trap

SIMPLE SALMON

With easy fishing access to the ocean, lakes and rivers, salmon is one of the most prominent foods in the region (p44). Freshly caught chinook, coho, chum, pink and sockeye are best here.

↑ FORAGE & FEAST

Whether it's foraging through mossy forests (p102), clamming along the coast (p177), tossing crab traps into the ocean (p176), or plating fresh meals, guided tours can usher you through every step of the process.

Best Seafood Experiences

▶ **Indulge in mouthfuls of mollusks on a shellfish farm in the San Juan Islands** (p84)

▶ **Sample sophisticated sushi with a West Coast twist at Tojo's in Vancouver** (p231)

▶ **Slurp raw oysters harvested from Puget Sound at Taylor Shellfish Oyster Bar** (p66)

▶ **Stop at South Beach Fish Market near Newport for Oregon's best fish and chips** (p183)

▶ **Try the tastiest fish tacos at Tacofino in Tofino, BC** (p238)

WANDERING WHALES

The rugged Pacific Northwest coastline is a migratory route for thousands of whales, including orcas, humpbacks and gray whales. They can be spotted year-round, but prime viewing season for each species depends on its specific migratory route.

WILDLIFE **ENCOUNTERS**

Birds, bears and whales, oh my! The wild Pacific Northwest boasts a bounty of beautiful creatures that thrive in their natural habitats. From the sea life that swims in the open ocean to the mammals that meander through the majestic mountains and towering trees, the protected nature parks, peaks and shores provide food and shelter for a diverse range of wildlife that can be easily spotted from a safe distance.

Left Humpback whale **Right** Sea lion **Below** Wild elk

→ MARINE LIFE

From shellfish to sea lions, and porpoises to puffins, marine life is abundant. But among the ocean's many creatures, whales take the title of most popular.

BIRDS OF PREY

Raptors rule the sky here, where towering trees provide the perfect perches for birds of prey. Spot red-tailed hawks, bald eagles and falcons soaring overhead.

↑ MAJESTIC MAMMALS

Mountain ranges and rainforest canopies provide shelter and sustenance for the bears, elk, foxes and other land mammals that call the Pacific Northwest home.

▶ For more Pacific Northwest beasts, birds and...slugs, see p216

Best Wildlife-Viewing Experiences

▶ **Find razor clams in the Tillamook Head tide pools on the Oregon Coast** (p176)

▶ **Get up close with gigantic gray whales on the open ocean of Tofino** (p239)

▶ **Behold the beauty of black foxes on the San Juan Islands** (p79)

▶ **Spot birds along the 'Pacific Flyway' of the BC Bird Trail** (p222)

▶ **Sleuth for legendary Sasquatch on Mt Rainier** (p112)

0 100 km
0 50 miles
Campbell River
Powell River
Vancouver Island
Parksville
Tofino
Ucluelet
Port Renfrew
Strait of Juan de Fuca
Neah Bay
Pacific Ocean
Ocean Shores
Manzanita
Tillamook

North Chesterman Beach

All-season surfing

Yes, you can surf in Canada. Known as Canada's surf capital, the town of Tofino (on Vancouver Island) is home to 20 miles of beaches, offering exposed coast and cold-water surfing swells for surfers of all skill levels – just don't forget your wetsuit.

45min from downtown Vancouver ▶ p239

Ecola State Park

Seaside hiking

Weave through tree-lined rainforest trails and soak in sea views along the Ecola Point to Indian Beach stretch of Oregon Coast Trail, or try the more challenging Tillamook Head Trail, a 6-mile trek taken by the Lewis and Clark expedition in 1806.

10min from Cannon Beach ▶ p184

ALPINE & **AQUATIC ADVENTURES**

Stunning shorelines and massive mountain ranges mean the Pacific Northwest provides unparalleled natural surroundings and endless opportunities for outdoor adventure. And most amazingly, outdoor enthusiasts can enjoy it all – from puddle to peak – in close proximity. Here, it's possible to surf the swells, ski the slopes and meander along mountain trails, by bike or foot, all in one day.

Whistler
Squamish
BRITISH COLUMBIA
Strait of Georgia
Vancouver
Nanaimo
Tsawwassen
CANADA
USA
Mt Baker
Duncan
Bellingham
San Juan Islands
Victoria
Anacortes
Sooke
Mt Vernon
Puget Sound
Port Angeles
Port Townsend
Everett
Mt Olympus
Olympic National Park
Seattle
Bremerton
Wenatchee
Columbia River
Tacoma
WASHINGTON
Aberdeen
Olympia
Ellensburg
Naches
Yakima
Mt St Helens National Volcanic Monument
Astoria
Longview
Mt St Helens
Mt Adams
Columbia River
The Dalles
Vancouver
Portland
Mt Hood
OREGON
Newberg

Whistler

Epic skiing & snowboarding

As North America's largest ski resort and home to the 2010 Winter Olympics, Whistler is a paradise for slope-side endeavors. There's also plenty of snow fun to be had off the hills, from ice-cave tours to tobogganing.

90min from downtown Vancouver

▶ p234

Lake Union

Urban kayaking & paddleboarding

Skyline views combined with lake-side fun make this urban oasis an outdoor playground. The freshwater lake, found within Seattle's city limits, is perfect for boating and paddleboarding, and watercraft rentals make it easy to hit the water.

5min from downtown Seattle

▶ p63

Mount Rainier

Mountaineering thrills

The glacier peaks of this active volcano engage mountaineers looking for a vertical challenge. Access the mountain by one of four trailheads, and then choose from among the more than 20 climbing routes.

2hr from downtown Seattle ▶ p111

Multnomah Falls

Waterfall walks

A cruise along the Columbia River Hwy leads to a series of waterfalls, including Wahkeena Falls and the magnificent Multnomah Falls (a 5-mile trail connects the two). Bring a camera because you'll want to snap a photo or ten while taking in the views.

40min from Portland ▶ p163

DISKO
ENTER

FESTIVALS FOR KIDS

Vancouver International Children's Festival (childrensfestival.ca)

Children's Film Festival Seattle (childrensfilmfestivalseattle.org)

Children's Festival in Jacksonville, OR (storytellingguild.org)

FAMILY **FUN**

Made up of a matchless mix of alpine adventures, seaside stops and urban pursuits, the Pacific Northwest has something for everyone, making the region an ideal choice for multigenerational travel. From guided kayak tours to awesome playgrounds, massive museums and old-school amusement parks, there's always a programming option that caters to kids.

Left Oaks Amusement Park (p142), Portland **Right** Ziplining near Whistler **Below** Architect Frank Gehry's Museum of Pop Culture (p57), Seattle

→ OUTDOOR ADVENTURES

From ziplining (p222) across mountain peaks to cold-water surfing in the Pacific Ocean (p184), nature's playground is sure to satisfy thrill-seekers of all ages.

PARKS & PLAYGROUNDS

Wide-open green spaces, nature-inspired playgrounds, and water play by beaches and lakes – in the Pacific Northwest, there's always somewhere for the kids to play.

▶ Discover some of the region's largest urban parks in Seattle (p65), Portland (p125) and Vancouver (p228)

↑ MODERN MUSEUMS

Focused on fun for the whole family, the region is teeming with family-focused museums that provide hands-on activities and engaging educational experiences.

Best Family Experiences

▶ **Shop and play at Kids Market on Granville Island** (p209)

▶ **Find outdoor adventures for families on Fidalgo Island** (p81)

▶ **Ride a rollercoaster at Oaks Amusement Park in Portland** (p142)

▶ **Look for lighthouses on a drive along the Washington Coast** (p106)

▶ **Marvel at music's biggest icons at the Museum of Pop Culture in Seattle** (p57)

Sepia Players

↘ CONNECTING COMMUNITIES

The Vancouver Mural Festival's Black Strathcona Resurgence Project (BSRP; pictured) focuses on Black story-telling through the visual impact of public murals, and aims to re-claim visibility for the city's Black community.

URBAN **ART**

Giving new meaning to 'painting the town,' the urban centers around the Pacific Northwest shine with soaring structures, colorful crosswalks, monumental murals and boundary-pushing public art displays. The urban art found around the region showcases both local and international talent in a way that makes art accessible for all, with most displays free to view.

Best Urban Art Experiences

- **Snap photos of stunning murals at the Vancouver Mural Festival** (p226)
- **Stroll across the artfully customized crosswalks of Seattle** (p59)
- **Admire outdoor art at San Juan Island Sculpture Park** (p87)
- **Wander In wonder through Price Sculpture Forest on Whidby Island** (p87)

ARTIST: ANTHONY JOSEPH; IMAGE: LISA WONG/VANCOUVER MURAL FESTIVAL ©

↘ NATURE INSPIRED

Many markets and boutiques found throughout the Pacific Northwest feature locally made keepsakes created using nature-sourced materials – the perfect way to bring home a piece of the coast.

CITY SHOPS **& STOPS**

Whether you're embarking on an adventurous escape outdoors, or wandering the city streets of a new-to-you urban epicenter, you'll want to preserve the most memorable moments by taking something home to remind you of your travels. Bring home a piece of the Pacific Northwest by purchasing locally made goods.

Best Shopping Experiences

- **Make your way through the maze of Seattle's Pike Place Market** (p48)
- **Head to Eugene's Woodburn Outlets for shopping with no sales tax** (p145)
- **Watch artists and shop at studios on Vancouver's Granville Island** (p208)
- **Browse the stalls of Portland's Saturday Market for handmade gifts and goodies** (p138)

THOMAS BARWICK/GETTY IMAGES ©

↘ COAST CRUISING

A scenic six-hour road trip along Hwy 101 (pictured) will take you from Vancouver to Portland, a curvy coastal drive with tons of must-see stops along the way.

HIT THE **ROAD**

From the coast to the city to the Cascades, there's so much to see and do in the region, you won't want to stay in one spot. Thanks to well-paved roads, you can see it all with a day trip or road trip that promises unparalleled pursuits found further afield.

Best Road Trips

- ▶ **Look for lighthouses along the Washington Coast** (p106)
- ▶ **Surf, SUP, soak and steam along the coast of Tofino, BC** (p238)
- ▶ **Taste the terroir in Oregon's wine-centric Willamette Valley** (p154)
- ▶ **See volcanoes, waterfalls, hot springs and lakes on a drive along Sisters Circuit** (p194)

↘ FOREST-BATHING BENEFITS

The Japanese practice of *shinrin-yoku* (or 'forest bathing') is more than just a walk in the woods. It's said to reduce stress, lower your heart rate and increase happiness.

BOB POOL/SHUTTERSTOCK ©

WILDERNESS WELLNESS

Yoga may be a popular pastime, but wellness goes beyond the indoor spas and studios in this region. Whether it's a meditative meander through an old-growth forest such as Cascadia State Park (pictured) or a silent soak and steam at a Nordic-style spa set in the woods, wellness is done differently in the Pacific Northwest.

Best Wellness Experiences

- **Meander on a mindful forest-bathing journey with Cascadia Forest Therapy** (p113)
- **Bathe in the bubbling Belknap Hot Springs pools in Central Oregon** (p195)
- **Soak and steam in the mountains at Scandinave Spa in Whistler** (p235)

→ Summer Season

The Pacific Northwest's summer unofficially runs from late May to early September. Everyone takes advantage of the sunshine with boating, picnics, hikes, BBQs and alfresco dining.

Demand for just about everything – hotel rooms, restaurant reservations, tours and activities – skyrockets in summer. Book well in advance.

↘ Portland Rose Festival

Stop and smell the roses at this festival, a series of parades, concerts and other events in Oregon's biggest city.

▸ rosefestival.org

Summer tends to be almost offensively beautiful along the coast and in the mountains, but be prepared for high heat east of the mountains.

JUNE

Average daytime max: 71°F
Days of rainfall: 8

JULY

The Pacific Northwest in SUMMER

FRANCESCO VANINETTI PHOTO/GETTY IMAGES ©, CHAITRA KUKANUR/SHUTTERSTOCK ©, STEVE BURCH/ALAMY LIVE NEWS/ ALAMY STOCK PHOTO ©, LIJUAN GUO/SHUTTERSTOCK ©, MPH PHOTOS/ SHUTTERSTOCK ©, SVETA IMNADZE/SHUTTERSTOCK ©

→ Celebration of Light

Catch Vancouver's signature summer festival – a fireworks competition held over three nights. The city gathers on beaches and boats to watch.

▶ hondacelebrationoflight.com

↓ Capitol Hill Block Party

Score tickets to this three-day music and art festival in Seattle, where top artists perform on stages set right on city streets.

▶ capitolhillblockparty.com

← World Naked Bike Ride

Don't avert your eyes. This iconic Portland event draws up to 10,000 participants.

▶ worldnakedbikeride.org

AUGUST

Average daytime max: 77°F
Days of rainfall: 5

Average daytime max: 79°F
Days of rainfall: 5

Packing notes

Hat, sunscreen, water bottle and a light jacket for nighttime cool spells.

Time to break out the raincoat: the coast's sunshine fades to drizzly gray in September. The cold, cloudy rain will likely last until late spring. The desert, east of the mountains, is still reliably dry.

Vancouver
International
Film
Festival
Vancouver
International
Film
Festival

↙ Vancouver International Film Festival

One of the world's largest showcases of Canadian film, VIFF also screens films from over 70 countries.

▸ viff.org

← Final Fruits of the Season

Farmers markets wrap up their season in the fall, so September can be a great chance to sample the last of the year's plums, pluots and quince.

→ Hood River Fly-In

Hundreds of antique airplanes go on display in Hood River at this annual Oregon event. Good fun for kids and plane enthusiasts.

SEPTEMBER

Average daytime max: 72°F
Days of rainfall: 8

OCTOBER

The Pacific Northwest in AUTUMN

→ Seattle Fresh Hop Beer Festival

Sample the season's favorite beer from around the Northwest, alongside local food and music.

▶ freshhop.com

Late August kicks off wet-hop beer time. Breweries around the region show off their suds, and most hops come from Washington's Yakima Valley.

→ Turning of the Leaves

The region is ablaze with fall colors throughout October, especially west of the mountains.

Average daytime max: 61°F
Days of rainfall: 14

NOVEMBER

Average daytime max: 52°F
Days of rainfall: 17

Packing notes

Rain jacket required. It should be lightweight, readily stowed and easy to layer over other clothing.

↙ Ski Season

Ski resorts generally have good powder December through February. The best include Washington's Mt Baker, Oregon's Mt Hood and BC's Whistler.

Northwesterners hunker down in winter. Days are short and often dark, with the sun dampened by rainclouds. Ideal for indoor hobbies or snow sports.

The odd snowstorm can pay the cities a visit.

↘ Oregon Shakespeare Festival

Winter is a great time to experience the nearly year-round series of Shakespeare plays in Ashland.

▶ osfashland.org

WELCOME TO THE OREGON SHAKESPEARE FESTIVAL

DECEMBER

Average daytime max: 47°F
Days of rainfall: 19

JANUARY

The Pacific Northwest in WINTER

JUANA NUNEZ/SHUTTERSTOCK ©, CHRIS ALLAN/SHUTTERSTOCK ©, AGAVE PHOTO STUDIO/SHUTTERSTOCK ©, DANITA DELIMONT/ALAMY STOCK PHOTO ©, OLEG MAYOROV/SHUTTERSTOCK ©, CASCADE CREATIVES/SHUTTERSTOCK ©

→ Dine Out Vancouver Festival

A 17-day celebration of the city's culinary scene, featuring special menu tastings, events, workshops and classes around the city.

▶ dineoutvancouver.com

HSBC

↓ Hmong New Year Celebration

Takes place at the Seattle Center, featuring traditional clothing, dance and food.

↘ Magic in the Market

Seattle's iconic Pike Place Market celebrates the holidays with this annual event, complete with caroling, eggnog and a lighting ceremony.

Seattle, p48

▶ pikeplacemarket.org

PUBLIC
MARKET
CENTER

FEBRUARY

Average daytime max: 48°F
Days of rainfall: 19

Average daytime max: 50°F
Days of rainfall: 16

Packing notes

You may need heavy winter gear; check the forecast. Otherwise, stick to rain gear, warm clothing and sturdy footwear.

→ Spring Blooms

Spring hits with a riot of flowers and foliage: cherry blossoms, tulips and daffodils, and bright green leaves. As winter thaws, this is a fantastic time to see the region in all its splendor.

↓ Vancouver Craft Beer Week

One of Canada's largest beer events, this pairs brews from more than 100 breweries with delicious eats, live music and lumberjack competitions.

▶ vancouvercraftbeerweek.com

↘ Bend Brewfest

Drink up at one of the largest beer festivals in Oregon; held in Bend's Old Mill District.

▶ bendbrewfest.com

MARCH

Average daytime max: 54°F
Days of rainfall: 17

APRIL

The Pacific Northwest in SPRING

↘ Seattle International Film Festival

Watch some of the best in international and independent films at this annual event.

▶ siff.net

2022 SEATTLE
INTERNATIONAL
FILM FESTIVAL

↓ Vancouver Cherry Blossom Festival

Shows off the city's 40,000 cherry blossom trees and includes live events, viewing tours and traditional Japanese festivities.

▶ vcbf.ca

In May farmers markets start waking up. Stock up on picnic supplies like fresh fruit, cheese, bread, pastries and prepared foods.

Spring crowds are thin, but they'll build as summer nears. If you don't mind occasional rain, you'll see the region at its best.

MAY

Average daytime max: 59°F
Days of rainfall: 12

Average daytime max: 66°F
Days of rainfall: 11

Packing notes

Unpredictable weather means layers. Nights will require a lightweight jacket. Bring a rain jacket too.

SEATTLE, THE CASCADES & BEND
Trip Builder

TAKE YOUR PICK OF MUST-SEES AND HIDDEN GEMS

An iconic West Coast stop for any traveler, Seattle sparks with energy and creativity. From the Emerald City to the Cascade Mountains and stretching down to Central Oregon, wine, beer, food and outdoor adventures await.

Trip Notes

Hub towns Seattle, Bend

How long Allow nine to 14 days

Getting around Explore Seattle using public transportation. Rent a car in Seattle, Seattle-Tacoma International Airport or Bend.

Tips Mountain regions can still have snow well into June; some roads and trails may be closed. Visit in April to May or September to avoid the bulk of the crowds.

Seattle
Dine on delicious market eats on Show Me Seattle's Taste Pike Place Market Food Tour, stroll along the waterfront and round out your day in Ballard's Brewery District.
5¾hr from Bend

Mt Rainier National Park
Take your time exploring the park. Hike trails like the Grove of the Patriarchs and the Paradise Meadow Trail. Or head to Crystal Mountain and ride Mt Rainier Gondola for spectacular summit views.
2hr from Seattle

Sisters
Make time to do nothing but soak your cares away at the soothing Belknap Hot Springs.
30min from Bend

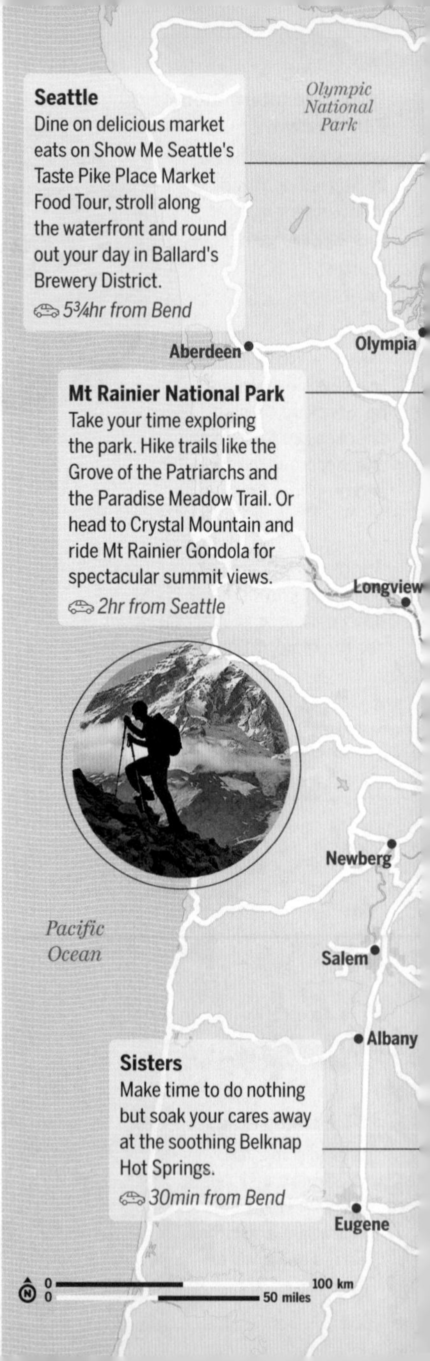
Olympic National Park
Aberdeen
Olympia
Longview
Newberg
Pacific Ocean
Salem
Albany
Eugene
0 100 km
0 50 miles

Everett
Puget Sound
Woodinville
Seattle
Tacoma
Chelan
Leavenworth
Wenatchee
Wenatchee National Forest
Moses Lake
Mt Rainier
Gifford Pinchot National Forest
WASHINGTON
Columbia River
Vancouver
Portland
Hood River
The Dalles
Maryhill
Arlington
Mt Hood National Forest
OREGON
Madras
Willamette National Forest
Sisters
Bend
Deschutes National Forest

Woodinville
Taste wines from Washington's first winery at Chateau Ste Michelle or sign up for a wine-blending class. Extend your stay to discover more about Washington Wine Country.
30min from Seattle

Leavenworth
Spend a leisurely afternoon floating down the Wenatchee River. Wrap up the evening with brats and beer at one of the German restaurants in this Bavarian-themed town.
2¼hr from Seattle

Mt St Helens
See the blast zone and learn about this volcanic event and the lives lost, at Johnston Ridge Observatory. Stick around to explore trails, lava caves and volcanic landscapes.
2¾hr from Seattle

Maryhill
Take the slow route to Bend along the Washington side of the Columbia River to explore this small town, which boasts a fine-arts museum, winery and replica of Stonehenge.
2½hr from Bend

Bend
Explore a landscape full of volcanic wonders, nature hikes, river floats and breweries – spend your days playing your way.
5¾hr from Seattle

VANCOUVER, WHISTLER & SAN JUAN ISLANDS Trip Builder

TAKE YOUR PICK OF MUST-SEES AND HIDDEN GEMS

Beloved for its vibrant urban culture and natural beauty, Vancouver offers big-city experiences with outdoor adventures in the city and beyond. Adding to its appeal, just 90 minutes north is the ski town of Whistler, and south across the US border are the San Juan Islands and the city of Seattle.

Trip Notes

Hub towns Vancouver, Seattle

How long Allow nine to 14 days

Getting around Vancouver and Seattle can be explored using public transportation. To explore outside the city, rent a car at Vancouver International Airport or Seattle-Tacoma International Airport.

Tips Visit December to March for the best powder on Whistler. Elsewhere, July and August herald beach and/or patio weather and a plethora of outdoor festivals.

Squamish
Horseshoe Bay
Vancouver
Strait of Georgia
Nanaimo
Vancouver Island
Tsawwassen
Gulf Islands
San Juan Island
Strait of Juan de Fuca

Vancouver
Spend the day in the city's beloved Stanley Park. Stroll or bike the waterfront, learn about Indigenous culture on the Talking Totems tour, snap your photo at the Hollow Tree.
3hr from Seattle

San Juan Island
Don't rush. Spend a couple of days exploring the island and keep an eye out for black foxes and whales. Explore parks. Enjoy the artistic vibes and local cuisine.
3¼hr from Seattle

Coupeville
Sample world-famous mussels at one of the town's restaurants. Explore Fort Casey Historical Park, climb the lighthouse tower and savor the Olympic Mountain views.
1¾hr from Seattle

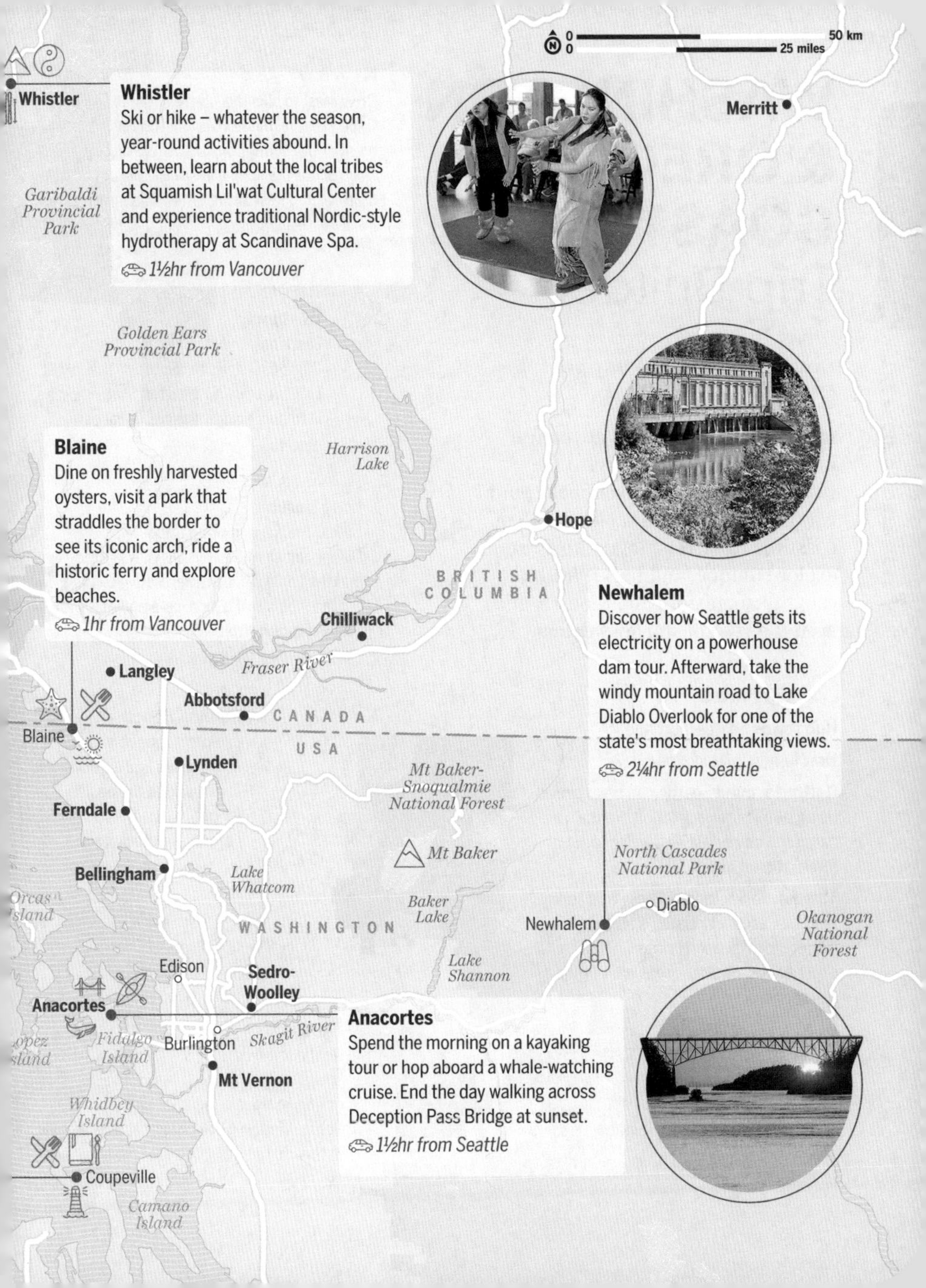
0 50 km
0 25 miles
Whistler
Merritt
Garibaldi Provincial Park
Golden Ears Provincial Park
Harrison Lake
Hope
BRITISH COLUMBIA
Chilliwack
Langley
Fraser River
Abbotsford
CANADA
Blaine
USA
Lynden
Mt Baker-Snoqualmie National Forest
Ferndale
Mt Baker
North Cascades National Park
Bellingham
Lake Whatcom
Orcas Island
Baker Lake
Diablo
Newhalem
Okanogan National Forest
WASHINGTON
Lake Shannon
Edison
Sedro-Woolley
Anacortes
Skagit River
Fidalgo Island
Burlington
Lopez Island
Mt Vernon
Whidbey Island
Coupeville
Camano Island

Whistler

Ski or hike – whatever the season, year-round activities abound. In between, learn about the local tribes at Squamish Lil'wat Cultural Center and experience traditional Nordic-style hydrotherapy at Scandinave Spa.

1½hr from Vancouver

Blaine

Dine on freshly harvested oysters, visit a park that straddles the border to see its iconic arch, ride a historic ferry and explore beaches.

1hr from Vancouver

Newhalem

Discover how Seattle gets its electricity on a powerhouse dam tour. Afterward, take the windy mountain road to Lake Diablo Overlook for one of the state's most breathtaking views.

2¼hr from Seattle

Anacortes

Spend the morning on a kayaking tour or hop aboard a whale-watching cruise. End the day walking across Deception Pass Bridge at sunset.

1½hr from Seattle

WASHINGTON & OREGON COAST
Trip Builder

TAKE YOUR PICK OF MUST-SEES AND HIDDEN GEMS

Start your coastal adventure in the city, then head west to the rugged wilderness. As you make your way along this remarkable stretch of coastline from Washington to Oregon, explore unique landmarks, freshly caught fish, historic lighthouses, and even the rush of stormy weather.

Trip Notes

Hub towns Seattle, Portland

How long Allow nine to 14 days

Getting around Seattle can be explored using public transportation. Rent a car in the city or at Seattle-Tacoma International Airport.

Tips July to September is dry and sunny, but book accommodations ahead. The winter storm season brings unique experiences. Remote areas have limited cell service.

Neah Bay
Drive west to hike the 1.5-mile trail to Cape Flattery, the northwesternmost point of the contiguous US. Afterward, learn about the local tribe at the Makah Cultural and Research Center Museum.
4½hr from Seattle

Westport
Learn how to surf or beachcomb. Climb 135 steps to the top of the tallest lighthouse in Washington State. Indulge in freshly caught fish at a local cafe.
2¼hr from Seattle

Long Beach
Spend the day exploring Cape Disappointment State Park; visit lighthouses and the Lewis & Clark Interpretive Center. Try razor clams at a local cafe and enjoy an evening beach stroll.
2¼hr from Portland

Cannon Beach
Explore boutique shops, art galleries and eateries. Then head to the beach for photo ops of its famous Haystack Rock.
1½hr from Portland

Pacific Ocean

Florence
Rent a sandboard or buggy and spend the day at the Oregon Dunes or hike to Heceta Lighthouse State Scenic Viewpoint. Recharge at a cafe in this characterful riverside town.
2¾hr from Portland

Vancouver Island
San Juan Islands
Anacortes
0 100 km
0 50 miles
CANADA
USA
Neah Bay
Victoria
Skagit River
Mt Vernon
Strait of Juan de Fuca
Whidbey Island
Port Angeles
Port Townsend
Everett
Mt Olympus
Olympic National Park
Puget Sound
Seattle
Bremerton
Olympic National Forest
Wenatchee
Wenatchee National Forest
Tacoma
Snoqualmie National Forest
Ocean Shores
Aberdeen
Olympia
Ellensburg
Westport
Willapa Bay
WASHINGTON
Long Beach
Astoria
Longview
Seaside
Columbia River
Cannon Beach
Manzanita
Vancouver
Hood River
Tillamook
Portland
Newberg
McMinnville
OREGON
Mt Hood National Forest
Lincoln City
Salem
Depoe Bay
Newport
Albany
Corvallis
Yachats
Siuslaw National Forest
Willamette National Forest
Sisters
Eugene
Florence
Springfield
Bend
Deschutes National Forest

Seattle
Spend the day at Seattle's Lake Union, where you can rent a boat, enjoy a picnic at Gas Works Park and discover the Emerald City's history at the Museum of History and Industry.
2¾hr from Portland

Astoria
Wander around America's oldest settlement west of the Mississippi; join the underground tour, climb the Astoria Column, and down burgers and beer when Fort George Brewery rings its bell.
1¾hr from Portland

Portland
Detour off the coast to explore Portland's hip vibe. Attend a show at Doug Fir Lounge, search for treasures at Portland Flea and savor a leisurely Sunday brunch at Radar.
2¾hr from Seattle

7 Things to Know About the PACIFIC NORTHWEST

INSIDER TIPS TO HIT THE GROUND RUNNING

1 Bites & Beverages

In cities like Portland, Bend, Seattle and Vancouver, BC, eating and drinking are a passion. From a quality meal at a locally owned restaurant to regionally grown seasonal produce at farmers markets, to coffee shops, kombucha or alcoholic beverages, the amount of great food and drink is overwhelming, and caters to all kinds of diets. Meat eaters, vegans, vegetarians and gluten-free eaters will not go hungry, nor will they be forced to eat at specialized fringe eateries.

LOCAL
FOOD

▸ For a snapshot on how Portlanders start the day, see p126

2 A Dog's World

Any visitor to the Pacific Northwest will soon observe that pretty much everyone has a dog. Fortunately for travelers with dogs, this has resulted in a plethora of dog-friendly hotels, bars, restaurants, parks, beaches and events. Whether you're stopping for brunch or having a beer, you'll see plenty of locals in the company of their beloved canine companions.

▸ Discover some wilder local creatures on p216

3 Leaves Aplenty

From plant-based foods to plant-filled rooms to forest bathing to legal cannabis leaf, Pacific Northwesterners are obsessed with plants and everything living and green.

▸ Understand the ins and outs of legal weed on p132

4 Green Scene

Reuse and recycle! People in the Pacific Northwest typically try to live 'green' by recycling, composting, reducing consumption, and keeping the air and water clean. Paper bags, reusable bags and refillable water bottles are staples.

▸ Find out more on p248

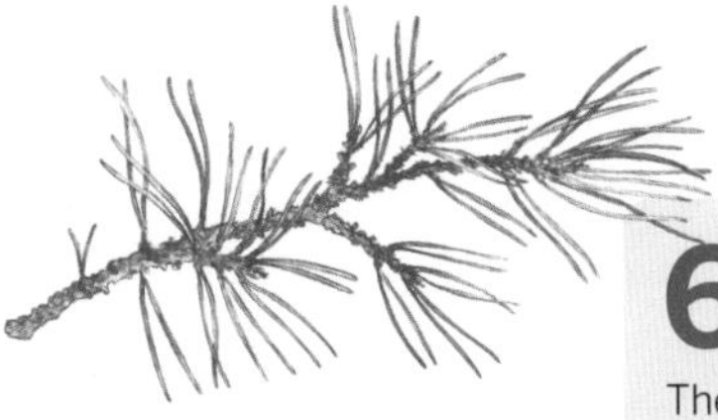

5 Full Cycle

Bikes are integral to Portland and Vancouver, as evidenced by their abundance of bike shops, bike rentals and trails. The Oregon Coast also has plenty of opportunity for summer rides that take advantage of prevailing winds, while Washington visitors should see the 8.5-mile Discovery Trail, and those in Bend, Oregon, can take on some of the best mountain-biking trails in the region.

▶ For more on getting around the Pacific Northwest, see p244

6 Parks & Outdoor Spaces

The Pacific Northwest boasts an incredible number of green spaces, waterways, forests and parks. Walking the loop around Green Lake is a must when visiting the Seattle area, as are Golden Gardens beach park, the San Juan Islands (via Deception Pass State Park), and a hike through the massive Discovery Park. Oregon's must-see nature areas include Sauvie Island, the Oregon Coast, Silver Falls State Park and the Columbia River Gorge National Scenic Area.

North of the border, Tofino in British Columbia is a Unesco Biosphere Region replete with ancient rainforests, ocean swells and sandy beaches. One of the world's great urban parks, 400-hectare Stanley Park offers seawall strolls, sandy beaches, heated pools and woodland trails only steps from Vancouver. On the far eastern edge of North Vancouver, Deep Cove is a premium site for kayaking, stand-up paddleboarding and surfskiing. Pick your craft and paddle along Indian Arm – North America's southernmost fjord.

▶ Let nature be your therapist with our step-by-step guide to forest bathing on p112

7 Art Central

Portland offers plenty of arts festivals and a slew of indie galleries. Travelers in Vancouver, BC, should check out the Bill Reid Gallery of Northwest Coast Art, while Washington visitors should make time for the Seattle Art Museum and indigenous art in the San Juan Islands' Friday Harbor.

▶ Discover an island dedicated to the arts on p208

Read, Listen, Watch & Follow

READ

The Art of Racing in the Rain (Garth Stein; 2008) Golden retriever Enzo narrates his life in this *New York Times* bestseller.

The Art of Racing in the Rain

Day Hikes in the Pacific Northwest (Don J Scarmuzzi; 2018) Pacific Northwest 'trails, loops and summit scrambles'.

Day Hikes in the Pacific Northwest
Don J Scarmuzzi

This is Portland: The City You've Heard You Should Like (Alexander Barrett; 2013) Witty guide to Portland culture.

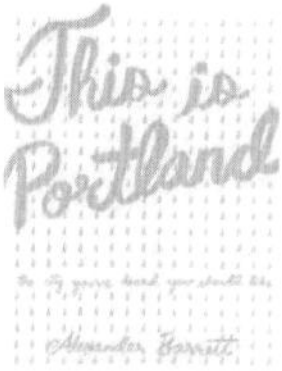
This is Portland
Alexander Barrett

Dune (Frank Herbert; 1965) Epic science fiction novel inspired by the windswept sand dunes of Florence, Oregon.

DUNE
FRANK HERBERT

LISTEN

On She Goes This podcast by and for women-of-color travelers brings on special guests, showing them the diverse experiences Portland has to offer.

Think Out Loud Oregon Public Broadcasting's daily show on politics and global issues also covers Pacific Northwest sports, music, books and the environment.

Spilled Milk Seattle writer Molly Wizenberg and comedian Matthew Amster-Burton tackle various culinary topics on each podcast episode, dissecting in granular detail.

Nevermind (Nirvana; 1991) This album (pictured: top row, second from left) was the apogee of grunge music, aka the 'Seattle Sound'.

BEST SELLERS
LONDON GRAMMAR

ELLY GODFROY/ALAMY STOCK PHOTO ©

Portland, Oregon (Jack White and Loretta Lynn; 2004) Lyrical song on Lynn's album *Van Lear Rose* about a dive-bar meetup and ensuing romance.

WATCH

Wild, Wild Country (2018) Captivating documentary about a 1980s commune in Antelope, Oregon (pictured right).

Eater's Guide to the World, Ep 1 (2020) Food critic Karen Brooks and narrator Maya Rudolph explore the pleasures of dining alone in the Pacific Northwest.

Oregon Experience (2006) Historical series exploring Oregon's past, co-produced by Oregon Public Broadcasting (OPB) and the Oregon Historical Society.

10 Things I Hate About You (1999; pictured right) Seattle teen romcom includes prom at the Paramount Theater and the Fremont Troll.

British Columbia: An Untold History (2021) Inclusive history of BC.

KATYA PALLADINA/STOCKIMO/ ALAMY STOCK PHOTO ©

RGR COLLECTION/ ALAMY STOCK PHOTO ©

FOLLOW

SeattleMet
Seattle Metropolitan Magazine (@SeattleMet) Seattle news, culture and lifestyle.

Portland Mercury (portlandmercury.com) Portland music, arts, and events coverage.

Eater Seattle (@eaterseattle) Comprehensive food coverage.

Travel Oregon (traveloregon.com) Oregon's visit-worthy destinations.

VANCOUVER
Vancouver Magazine (vanmag.com) Coverage of food, drink, entertainment and more.

SEATTLE

CULTURE | CRAFT BEER | URBAN OUTDOORS

Experience
Seattle
online

SEATTLE
Trip Builder

Seattle is a city of creatives, doers, adventurers and brilliant minds, who have opened enticing restaurants, carved out cultural hubs and otherwise spoken up for their passions and projects. It's all set against a landscape that inspires awe – and impressive efforts to protect and honor it.

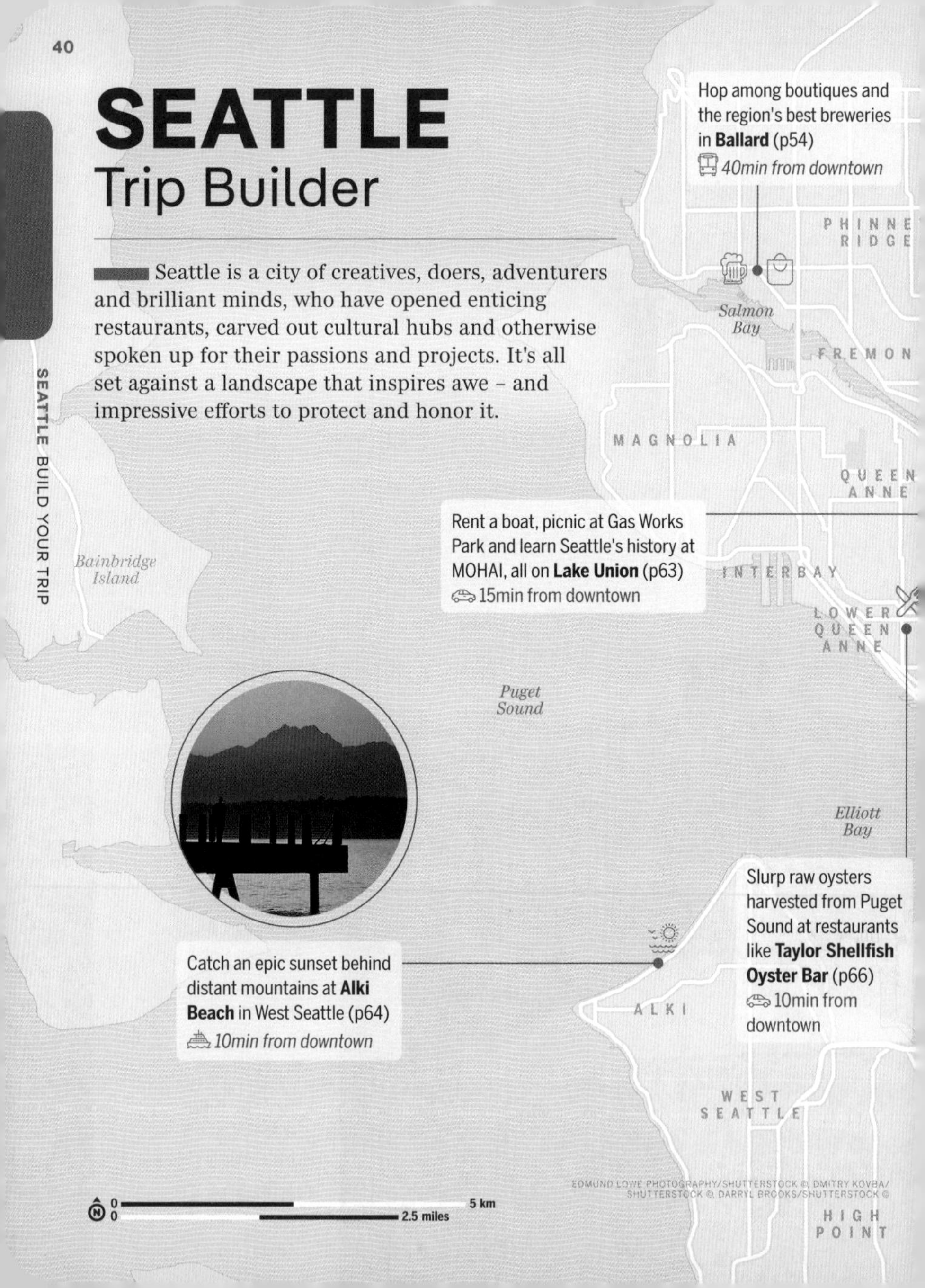
PHINNEY RIDGE
Salmon Bay
FREMONT
MAGNOLIA
QUEEN ANNE
INTERBAY
LOWER QUEEN ANNE
Bainbridge Island
Puget Sound
Elliott Bay
ALKI
WEST SEATTLE
HIGH POINT
0 5 km
0 2.5 miles

Hop among boutiques and the region's best breweries in **Ballard** (p54)
40min from downtown

Rent a boat, picnic at Gas Works Park and learn Seattle's history at MOHAI, all on **Lake Union** (p63)
15min from downtown

Catch an epic sunset behind distant mountains at **Alki Beach** in West Seattle (p64)
10min from downtown

Slurp raw oysters harvested from Puget Sound at restaurants like **Taylor Shellfish Oyster Bar** (p66)
10min from downtown

EDMUND LOWE PHOTOGRAPHY/SHUTTERSTOCK ©, DMITRY KOVBA/SHUTTERSTOCK ©, DARRYL BROOKS/SHUTTERSTOCK ©

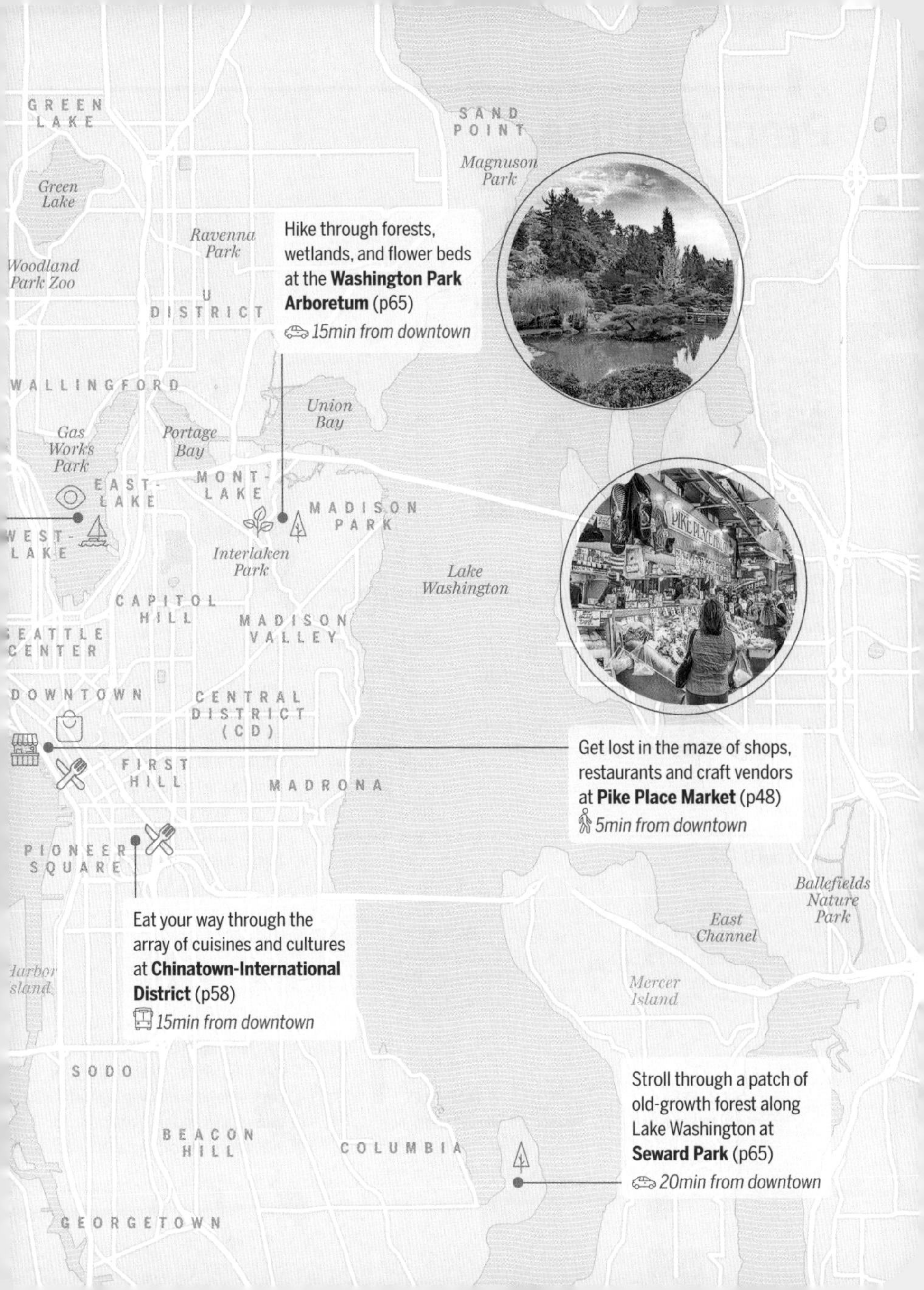
GREEN LAKE
Green Lake
Woodland Park Zoo
Ravenna Park
U DISTRICT
SAND POINT
Magnuson Park
WALLINGFORD
Gas Works Park
Portage Bay
Union Bay
EASTLAKE
MONTLAKE
MADISON PARK
WESTLAKE
Interlaken Park
Lake Washington
CAPITOL HILL
MADISON VALLEY
SEATTLE CENTER
DOWNTOWN
CENTRAL DISTRICT (CD)
FIRST HILL
MADRONA
PIONEER SQUARE
Harbor Island
Ballefields Nature Park
East Channel
Mercer Island
SODO
BEACON HILL
COLUMBIA
GEORGETOWN

Hike through forests, wetlands, and flower beds at the **Washington Park Arboretum** (p65)

15min from downtown

Get lost in the maze of shops, restaurants and craft vendors at **Pike Place Market** (p48)

5min from downtown

Eat your way through the array of cuisines and cultures at **Chinatown-International District** (p58)

15min from downtown

Stroll through a patch of old-growth forest along Lake Washington at **Seward Park** (p65)

20min from downtown

Practicalities

EQROY/SHUTTERSTOCK ©

ARRIVING

Seattle-Tacoma International Airport This is the region's major hub. A ride to downtown Seattle on the Link light rail takes an hour and costs $3 (adult ticket). Buy tickets on the ground floor of the station, which is connected to the 4th floor of the airport parking garage. Flat-rate taxis cost $40 for a ride to downtown Seattle; Lyft and Uber rides are comparable in cost.

HOW MUCH FOR A...

cup of coffee
$4

pint of beer
$6

dozen oysters
$25

WHEN TO GO

JUN–SEP
Sunny, warm, and busy. All of Seattle seems to live outside

OCT–NOV
Cooler days and fall colors. Rainy season starts

DEC–FEB
Clouds and rain are common. Perfect for indoor activities

MAR–MAY
The city perks up for spring and the return of the sun

GETTING AROUND

Light rail Seattle's Link light rail threads through the city's major hubs, from the airport to the stadiums to downtown, Capitol Hill and the University District. Adult tickets cost $2.25 to $3.50 depending on trip distance.

Bus King County Metro's extensive bus system links the city's neighborhoods. You can pay the adult fare of $2.75 by depositing cash in the fare box on board. Or download the Transit GO app, where you can buy tickets for the bus, water taxi and streetcar.

Walking One of the best ways to see Seattle is on foot. The city has ample infrastructure for pedestrians, including signed crosswalks and well-maintained sidewalks and other paved paths.

EATING & DRINKING

hello em

Seattle boasts a robust and diverse dining scene, where high-price restaurants sling multi-course meals next to take-out windows, fast food and breweries hosting food trucks. The city benefits from Washington State's rich agricultural production, the wealth of seafood from surrounding waterways, and deep links with an array of food traditions. And, yes, the city's reputation for coffee snobbery is rooted in reality: with perfectly brewed coffee widely available. Ditto craft beer – outstanding breweries abound.

Best Vietnamese coffee
Hello Em (p67; pictured top)

Must-try tacos
Marination Ma Kai (p61)

CONNECT & FIND YOUR WAY

Wi-fi Seattle has plenty of free wi-fi hotspots at public libraries, community centers, and a smattering of landmarks and public buildings. The city has a map of these at seattle.gov.

Navigation Many streets are numbered and include a directional (north, southwest, east etc), except when downtown, so it's fairly easy to orient yourself.

FREE MUSEUM DAYS

Many of Seattle's museums offer free admission on the first Thursday of each month. Participating museums include the Museum of History and Industry, Seattle Art Museum and the National Nordic Museum.

WHERE TO STAY

Seattle's collection of neighborhoods have distinct personalities. Stay downtown if you want convenience or a hotel. Otherwise, pick a neighborhood and opt for a short-term rental.

Neighborhood	Pro/Con
Capitol Hill	Central location full of bars and restaurants. Crowded and loud on weekend nights.
Downtown	Easy access to major attractions. Somewhat soulless after dark.
Fremont	Quirky and lively canal-side neighborhood with great boutiques. Crowded.
Ballard	Breweries, shops and top-notch restaurants. Not centrally located.
West Seattle	Scenic beaches and restaurants aplenty. Isolated and inaccessible via transit.
Columbia City	Light rail access to a small town-like 'downtown' strip of businesses. Further afield.

MONEY

Cash is rarely a necessity in Seattle, though you may want to carry some if you plan to take the bus.

01 Salmon in the CITY

NATURE | CONSERVATION | OUTDOORS

Most visitors to the Northwest expect to find salmon, though most look for it on a dinner plate. Unfortunately, the region's signature fish is struggling. But protection efforts are underway, and salmon do still return to their natal streams throughout the region. Some routes thread through Seattle, so it's possible to catch a glimpse of this iconic animal, right in city limits.

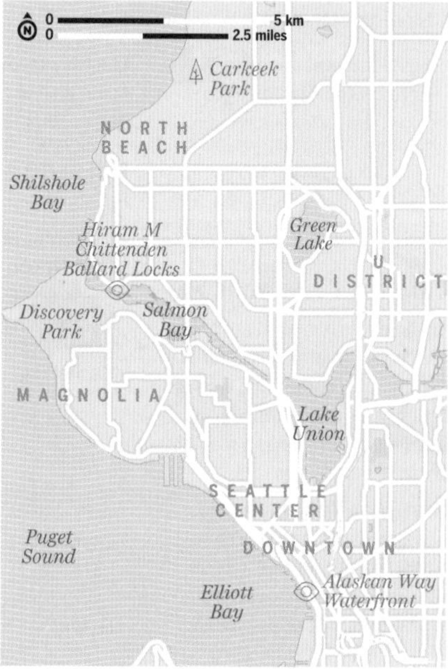
0 5 km
0 2.5 miles
Carkeek Park
NORTH BEACH
Shilshole Bay
Hiram M Chittenden Ballard Locks
Green Lake
U DISTRICT
Discovery Park
Salmon Bay
MAGNOLIA
Lake Union
SEATTLE CENTER
Puget Sound
DOWNTOWN
Elliott Bay
Alaskan Way Waterfront

How to

Getting here & around Most of these spots are accessible via public transit, as well as through ride-hailing companies.

When to go July to November is the best time to spot adult salmon in creeks and streams.

Viewing spots Places along the Cedar River and Issaquah Creek. On scheduled days, the Seattle Aquarium's naturalists are set up along the Cedar River banks to help visitors find salmon.

Visit the **Hiram M Chittenden Ballard Locks**, a fascinating feat of engineering in its own right. After you watch all manner of sailboats, kayaks and tugboats float through the locks, head to the Fish Ladder Viewing Room, where you might spot migrating sockeye, chinook and coho. Keep an eye out for the seals that gather nearby, snagging passing salmon as they queue up to climb the ladder around the locks.

Tucked under the busy **Alaskan Way waterfront** of ferry docks and souvenir shops sits an improbable ecosystem. When the city made seismic upgrades to the Elliott Bay seawall downtown, to better protect the city against earthquakes, it also added considerations for salmon. Now, there's textured walls providing habitat for young salmon, plus glass skylights on the sidewalk to enable the fish to better see

their prey darting along the living walls.

In late October through early December, hike north Seattle's **Carkeek Park** to spot salmon heading up Piper's Creek and Venema Creek to spawn. Historically, this salmon run has been hit hard, spurning an impressive citizen-led conservation effort. The trails through the park's deep ravines lead to a scenic beach along Puget Sound, and there are several chances to peek into the creeks along the way to look for fish.

Volunteer Opportunities

Carkeek Watershed Community Action Project puts volunteers to use from late October through early December during the salmon run. It counts, measures and identifies live and dead fish.

Washington Department of Fish and Wildlife has a long list of volunteer opportunities, including chances to work on creek restoration.

Long Live the Kings, a wild salmon restoration nonprofit, sends out volunteer field opportunities through the email list on its website.

As with any volunteering opportunities, do your research before signing up.

Above Fish ladder, Hiram M Chittenden Ballard Locks

Salmon Under Threat

CAN WE SAVE THE NORTHWEST'S ICONIC FISH?

Most visitors associate the Pacific Northwest with seafood - salmon in particular. But the area's iconic fish is under threat, and often the salmon on local menus isn't from local waters. Efforts to protect the fish that remain fight against enormous odds, but there's hope.

DANITA DELIMONT/SHUTTERSTOCK ©

Left Salmon, Issaquah Creek **Middle** Salmon jumping upstream **Right** Sound Salmon Solutions volunteers

Once Epic Runs

Pre-contact Indigenous communities living along the Northwest's coasts and rivers harvested great quantities of salmon for millennia. These anadromous fish are born in freshwater streams and rivers before they migrate to salt-water, where they live out their adult lives until they return to their natal streams to spawn and die. That once-healthy cycle resulted in legendary salmon runs, with waterways so choked with fish, the saying goes, 'you could walk across the river on their backs.' The fish were – and still are – a central part of Indigenous Northwest cultural identity.

A Fish in Trouble

Salmon are a linchpin in a healthy ecosystem – a so-called 'keystone species.' In addition to being delicious for human consumption, they're a vital food source for animals like orca, bears, eagles and otters. Some 137 other species depend on this fish for survival. And, when salmon return to their birthplaces to reproduce and die, their decomposing bodies bring critical nutrients from the ocean deep into the forest, where they essentially become fertilizer. Without salmon, the delicate web of life in the Northwest cannot thrive.

When Euro-Americans started settling in the North-west in the mid-1800s, they industrialized the region and began altering the environment to the detriment of salmon. They opened large canneries up and down the coast, harvesting more salmon than was sustainable and turning the fish into big industry. They logged the forests extensively, degrading habitat. They built dams on the region's rivers, preventing salmon from reaching their spawning grounds.

CAVAN IMAGES/ALAMY STOCK PHOTO ©

WWW.SOUNDSALMONSOLUTIONS.ORG ©

Today, salmon continue to face a barrage of human-generated threats: ocean acidification, rising sea levels, water pollution and more. And their dwindling numbers are evident; it's rare to find Puget Sound salmon on a restaurant menu or in a grocery store; most wild-caught salmon comes from Alaska, and other fish comes from environmentally questionable fish farms.

Salmon are a linchpin in a healthy ecosystem – a so-called 'keystone species.' Without salmon, the delicate web of life in the Northwest cannot thrive.

And the region's beloved Southern Resident orca are struggling. These animals' diets lean heavily on Chinook salmon, but it's hard for them to find enough food to fill their giant bellies. Coupled with other environmental threats, this means these iconic creatures are on the brink of extinction.

Protection Efforts

Several species of the area's salmon are now protected by the federal Endangered Species Act, and a slew of restoration efforts are underway. Salmon fishing is greatly curtailed, and more sustainable fishing methods are being developed. Dam removal on rivers has helped give the fish access to their historic spawning grounds. River habitat restoration has helped returning adults and outgoing juvenile salmon. An array of projects to make Puget Sound healthier for all inhabitants provides stability for salmon, if indirectly.

As the region's human population continues to grow, these efforts take on dire importance. Although we may never again walk across the backs of salmon, there is hope we can regain some of what was lost.

Restoriation Organizations

A variety of organizations are working on restoration efforts around Puget Sound. **Sound Salmon Solutions** works on habitat restoration and education, plus leads volunteer projects. **Long Live the Kings** focuses on fieldwork and evidence-based solutions to build conservation partnerships and rebuild salmon and steelhead populations. The **Nature Conservancy** puts its efforts toward rivers and their floodplains, working to create a healthier Puget Sound watershed. **Puget Sound Restoration Fund** undertakes habitat restoration projects around the sound, which indirectly benefit salmon. And **Puget Soundkeeper** protects Puget Sound's water quality through monitoring and public policy.

02 Hidden Pike PLACE

SHOPPING | HISTORY | CULTURE

Pike Place Market – one of the oldest continuously operating public farmers markets in the country – is in many ways the beating heart of Seattle, where artists and artisans come together to represent the city's robust personality. With a little creativity, it's possible to experience the best of the market beyond the scrum.

Song of the Farmers

How to

Getting here The market's downtown location is easy to reach via public transit. The major bus artery of Third Ave and the Westlake light-rail station are nearby.

When to go Pike Place is mobbed on summer weekends. For quieter visits, come October to May, avoid weekends and arrive around 9am.

Roll call At 9am day-stall vendors gather on the Virginia St side of North Arcade for 'roll call,' a tradition that divvies up table space and opens the market.

GHOST ALLEY ESPRESSO
1499

PUBLIC
MARKET
MEET THE PR
FARMERS MARKET
INFORMATION
MARKET THEATER

What Many People Miss

Pike Place Market's sprawling collection of craft booths, produce and seafood vendors, restaurants and shops draws visitors in throngs. This iconic market can at times feel overrun, a flooded river of humanity. That tracks: Pike Place is Seattle's most popular attraction and the 33rd most visited in the world, logging 10 million visitors a year.

Most visitors are so enchanted with the Public Market Center sign at the market's Pike St and Pike Pl entrance that they miss the **Aki Sogabe mural** tucked under the roofline. *Song of the Earth* is an homage to the market's Japanese farmers, who ran two-thirds of the stalls here before they were sent to internment camps during World War II.

The street-level **Main Arcade** is often the most mobbed. Try heading to the market's lower levels, where quirky shops are tucked away in a maze of hallways. Then cross Pike Pl to the **Sanitary Market**, where more shops and vendors sit just off the main drag.

Go with a Guide

Try a tour with **Public Market Tours**, which leads visitors on a one-hour stroll through the market's highlights and history. **Friends of the Market** hits the lesser-known nooks. Or eat your way through the market on the Taste Pike Place Market Food Tour hosted by **Show Me Seattle**.

Above left Pike Place Market **Far left top** Aki Sogabe's *Song of the Earth* **Far left bottom** Ghost Alley Espresso

Food & Drink

Carved out of one of the first public restrooms on the west coast, **Ghost Alley Espresso** is 147 sq ft of history and charm. Be sure to ask about the resident ghost that the business' name hints at.

The counter at **Mee Sum Pastry** has been slinging Chinese bites for 30 years. The highlight is the barbecue pork *hum bao*, a perfect walking snack.

Honest Biscuit has perfected the biscuit sandwich. Stuff your face with these delights, which come loaded with fillings such as fried chicken, local cheese and meat, jam, honey and more.

03 Seattle STAIRS

URBAN HIKES | OUTDOORS | HISTORY

Seattle's neighborhoods cling to hilly – and frequently steep – terrain. The hills are often linked by long sets of stairs, many built more than a century ago. These stairways offer a thigh-burning means of discovering the city: exploring hidden pockets, tapping into its history and personality, and enjoying its overlooked aspects. Of Seattle's 650 accessible stairways, here are a few standouts.

AARON MCCOY/GETTY IMAGES ©

How to

Getting around Many stairs are accessible via public transport. Check route guides and schedules for more information.

When to go Year-round. Seattle's stairways are accessible in any season, and there's always something to see. Spring and summer are saturated with greenery, but winter's bare tree branches open up distant views from these hillside perches.

Seattle's longest With 388 steps over 13 flights and a 160ft elevation, the Howe Street Stairs are not for the fainthearted.

HEIDI IHNEN PHOTOGRAPHY/SHUTTERSTOCK ©

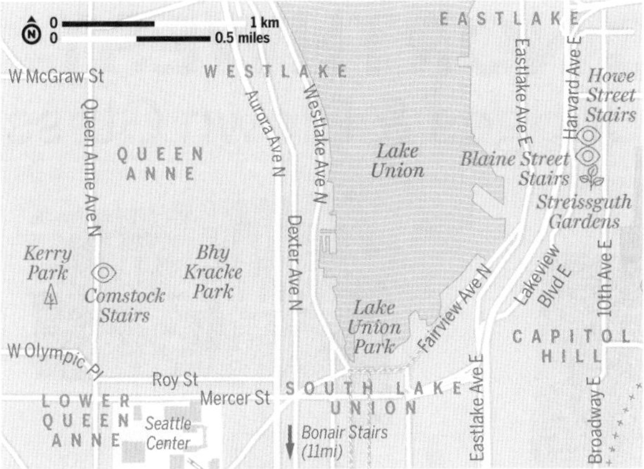

0 1 km
0 0.5 miles
EASTLAKE
W McGraw St
WESTLAKE
Queen Anne Ave N
QUEEN ANNE
Aurora Ave N
Westlake Ave N
Lake Union
Eastlake Ave E
Harvard Ave E
Howe Street Stairs
Blaine Street Stairs
Streissguth Gardens
Dexter Ave N
Kerry Park
Comstock Stairs
Bhy Kracke Park
Lake Union Park
Fairview Ave N
Lakeview Blvd E
10th Ave E
CAPITOL HILL
W Olympic Pl
Roy St
Mercer St
SOUTH LAKE UNION
LOWER QUEEN ANNE
Seattle Center
Bonair Stairs (11mi)
Eastlake Ave E
Broadway E

Howe St & Blaine St The **Howe Street Stairs** and the parallel **Blaine Street Stairs** sit just one block apart and once served as connectors for streetcar lines running at the summit and base of Capitol Hill. They're incredibly scenic, ducking into tree-covered shade and emerging at viewpoints that extend across Lake Union. The 293-step Blaine Street Stairs run alongside **Streissguth Gardens**, a charming one-acre green space that's home to vegetable-garden plots and ornamental plantings.

Comstock Trees and vines all but envelop the **Comstock Stairs**, one of the oldest stairways in the city. This 1909 structure – nicknamed the Comstock Grand Dame – winds up the side of Queen Anne Hill. The curves, landings and greenery bathe this 85-step staircase in romance. While you're in the area, stop at **Kerry Park** for one of the best views in the city, with the Space Needle front and center and, on a clear day, Mt Rainier looming behind the skyline.

Bonair The 109-step **Bonair Stairs** climbs up the hill of West Seattle, where you'll score views out across Puget Sound and of Alki Beach below. Winter, when the trees are bare, brings the most expansive views. In spring, foliage envelops the stairs, and come late summer there will be ripe blackberries to snack on.

Far left top Stairway, Queen Anne neighborhood **Far left bottom** Kerry Park

Take the Stairs

Seattle's stairways, roughly 650 of them, allow exploration of many out-of-the-way neighborhood byways and attractions. In a city that was built around water and hills, the stairs connected neighborhood enclaves to transit, parks and jobs. Today these same stairs remind us of our past and lead us to the exciting new sights of our growing city. To really discover Seattle, head for the stairs!

■ **Recommended by Cathy and Jake Jaramillo,** *authors of the book* Seattle Stairway Walks

PACIFIC NORTHWEST
Buildings, Bridges & Blown Glass

01

POSTCARD
PLACE STAMP HERE
FROM:

02

03

04

05

06

01 Glass sculptures

Seek out Dale Chihuly's sensual, multi-colored glass creations around Seattle and Tacoma.

02 Bavarian beauty

Channel *A Sound of Music* amid the faux-German buildings of Leavenworth, WA.

03 Hawthorne Bridge

This 1910 stunner in Portland is the world's oldest vertical-lift bridge.

04 Portland Building

Plagued with structural issues, this postmodern behemoth is guarded by an immense statue of the Goddess of Commerce.

05 Mt Angel Abbey

This Benedictine monastery located outside Salem, OR, boasts not only an Alvar Aalto–designed library but also a 2.5lb pig hairball.

06 VPL Central

Vancouver seduces readers and tourists alike with the Colosseum-like facade of its central library branch.

07 Burrard Bridge

Vancouver's Lions Gate Bridge may garner the lion's share of attention, but this elegant span offers an art deco gateway to downtown.

07

10

11

08

09

12

08 Port Townsend

A Victorian-lover's dream, this pretty Washington town is replete with architectural delights, including the 1890 Hastings Building.

09 Columbia Center

Towering over the Space Needle, though perhaps not quite as pretty, this Seattle skyscraper is the Pacific Northwest's tallest building.

10 Portland's Oregon Convention Center

Spot the twin spire towers, then discover the world's largest Foucault pendulum inside.

11 Tacoma Narrows Bridge

This pair of twin suspension bridges is known less for its current state and more for its infamous beginnings – the original span collapsed in 1940, only four months after completion.

12 Cloudraker Skybridge

This 130m-long suspension bridge – with see-through base – connects the top of Whistler Peak with the Raven's Eye viewing plaform. Not one for the faint of heart!

04 Ballard Brewery DISTRICT

CRAFT BEER | DINING | CULTURE

Seattleites are serious about their beer, and it's easy to find a brewery taproom just about anywhere here. But Ballard is home to the highest concentration of breweries, allowing enthusiasts to hop from one to the next, sampling some of the best brews the Northwest has to offer.

STOUP
BREWING

BRIAN LOGAN PHOTOGRAPHY/SHUTTERSTOCK ©

How to

Getting here & around Ballard is accessible via King County Metro bus. Once you're here, move from brewery to brewery on foot, or pick up a shared scooter or electric bike.

When to go Breweries are open year-round, but tend to be more crowded on weekend evenings.

Stay fed Many breweries don't serve food, but allow patrons to bring in meals, or get takeout delivered to the taproom. Some host food trucks; schedules can be found on brewery websites.

BALLARD

VDB PHOTOS/SHUTTERSTOCK ©

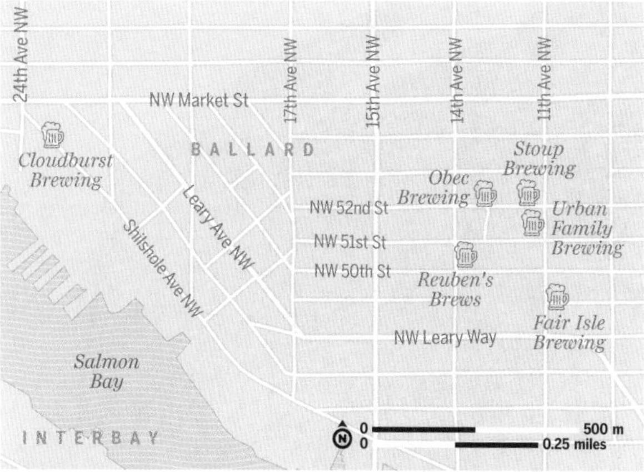

24th Ave NW
NW Market St
17th Ave NW
15th Ave NW
14th Ave NW
11th Ave NW
BALLARD
Cloudburst Brewing
Stoup Brewing
Obec Brewing
Urban Family Brewing
NW 52nd St
NW 51st St
NW 50th St
Leary Ave NW
Shilshole Ave NW
Reuben's Brews
Fair Isle Brewing
NW Leary Way
Salmon Bay
INTERBAY
0
500 m
0
0.25 miles

Far left top Stoup Brewing **Far left bottom** Ballard neighborhood boundary indicator

Drink Up

The Ballard neighborhood's modern history as a nerve center for the maritime and lumber industries means it has something breweries need: large warehouse spaces near population centers. As Ballard transitioned to a more residential neighborhood, breweries moved in, too.

The Ballard brewery district, in its modern form, got its start in 2012, with the opening of **Reuben's Brews**. Here, visitors will find an impressive range of beers, all well crafted, and a popular patio. Another early entrant to the scene was **Stoup Brewing**, beloved for its expansive patio, West Coast–style IPAs and sour beers, and consistent food-truck presence.

Things get funky at **Fair Isle Brewing**, where saisons and farmhouse ales rule the beer list, and wild fermentation is at the heart of the operation. Ditto **Urban Family Brewing**, where sour beer stands front and center, complemented by porters and IPAs.

IPA lovers shouldn't miss **Cloudburst Brewing**, where the hoppy style reigns supreme. The on-site food truck from **Plenty of Clouds** serves Chinese dim sum fare in the beer garden. Less aggressively hopped are the English and Czech beers at **Obec Brewing**.

Beyond Ballard

Many outstanding breweries are spread across the city. Other standouts beyond Ballard include **Holy Mountain Brewing Company**, arguably one of the best in the country.

Another mainstay is **Rooftop Brewing Company**, where beloved styles – Belgian *wit*, Mexican lager and hazy IPAs – get the attention they deserve.

The always-excellent **Standard Brewing** slings a range of styles, but hops-forward beers and funky, wild experimentations are the focus.

Over in West Seattle, the **Good Society Brewery** pours with a purpose: each pint benefits a social or environmental cause.

05 Culture of SEATTLE

MUSEUMS | FESTIVALS | FOOD

Seattle's cultural history dates to the original inhabitants, Native Americans, and continues on to present-day immigrant groups and communities of color contributing to the city's tapestry. Add in other affinity groups that thrive here, like Seattle's queer community, and there's much to celebrate.

ARCHITECT: FRANK GEHRY; CK FOTO/SHUTTERSTOCK ©

How to

Getting here & around Each of these events and locations are on or near bus lines and the light rail. They're also accessible via ride-hailing companies.

When to go Year-round, though for one-time events, you can plan ahead and buy tickets in advance.

Hendrix fans As well as the Museum of Pop Culture, Hendrix fans can also visit Jimi Hendrix Park in the Central District, as well as a statue of the musician along the sidewalk on Broadway near Pike.

Burke Museum
Union Bay
Lake Union
Museum of Pop Culture
Frye Art Museum
Seattle Art Museum
Langston Hughes Performing Arts Institute
Elliott Bay
Wing Luke Museum
Lake Washington
Northwest African American Museum
Harbor Island
Duwamish Longhouse and Cultural Center
0 2 km
0 1 mile

First Americans Humans have called Puget Sound home for more than 10,000 years. That incredible cultural legacy has an important presence around Seattle today. The city itself is named for the hereditary chief of the Suquamish and Duwamish people.

Shop for goods from local Native American artisans at **Eighth Generation** in Pike Place Market. View Northwest Coast and Coast Salish masks, textiles and sculptures at the **Seattle Art Museum**. Learn about the region's human history at the **Burke Museum**, where there's also an Indigenous-owned cafe, **Off the Rez**. The **Duwamish Longhouse and Cultural Center** is home to the first new tribal longhouse built in 150 years in Seattle. The center has a museum and hosts events throughout the year.

Music & art Seattle has long been a proving ground for some of the world's most noted figures in music, like Jimi Hendrix and Nirvana. Learn more about these and other musical influences at the **Museum of Pop Culture**.

Left Jonathan Borofsky's *Hammering Man* (1991), Seattle Art Museum **Above left** Museum of Pop Culture

Local and global artworks are on display at the always-free **Frye Art Museum**.

Shop for jewelry, ceramics, desserts, vintage clothing and more from independent retailers at the **Georgetown Trailer Park Mall**. And visit the immersive installations at the offbeat **Museum of Museums**, where even the bathrooms are works of art. The **Fremont Sunday Market** is another hub for handmade items and vintage finds.

Culture on the plate Seattle's cultures are perhaps most present in its restaurant scene. There's a vibrant collection of Ethiopian restaurants in the Central District neighborhood, for example – **East African Imports & Restaurant** and **Meskel Restaurant** are two of the best.

In the Chinatown-International District, Seattle's Asian communities show off their cuisines at restaurants that serve bubble

Central Area Arts & Culture District

Seattle has several designated arts and culture districts, including one in the Central Area. This neighborhood has long been important to Seattle's Black community, which suffered widespread discrimination and found a toehold in this part of the city. Many Black residents and businesses have been forced out by gentrification, but recent preservation efforts have helped stem that trend. Black-owned restaurants (like **Communion** and **Fat's Chicken and Waffles**) have a noticeable presence, as do cultural cornerstones like the **Northwest African American Museum** and the **Langston Hughes Performing Arts Institute**.

Crosswalks

Customized crosswalks – painted to emulate a specific neighborhood's heritage – are popping up around Seattle. In the 'gayborhood' of Capitol Hill, there are 11 rainbow crosswalks. In the Central Area, there are crosswalks bearing the colors of the Pan-African flag. In Rainier Beach, there's one decorated to match the Ethiopian flag.

tea, sushi, dim sum and more. It's hard to go wrong here, but if the choices are overwhelming, book a food tour through the **Wing Luke Museum**. There's a rotating calendar of tours built around a theme like dumplings or rice. Before your tour, save time to visit the museum and survey neighborhood history.

Festivals A full slate of festivals celebrate a range of creative talents, including **Northwest Folklife Festival**, an annual celebration of folk arts and cultures from around the Pacific Northwest. The annual **Seattle Pride Fest** celebrates queer culture with parties, marches, parades and outdoor festivals each June. And the **Seattle Queer Film Festival** is the largest of its kind in the region. The huge and wide-ranging **Bumbershoot** festival celebrates all things art, including film, dance, comedy, music and visual arts.

There's no doubt Seattle is a quirky place. This is evident at events like the **Moisture Festival**, which combines circus, burlesque and comedy performances. The annual **Fremont Solstice Parade** involves stilt walkers, giant puppets and cyclists wearing nothing but body paint. The accompanying **Fremont Fair** sprawls across six city blocks with some 300 craft vendors.

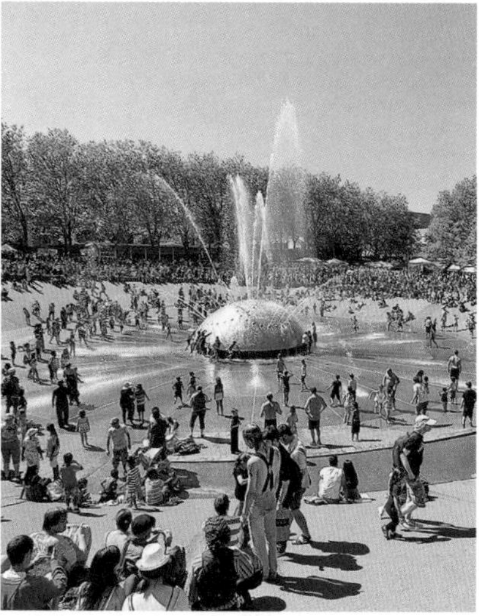

Left Northwest African American Museum **Above top** Rainbow crosswalk, Capitol Hill **Above** Northwest Folklife Festival attendees at the International Fountain

06 West Seattle by WATER

FERRY | OUTDOORS | FOOD

Zip away from the waterfront skyscrapers of downtown Seattle and cross Elliott Bay on the West Seattle water taxi. Short but scenic, the pedestrian ferry drops off near a waterfront path leading to restaurants, kayak and bike rentals, and panoramic downtown views.

TRONG NGUYEN/SHUTTERSTOCK ©

Trip Notes

Getting here & around The West Seattle water taxi departs downtown from Pier 50, at the foot of Yesler Way. Boats leave every 30 to 60 minutes and the trip takes about 10 minutes. Once you land, head to Alki Kayak Tours next to the ferry dock to rent kayaks, paddleboards, bikes and even in-line skates.

When to go Summer weekends are busy. Go during the week or outside summer to avoid crowds and to be more likely to spot wildlife.

Top tip Once onboard, climb to the top deck for the best skyline views. Time your return trip with sunset and keep the camera handy.

Views from the Water

From the water taxi, you can see all that makes up this vibrant city, including the Puget Sound, Seattle skyline, Seattle Seahawks Lumen Field, Seattle Mariners T-Mobile Park, and the iconic Space Needle.

Kamala Saxton, *co-owner of Marination Ma Kai fusion restaurant @curb_cuisine*

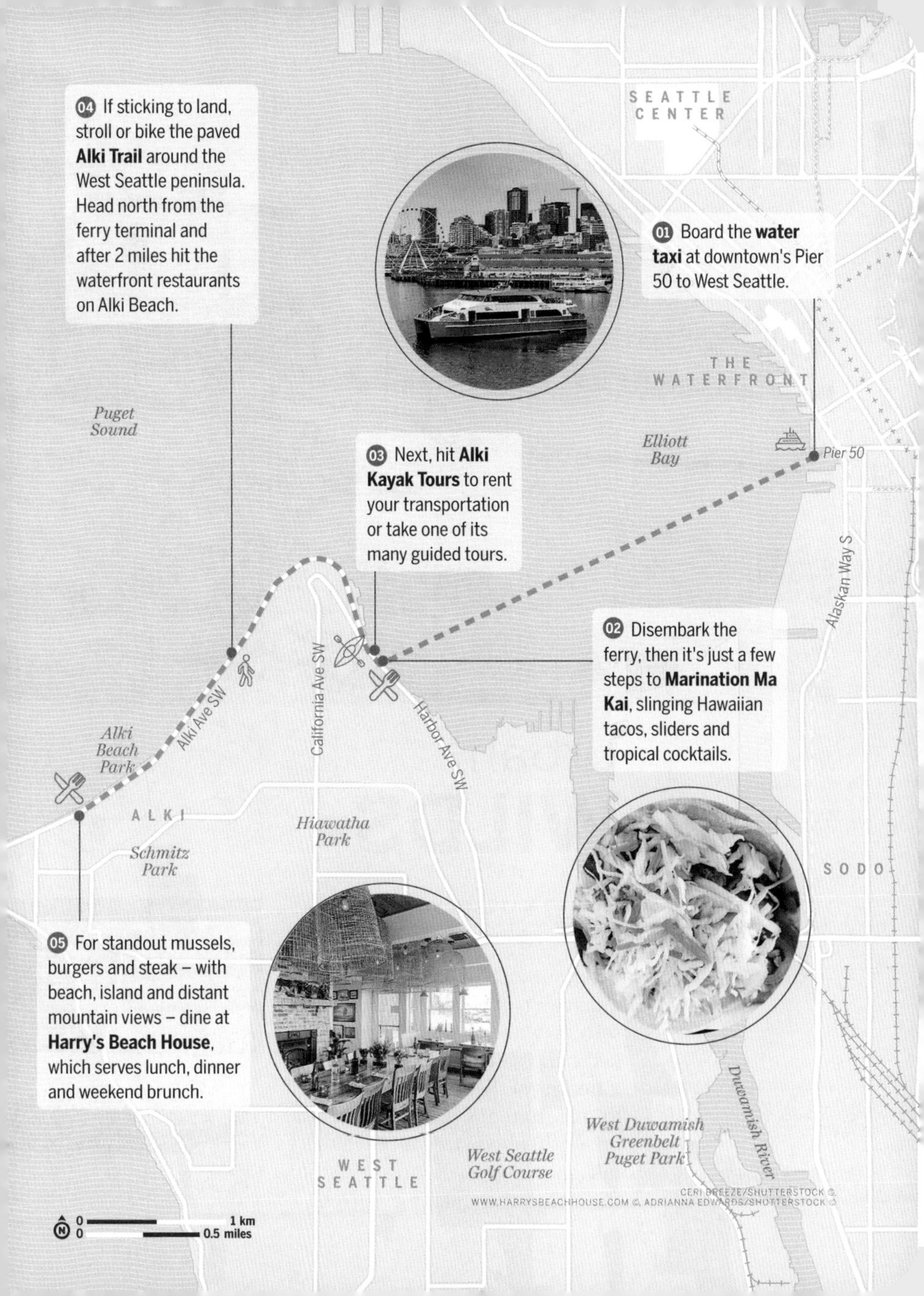
SEATTLE CENTER
THE WATERFRONT
Elliott Bay
Pier 50
Puget Sound
Alaskan Way S
Alki Ave SW
California Ave SW
Harbor Ave SW
Alki Beach Park
ALKI
Schmitz Park
Hiawatha Park
SODO
Duwamish River
West Duwamish Greenbelt Puget Park
West Seattle Golf Course
WEST SEATTLE
0 1 km
0 0.5 miles

04 If sticking to land, stroll or bike the paved **Alki Trail** around the West Seattle peninsula. Head north from the ferry terminal and after 2 miles hit the waterfront restaurants on Alki Beach.

01 Board the **water taxi** at downtown's Pier 50 to West Seattle.

03 Next, hit **Alki Kayak Tours** to rent your transportation or take one of its many guided tours.

02 Disembark the ferry, then it's just a few steps to **Marination Ma Kai**, slinging Hawaiian tacos, sliders and tropical cocktails.

05 For standout mussels, burgers and steak – with beach, island and distant mountain views – dine at **Harry's Beach House**, which serves lunch, dinner and weekend brunch.

07 Urban WILDS

HIKING | NATURE | VIEWS

Seattle has many things going for it. Chief among its best qualities is the city's spectacular setting, where steep hills meet lakes and saltwater, and where glimpses of distant mountains add drama. Here it's possible to stand on a driftwood-strewn beach or hike an old-growth forest right in the city limits – just for starters.

GARY IVES/SHUTTERSTOCK ©

How to

Getting here & around All of these experiences are set within Seattle city limits, making them accessible via public transport or ride-hailing companies.

When to go It's nearly always a great time to visit a park in Seattle, but you'll want to save picnics and water activities for warmer weather.

Brave the rain Bring good rain gear with you if you visit outside summer. If you don't mind going outdoors when it's damp, your fortitude will be rewarded with quieter trails and more chances to spot wildlife.

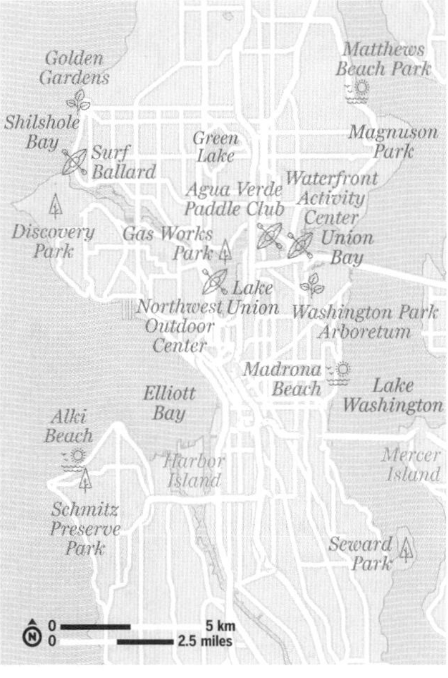
Golden Gardens
Matthews Beach Park
Shilshole Bay
Surf Ballard
Green Lake
Magnuson Park
Waterfront Activity Center
Agua Verde Paddle Club
Discovery Park
Gas Works Park
Union Bay
Lake Union
Northwest Outdoor Center
Washington Park Arboretum
Madrona Beach
Lake Washington
Elliott Bay
Alki Beach
Harbor Island
Mercer Island
Schmitz Preserve Park
Seward Park
0 5 km
0 2.5 miles

Get on the Water

There are so many ways to get on a boat in Seattle. Paddle a canoe or kayak from the University of Washington's **Waterfront Activity Center** over to the marshes of the Arboretum, keeping an eye out for bald eagles and otters.

The **Green Lake Boathouse** rents an array of watercraft on this small lake ringed by a park and walking path. Try kayaks, pedal boats, paddleboards and water bikes. Or if lounging is more your speed, there are also water hammocks for rent.

With a view of the skyline and floatplanes zipping overhead, **Lake Union** often feels like the city's playground. Explore its houseboat-studded shorelines via kayak or paddleboard from the **Northwest Outdoor Center** or from **Agua Verde Paddle Club** – whose sibling restaurant is a great spot for Mexican food after your paddle.

Left Kayakers, Lake Union
Above left West Point Lighthouse (p65)

Near the edge of Puget Sound, **Surf Ballard** rents kayaks and stand-up paddleboards. From here, paddle in view of the Olympic Mountains and try to spot friendly harbor seals.

Have a Picnic

Picnics at **Gas Works Park** are lovely any day the sun's out, but time your visit with the costumed Duck Dodge regatta every Tuesday night from May through September. Otherwise, the Seattle skyline, Kite Hill and the steampunk-esque former gasification plant are worthy draws.

Sunsets at **Golden Gardens** are practically legendary in Seattle. Set up on the sandy beach and prepare to watch the sun slip behind the Olympic Mountains.

The many stretches of grass at **Volunteer Park** are complemented by huge shade trees. There are plenty of picnic tables here, and enough room to toss a football or Frisbee.

Hit the Beach

A long stretch of sand facing Puget Sound, **Alki Beach** and the accompanying multi-use path frequented by roller skaters call to mind images of Southern California. It's a great place to walk, beachcomb or eat an ice cream.

Lake Washington's many beaches include **Madrona Beach**, a patch of sand with a lifeguard posted in summer. The water hits the perfect temperature in late summer.

Another gem fronting Puget Sound, **Lincoln Park** has a paved beach walkway and plenty of benches and picnic space for lingering.

Billed as the city's largest freshwater bathing beach, **Matthews Beach Park** on Lake Washington has 100ft of sandy shoreline.

It's Wild Out There

Seattle's many green spaces harbor a range of wildlife. Sharp-eyed visitors might spot seals, otters, bald eagles, coyotes, beavers, foxes and bats throughout the city – but especially in the parks. There are even occasional reports of mountain lions in Discovery Park, but not to worry: chances of actually meeting one are very low.

CAPTIVE COOKIE/SHUTTERSTOCK ©

Take a Hike

The **Washington Park Arboretum** occupies a verdant swath of central Seattle. There's something to see year round here, with trails that traverse through winter gardens, incredible displays of spring and summer flowers, and plenty of fall color. There are also boardwalks through wetlands on the northern fringe of the park.

Sticking out like a thumb into Lake Washington, the 300 forested acres of **Seward Park** feel remote. That's thanks to old-growth trees and quiet trails, where hikers have plenty of room to spread out. Don't miss the views of Mt Rainier from near the tennis courts.

Seattle's largest city park at 534 acres, **Discovery Park** has many trails, windswept bluffs, **West Point Lighthouse** and driftwood beaches that give it a wild personality.

The trails at **Schmitz Preserve Park**, wedged in a deep ravine in West Seattle, follow idyllic Schmitz Creek through mossy old growth.

DENISE LETT/SHUTTERSTOCK ©

Left Lincoln Park **Above top** Bald eagle **Above** Washington Park Arboretum

Listings

BEST OF THE REST

Seafood & Oysters

Local Tide $$

Various seafood-centric indulgences like a salmon BLT, an over-stuffed crab roll, and fried oysters are the draw here. Also offers a few lighter dishes and a darn good smash burger for anyone not feeling fish.

RockCreek Seafood & Spirits $$$

Seafood gets upscale treatment at RockCreek, which is designed to look like a fancy fishing lodge. Beautifully plated crab, bass, prawns and oysters pair with top-notch cocktails.

Walrus and the Carpenter $$$

Come early and be patient; the food is worth the wait. Piles of raw oysters, fancy approaches to locally sourced seafood, European cheeses and local vegetables are all noteworthy.

Taylor Shellfish Oyster Bar $$

Slurp locally raised oysters (and a range of other shellfish) paired with local wine and beer. The experts here know their stuff and can guide your experience.

Seattle Fish Guys $$

This small market sells Hawaiian poke bowls, clam chowder, oyster shooters, smoked salmon on baguette with cream cheese, and sashimi. The shop can also overnight anything you buy fresh.

Manolin $$

The flavors of the Yucatan shine here, with dishes like tuna tartare with peppers and jicama, and rockfish ceviche with avocado. Save room for dessert: the caramelized banana cake with rum whip is tops.

Caffeine Purveyors

Tougo Coffee $

In addition to straight-up coffee, Tougo also crafts coffee cocktails (booze-free), with various bitters and other mix-ins. There's also a great selection of baked goods from local artisans.

Boon Boona Coffee $

Eritrea-born owner Efrem Fesaha wants to put African coffee culture front and center. That means sourcing beans from small farms in Africa, which the company roasts in its facility south of the city.

Cafe Avole $

Focusing on Ethiopia's rich coffee culture, Cafe Avole uses a traditional *jebena* (coffee-pot) to steep its grounds, resulting in a bold but clean flavor.

Espresso Vivace $

One of the mainstays of Seattle coffee, Espresso Vivace absolutely nails espresso. The Cafe Nico is sublime with its additions of orange, vanilla and cinnamon.

Dungeness crab, Taylor Shellfish Oyster Bar

Phin $

There's no espresso machine here, just the namesake *phin*, a coffee filter used widely in Vietnam. It's accompanied by housemade ingredients like condensed milk and yogurt.

Hello Em $

This spot draws a line consistently, but it's worth the wait for indulgent *ca phe trung*, a Vietnamese specialty of coffee topped with sweetened egg cream. Don't miss the banh mi sandwiches and pastries.

Milstead and Co $

The big windows framing the steel undergirding of the Aurora Bridge are one draw, but the coffee is also consistently fantastic.

Fabulous Viewpoints

Kerry Park

Crowds descend on Kerry Park's viewpoint on sunny days. From here, the Space Needle sits front-and-center amid downtown's highrises, and Mt Rainier's glacier-studded cliffs loom large in the background. Its alpenglow adds drama during sunset.

Smith Tower

This historic, pencil-shaped building oozes vintage charm. The observation deck has 360-degree city views and a speakeasy bar.

Space Needle

Seattle's architectural icon has been remodeled and outfitted with a glass floor, so in addition to sweeping views, you can also stare down the startling 600ft to the ground.

Sky View Observatory

The observation level at the imposing onyx Columbia Tower claims the title as the tallest in the Pacific Northwest. Any visit is sure to impress, but come for sunset to ogle the 360-degree views from this incredible place.

JON BILOUS/SHUTTERSTOCK ©

Kerry Park

Volunteer Park Water Tower

Climb 107 steps to the top of this 1906 structure. Peek out over the surrounding Capitol Hill neighborhood to spot distant mountains.

In-Demand Dining

Saint Bread $$

Set in a former waterfront machine shop, Saint Bread praises all things carbohydrate. The tricked-out toasts and sandwiches complement the selection of pastries. Order to-go or eat at the covered picnic tables.

Rachel's Bagels and Burritos $$

Seattle is gripped by bagel mania, and some of the best can be found at Rachel's. And then there are the burritos, which come stuffed with an entire pound of goodness.

Kamonegi $$

Diners pack in tight for handmade soba noodles and tempura, all perfectly executed. Try the sake and fermented snacks next door at the sibling bar, Hannyatou.

Off Alley $$

Wedge yourself into this narrow space, where you'll sit at a counter with just a few others and partake of an ever-changing menu that puts underappreciated cuts of meat and offal on center stage.

Musang $$

Musang's focus is flavors from the Philippines, which it transforms to great effect in creative dishes. Weekend brunch, lunch and dinner timeslots are highly sought after.

Stateside $$

Southeast Asian flavors get modern plating and innovative twists here, with standouts like the crispy duck fresh rolls, chili cumin pork ribs, and goat curry. The cocktails are likewise tropical.

Zylberschtein's $$

This north Seattle Jewish deli has built a following for its fantastic menu of sandwiches, bagels and pastries. The meaty Reuben sandwich is a major draw: there's also a vegan tofu version.

Meesha $$

Meesha makes modern Indian food that eschews the dishes you can easily find elsewhere. Instead, you'll find Indian ingredients and additions borrowed from other cultures, too, like burrata and shishito peppers.

Joule $$

This steakhouse leans on bold Korean flavors, and sharing a table full of plates is encouraged. Kalbi short ribs with grilled kimchi, black cod with a gochugaru crust, and spicy rice cakes with chorizo are standouts.

Communion $$

This boisterous restaurant presents a mash-up of Seattle influences, from Asian to African American to Pacific Northwest. That translates to a catfish po-boy/banh mi, sauteed clams and mussels, and chili sauce wings.

Phnom Penh Noodle House $$

Long-running Phnom Penh Noodle House celebrates the flavors of Cambodia, with top dishes like chicken wings, noodle soups and crab fried rice.

Nue $$

This globe-trotting restaurant serves a handful of global street-food favorites consistently (like South African bunny chow, pineapple cornbread, Chengdu chicken wings, and Balinese BBQ spare ribs) alongside exciting specials. Stellar cocktail list.

Lady Jaye $$

Lady Jaye enthusiastically smokes everything from its burgers to its bourbon. Some dishes are reminiscent of traditional BBQ, but gussied up, like the bulgogi short-rib melt, smoked tofu chili, and smoked jalapeno kale caesar.

Jewelry & Vintage Clothing

Baleen

This jewelry store's specialty is modern and minimalist hoop earrings and layering chain necklaces. The shop uses recycled materials and saves scrap pieces for more recycling.

Throwbacks NW

Specializing in vintage sportswear, Throwbacks NW stocks quality jerseys, hats and memorabilia from bygone teams and eras. Seattle sports is at the center, but you'll find plenty of other cities represented, too, plus the occasional non-sports item.

FREMONT VINTAGE MALL ©

Fremont Vintage Mall

Fremont Vintage Mall

Packed with a range of vintage wonders. Whether you're hunting for those Disney mugs your grandmother had, an ironic cat sculpture or a great pair of cowboy boots, this place has a little bit of everything.

Lucky Dry Goods

Get nostalgic for your '80s prom dress at Lucky Dry Goods, where dressier vintage items rule the shop. The well-curated collection means shoppers avoid endless rack-sorting. For more casual wear, try the sibling Lucky Vintage shop.

Hitchcock Madrona

Specializing in jewelry and clothing, Hitchcock has honed its vision over the years to focus solely on items designed by its two owners. They change the entire space on a yearly basis, so just visiting to browse is an adventure in itself.

Supply Chain

Female artists are the focus at Supply Chain, which sources jewelry, bags and scarves from around the world. Local craftswomen also have a significant presence.

Cocktail Destinations

Deep Dive $$

This high-end cocktail lounge draws inspiration from hotel bars, with dark wood and upholstered banquets. The cocktails are also well designed, with a good nonalcoholic selection too.

Rumba and Inside Passage $$

Seven hundred rum options line the walls at Rumba, a 1950s island-inspired bar with a food menu of tacos and empanadas. Hidden behind Rumba is sibling bar Inside Passage, where you'll sip tiki cocktails under a giant octopus sculpture.

HARIS KENJAR/DEEP DIVE BAR ©

Deep Dive

Life on Mars $$

Life on Mars spins vinyl at the bar, and guests are encouraged to pick a record from the wall to help set the mood. The alcoholic cocktails are great, while the nonalcoholic options are thoughtful. The food menu – entirely vegan – caps it off.

Hotel Albatross $$

Over-the-top tiki drinks are served in ridiculous vessels that are as much a conversation starter as the dangerously drinkable booze. Wide-ranging food menu.

Rob Roy $$

Rob Roy mixes classic cocktails in a dark lounge space. This is where booze snobs and cocktail purists can get their fix. There are also playful touches like Goldfish crackers and instant ramen as snacks.

Navy Strength $$

Navy Strength leans into its tropical decor with plenty of rum drinks and mai tais. The rotating 'travel' menu traverses the globe, stopping off in places like the Mississippi Delta and Brazil to inspire new drinks and food.

Scan to find more things to do in Seattle online

NORTHWEST WASHINGTON & SAN JUAN ISLANDS

FOOD | NATURE | DAY TRIPS

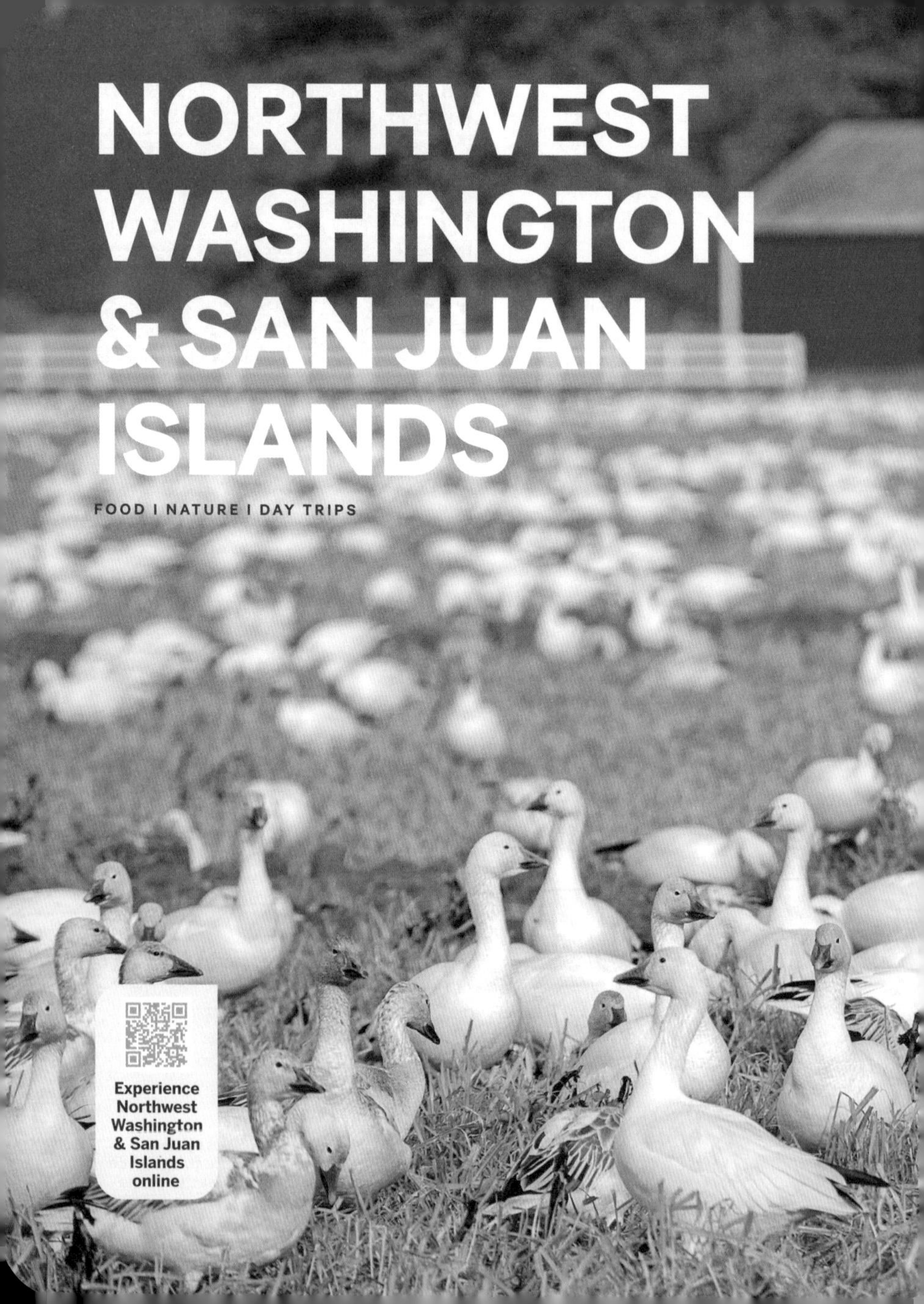

Experience Northwest Washington & San Juan Islands online

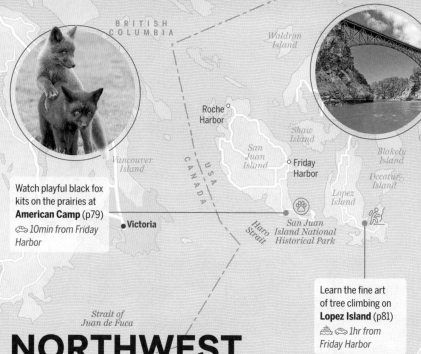

BRITISH COLUMBIA
Waldron Island
Roche Harbor
Shaw Island
San Juan Island
Friday Harbor
Blakely Island
Cypress Island
Decatur Island
Vancouver Island
USA
CANADA
Lopez Island
Victoria
Haro Strait
San Juan Island National Historical Park
Strait of Juan de Fuca
Coupeville
Freshwater Bay
Port Townsend

Watch playful black fox kits on the prairies at **American Camp** (p79)
10min from Friday Harbor

Learn the fine art of tree climbing on **Lopez Island** (p81)
1hr from Friday Harbor

Wander the meditative spaces at **Earth Sanctuary** (p87)
25min from Coupeville

NORTHWEST WASHINGTON & SAN JUAN ISLANDS

Trip Builder

Forested mountain foothills give way to rich farmlands and a scenic coastline dotted with islands and dramatic sunsets. Charming towns feature a myriad of pleasures that engage the senses, from artistic attractions to nature adventures and locally grown culinary delights.

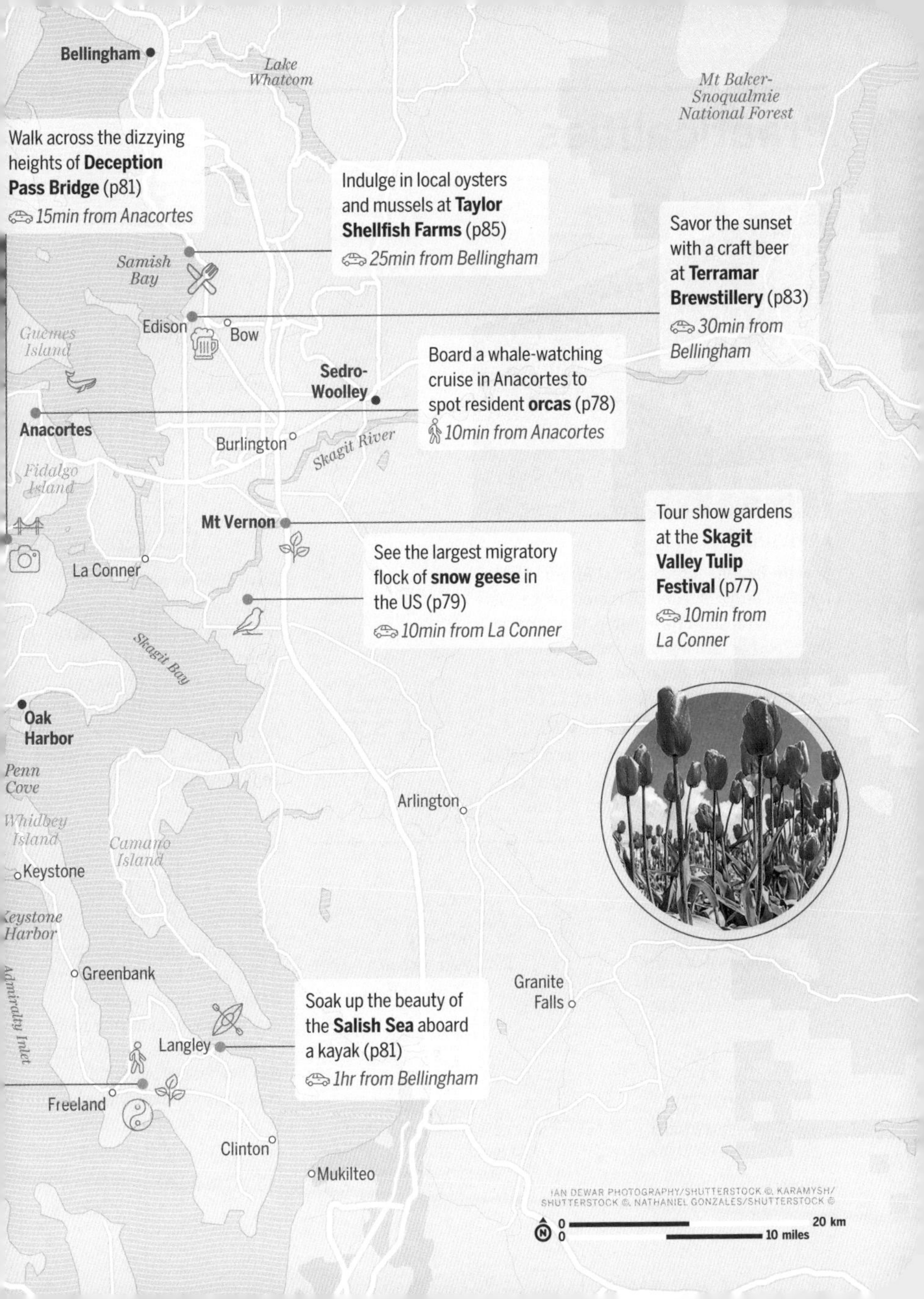
Bellingham
Lake Whatcom
Mt Baker-Snoqualmie National Forest
Walk across the dizzying heights of **Deception Pass Bridge** (p81)
15min from Anacortes
Indulge in local oysters and mussels at **Taylor Shellfish Farms** (p85)
25min from Bellingham
Savor the sunset with a craft beer at **Terramar Brewstillery** (p83)
30min from Bellingham
Samish Bay
Edison
Bow
Guemes Island
Sedro-Woolley
Board a whale-watching cruise in Anacortes to spot resident **orcas** (p78)
10min from Anacortes
Anacortes
Burlington
Skagit River
Fidalgo Island
Mt Vernon
Tour show gardens at the **Skagit Valley Tulip Festival** (p77)
10min from La Conner
La Conner
See the largest migratory flock of **snow geese** in the US (p79)
10min from La Conner
Skagit Bay
Oak Harbor
Penn Cove
Whidbey Island
Camano Island
Arlington
Keystone
Keystone Harbor
Greenbank
Admiralty Inlet
Granite Falls
Soak up the beauty of the **Salish Sea** aboard a kayak (p81)
1hr from Bellingham
Langley
Freeland
Clinton
Mukilteo
0 20 km
0 10 miles

Practicalities

Seattle-Tacoma Internation
Gate 8

MAX.KU/SHUTTERSTOCK ©

ARRIVING

Seattle-Tacoma International Airport Most travelers arrive here, which is around two hours from Northwestern Washington. Rent a car at the airport or take a shuttle (airporter.com) from the airport or downtown Seattle with drop-offs at Burlington, Anacortes, La Conner and Bellingham ($47 to $55 one-way).

Other points of entry To land on its doorstep, choose Bellingham International Airport or Paine Field. Amtrak also services the area.

HOW MUCH FOR A...

latte
$6

craft cocktail
$12

burger
$12

WHEN TO GO

JUL–SEP
Clear skies, warm, with occasional rain and wildfire smoke

OCT–DEC
Temperate with rain, possibly snow

JAN–FEB
Rainy and cold, possibly snow

MAR–JUN
Mix of sunshine and rain, mild temperatures, good for avoiding crowds

GETTING AROUND

Car Renting a car is the most convenient way to get around.

Ferry The only way to get to the islands (unless you have a boat); car, bike, motorcycle and walk-on options. All San Juan Island ferries (wsdot.wa.gov) depart from Anacortes (make reservations) and arrive at Friday Harbor, Orcas Island, Shaw Island and Lopez Island.

Train & bus Amtrak has stops in Stanwood, Mount Vernon and Bellingham. Buses serve the region's main communities with regular service via Skagit Transit, San Juan Transit and Whatcom Transportation Authority. Buses offer bike racks. Orcas Island Shuttle offers on-demand requests.

EATING & DRINKING

Puget Sound spot shrimp is the largest shrimp in the sound. It can be grilled, sauteed and fried, but locals prefer boiled to perfection and ready to peel and eat. A Pacific Northwest staple, mussels add flavor to chowders and elegant pasta dishes with white-wine sauce. Whether it's smoked, grilled or pan-fried, salmon is the ultimate signature seafood of the Pacific Northwest. The love of craft beer runs deep; sample a pint from one of the area's many craft breweries.

Best seafood
Shrimp Shack (p81; pictured top)

Must-try mead
Garden Path Fermentation (p83)

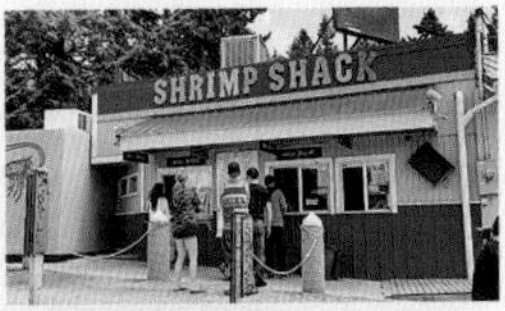
SHRIMP SHACK

CONNECT & FIND YOUR WAY

Wi-fi There is good reception throughout most of the region with the exception of some places in the islands and the Cascades.

Navigation Tourist centers and visitor bureaus offer useful information, including brochures on things to do, itineraries and maps.

STATE PARK PASSES

Get full access to state parks and order online or purchase at select parks. Discover Pass ($35 annual; discoverpass.wa.gov); day pass ($11.50).

WHERE TO STAY

With its wide mix of accommodations, Bellingham makes for a good home base. In destination towns like Anacortes, La Conner and Friday Harbor, accommodations book up fast in summer.

Location	Pro/Con
Anacortes	Historic waterfront town with shopping, dining and marina. Most accommodations on main street. Pricey in-season. Nightlife ends early.
La Conner	Waterfront town that's a good base for Skagit Valley exploration. A handful of B&Bs and inns. Pricey in season. Don't expect late-night nightlife.
Friday Harbor	Most island accommodations based here. Walking distance from ferry, shops and dining. Pricey in season.
Bellingham	Mix of accommodations at all price points. Can get very busy.

MONEY

Most businesses accept credit cards and ATMs are plentiful. Cash is good to have on hand for farmers markets, park day passes, and vendors who do not accept cards.

08 Floral BONANZA

NATURE | FAMILY | DAY TRIP

Discover the joys of tiptoeing through spring flowers in the Skagit Valley and beyond. First to arrive are daffodils, more than 1000 acres of bright-yellow petals. Then, tulips in every color imaginable, painting the fields like a canvas. Come July, the heavenly blossoms move to San Juan Island, where you can bask in fragrant fields of velvety lavender.

THE IMAGE PARTY/SHUTTERSTOCK ©

How to

Getting around It's best to experience the fields by car. In summer, a trolley stops at the lavender farm (fridayharborjolly trolley.com).

When to go Daffodils March, tulips April, lavender July. Check the RoozenGaarde Bloom Map (tulips.com/bloommap). Visit tulip fields on weekdays to avoid crowds.

Tulip fun Explore the month-long tulip festival activities (tulip festival.org).

Other info Come prepared with a rain jacket and suitable boots. Tulip show gardens charge a fee ($5 to $15 based on age).

OLESEATTLE/SHUTTERSTOCK ©

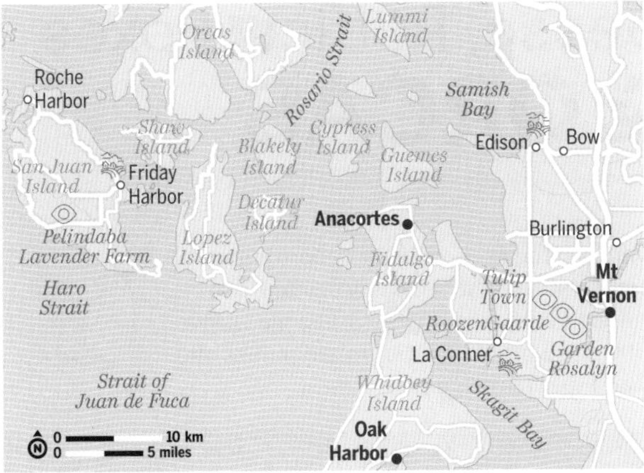
Orcas Island
Lummi Island
Roche Harbor
Rosario Strait
Samish Bay
Shaw Island
Cypress Island
Blakely Island
Guemes Island
Edison
Bow
San Juan Island
Friday Harbor
Decatur Island
Anacortes
Burlington
Pelindaba Lavender Farm
Lopez Island
Fidalgo Island
Mt Vernon
Haro Strait
Tulip Town
RoozenGaarde
La Conner
Garden Rosalyn
Strait of Juan de Fuca
Whidbey Island
Skagit Bay
Oak Harbor
0 10 km
0 5 miles

Daffodils With no official walking fields of the daffodil varieties grown (Dutch Master, Flower Cart and Standard Value), you'll need to explore on your own self-guided driving route. Make a day of it by touring the fields in the morning, then grabbing lunch in the charming town of **La Conner**. Afterward, explore boutique shops or participate in the #laconnerdaffodils photo contest.

Tulips The **Skagit Valley Tulip Festival** draws up to 500,000 visitors each April, and with good reason: the rows of tulips are stunning. While the fields are free to view, pay a little extra to walk the tulip fields and tour the world-class show gardens at **RoozenGaarde**, **Tulip Town** or **Garden Rosalyn**. Go petal deep by signing up for an all-day photograph pass for exclusive access to the fields or a mini tulip-picking workshop taught by the pros (tuliptown.com; tulips.com). Join a guided 2½-hour bicycle ride through the fields, meet local artists, taste local ales and eats (expint.org).

Lavender Open 24 hours, the fields at **Pelindaba Lavender Farm** (pelindabalavender.com) offer plenty of opportunities to capture that dreamy Instagram-worthy photo. While lavender nibbles – lemonade, ice cream, cookies – are available for purchase at the farm, there are no cafes nearby. Grab a bite to-go in **Friday Harbor** and enjoy a picnic among the blooms. The farm store brings more aromatic delights with handcrafted lavender products and demonstrations.

Far left top Tulips, RoozenGaarde **Far left bottom** Pelindaba Lavender Farm

Edison

Don't miss this charming town tucked within the Skagit Valley's agricultural heartlands, where you can pick up an award-winning loaf of bread at the **Breadfarm**; see some of the best Pacific Northwest art around at **Smith & Vallee Gallery**; and enjoy locally sourced gourmet food, such as wood-fired pizzas made with local grains and toppings at **Terramar Brewstillery** – not to mention beer, cider and spirits, all made with seasonal ingredients. On a sunny day, find a spot outside and take in the views of Samish Bay. The best part – you can visit all three within a two-minute walk! For a unique and fun event, come to the **Edison Chicken Parade** in February.

■ **Tips from Connor Harron,** *Director, Bike Northwest, Experience International, Rural Whatcom County @experienceintl*

09 Geese, Puffins, Foxes **& ORCAS**

WILDLIFE I ISLANDS I NATURE

Nature enthusiasts will love the extraordinary opportunities to see wildlife in their natural habitat. Some are easily spotted, like snow geese, trumpeter swans, and bald eagles. Others, like the elusive black fox, require good timing and a bit of luck. For tufted puffins and orcas, a sea adventure with an experienced guide is a must.

ZZ PHOTOGRAPHY/SHUTTERSTOCK ©

How to

When to go Snow geese, October to February. Tufted puffins, April to August. Whale-watching cruises, typically February to October.

Before you arrive Download the Great Washington State Birding Trail map (wa.audubon.org). Discover the special role Washington's Southern Resident Killer Whales have in the Salish Sea ecosystem and conservation efforts (whaleresearch.com).

On the water Wear layers as temperatures can drop more than 10 degrees. Bring binoculars, a camera and sunscreen.

DANITA DELIMONT/SHUTTERSTOCK ©

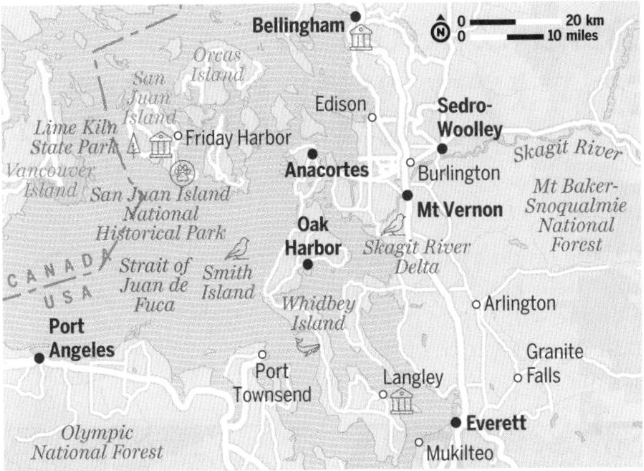
Bellingham
0 20 km
0 10 miles
Orcas Island
San Juan Island
Edison
Sedro-Woolley
Lime Kiln State Park
Friday Harbor
Skagit River
Vancouver Island
Anacortes
Burlington
San Juan Island National Historical Park
Mt Vernon
Mt Baker-Snoqualmie National Forest
Oak Harbor
Skagit River Delta
CANADA
USA
Strait of Juan de Fuca
Smith Island
Whidbey Island
Arlington
Port Angeles
Granite Falls
Port Townsend
Langley
Everett
Olympic National Forest
Mukilteo

Birding haven More than 362 species of birds migrate to **Skagit River Delta** each winter. With numbers reaching 50,000, snow geese make the largest gathering in North America. White with black wingtips and a wingspan of more than 4ft, they dominate the fields. Learn from birding experts through educational programs, tours and hikes (skagit audubon.org; birdsofwinter.org; skagitguidedadventures.com).

Get educated about migration and conservation through a priceless mounted bird collection at the John M Edson Hall of Birds in the **Whatcom Museum** in Bellingham.

Puffin' around Scout for these colorful sea parrots who nest on **Smith Island** on a naturalist-led boat tour (whales.com).

Extraordinary creatures San Juan Island is home to an unusual sight – black foxes. Glimpse this rare color variation at **San Juan Island National Historical Park** in the spring. Bring your binoculars and scan several dens stretching from American Camp to South Beach as the kits (red and black) come out to play.

Whale signs Behold the gentle giants of the sea on a whale excursion with **Island Adventures** or **Deception Pass Tours**, or onshore at **Lime Kiln State Park**. Visit the **Whale Museum** in Friday Harbor and **Langley Whale Center** to learn more about Washington's resident orca whales, names and family trees.

Far left top Orcas, Puget Sound
Far left bottom Snow geese, Skagit River Delta

Whalabration

With at least five official Whale Trail stops (the whaletrail.org), up your odds of a whale encounter from shore on scenic **Whidbey Island** (whidbeycamanoislands.com). Hop aboard a whale excursion with Deception Pass Tours for a glimpse water-side. In Langley (visitlangley.com), learn the mysteries of whales at the **Langley Whale Center** from Orca Network (orcanetwork.org) volunteers. Check out the whiteboard that notes daily whale sightings. In spring, join the celebration of the gray whale migration in the **Welcome the Whales** parade. Every year, they stop in Saratoga Passage on their journey from the Baja Peninsula to the Bering Sea. If you see a whale, ring the town's whale bell!

Tips by Sherrye Wyatt, *Writer, Whidbey Island*
@gowhidbeycamanoislands

10 Inland & Island ADVENTURES

LAND I WATER I ADVENTURE

Thrill-seeking families and outdoor enthusiasts are sure to find an adventure that suits their mood. Swoop down a 660ft zipline. Unleash your inner Viking with a spot of axe throwing. Test your climbing skills on a 200ft tree. Hike one of the many scenic trails. Or spend an idyllic day out on the water kayaking.

ADVENTURETERRA ©

How to

Getting around The best way to get around is by driving.

Ferry Reserve your spot for travel to the islands in advance (wsdot.wa.gov). Arrive 45 minutes before departurc; they will give spots away.

Hiking dos Be prepared. Wear sturdy shoes and sunscreen. Bring plenty of water and a hat.

Passes A day pass ($11.50) or Discover Pass ($35; discoverpass.wa.gov) is required to visit state parks.

EDMUND LOWE PHOTOGRAPHY/SHUTTERSTOCK ©

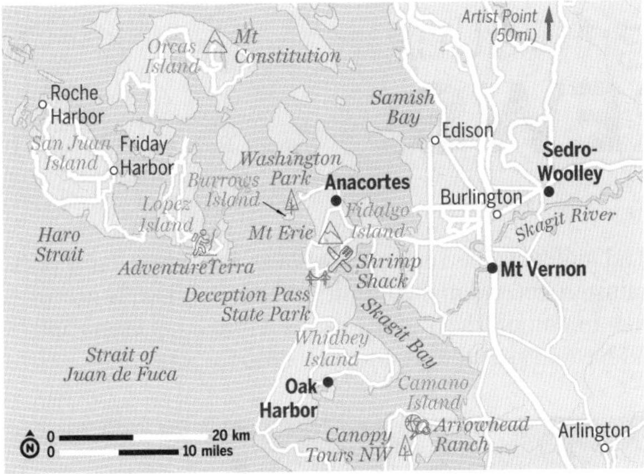

Artist Point (50mi)
Orcas Island
Mt Constitution
Roche Harbor
Samish Bay
Edison
San Juan Island
Friday Harbor
Sedro-Woolley
Washington Park
Burrows Island
Anacortes
Burlington
Lopez Island
Fidalgo Island
Skagit River
Haro Strait
Mt Erie
AdventureTerra
Shrimp Shack
Mt Vernon
Deception Pass State Park
Skagit Bay
Whidbey Island
Strait of Juan de Fuca
Oak Harbor
Camano Island
Arrowhead Ranch
Arlington
Canopy Tours NW
0 20 km
0 10 miles

Scenic thrills Undoubtedly one of the best viewpoints in the state, **Artist Point** offers views of Mt Baker and Mt Shuksan. Snow lasts through early summer, so be prepared to hike to the upper parking lot. Located on two islands (Whidbey and Fidalgo), **Deception Pass State Park** is connected by **Deception Pass Bridge**, the most photographed bridge in the state. Walk across its dizzying heights or hike one of the park's trails. Grab lunch at the **Shrimp Shack**. Drive or hike up to **Mt Erie**, where you can gaze over valleys, mountains and islands. No trip to the San Juan Islands (visitsanjuans.com) is complete without driving to the top of **Mt Constitution**. From the highest point in the islands, the spectacular views may just inspire you to extend your trip.

Land Thrills Take your love of trees to a limb level by learning the fine art of tree-canopy climbing with **AdventureTerra** (adventureterra.com) on Lopez Island. Discover the thrill of axe throwing at **Arrowhead Ranch** (arrowheadranchcamano.com) on Camano Island, or experience heart-pumping ziplines through a lush forest at **Canopy Tours NW** (canopytoursnw.com). Afterward eat at **Tapped Camano**.

Water thrills Soak up the beauty of the Salish Sea by kayak. Many guides offer day and multi-day tours, and some like **Anacortes Kayak Tours** (anacorteskayaktours.com) and **Whidbey Island Kayaking** (whidbeyislandkayaking.com) also offer bioluminescence tours.

Far left top AdventureTerra tree-canopy climbing **Far left bottom** Kayaking, Salish Sea

Island Playground

Families and outdoor adventurers will love **Fidalgo Island**. Join a guided sea-kayak adventure around uninhabited **Burrows Island** and enjoy incredible views, including of a lighthouse, while searching for whales. Head to **Deception Pass State Park** for a professionally guided sea-kayak trip at **Bowman Bay** and look for marine mammals and other wildlife. On the Whidbey Island side of the park, rent paddleboards or kayaks to explore **Cranberry Lake**. Back on Fidalgo Island, make the short hike to **Whistle Lake**, the locals' favorite swimming hole. Bring a picnic and hike the trails. **Washington Park** has quiet forest paths with gorgeous panoramic vistas of the San Juan Islands.

■ **Tips by Megan Schorr,** *owner, Anacortes Kayak Tours*
@anacorteskayaktours

11 Skagit Valley BREWS

BEER I CULINARY I DAY TRIP

If the Skagit Valley had an official beverage, it'd be beer. But not just any beer. It'd be a pint made with grains grown and malted right in the valley, locally grown hops, and water sourced from mountain rivers and streams. From crisp lagers and silky stouts to hazy IPAs and barrel-aged saisons, there's a drop for all palates.

WWW.TERRAMARCRAFT.COM ©

Trip Notes

Getting around The ale trail runs from the Cascade foothills to Fidalgo Island. Pick a home base, and explore safely by car.

Home base The majority of breweries are tucked between the towns of Burlington, Mount Vernon and La Conner.

Get stamped! Gamify your beer-hopping and earn a souvenir with passport stamps (skagitfarmtopint.com); purchase is not necessary.

Paws & pints Most breweries on the ale trail are fido-friendly.

Hop-Story

Washington State is the nation's top hops producer, with most crops grown in Eastern Washington. Local farmers are reviving the tradition in the Skagit Valley (hopskagit.com). Washingtonian State boasts more than 400 craft breweries, and a little over a dozen are located in the Skagit Valley.

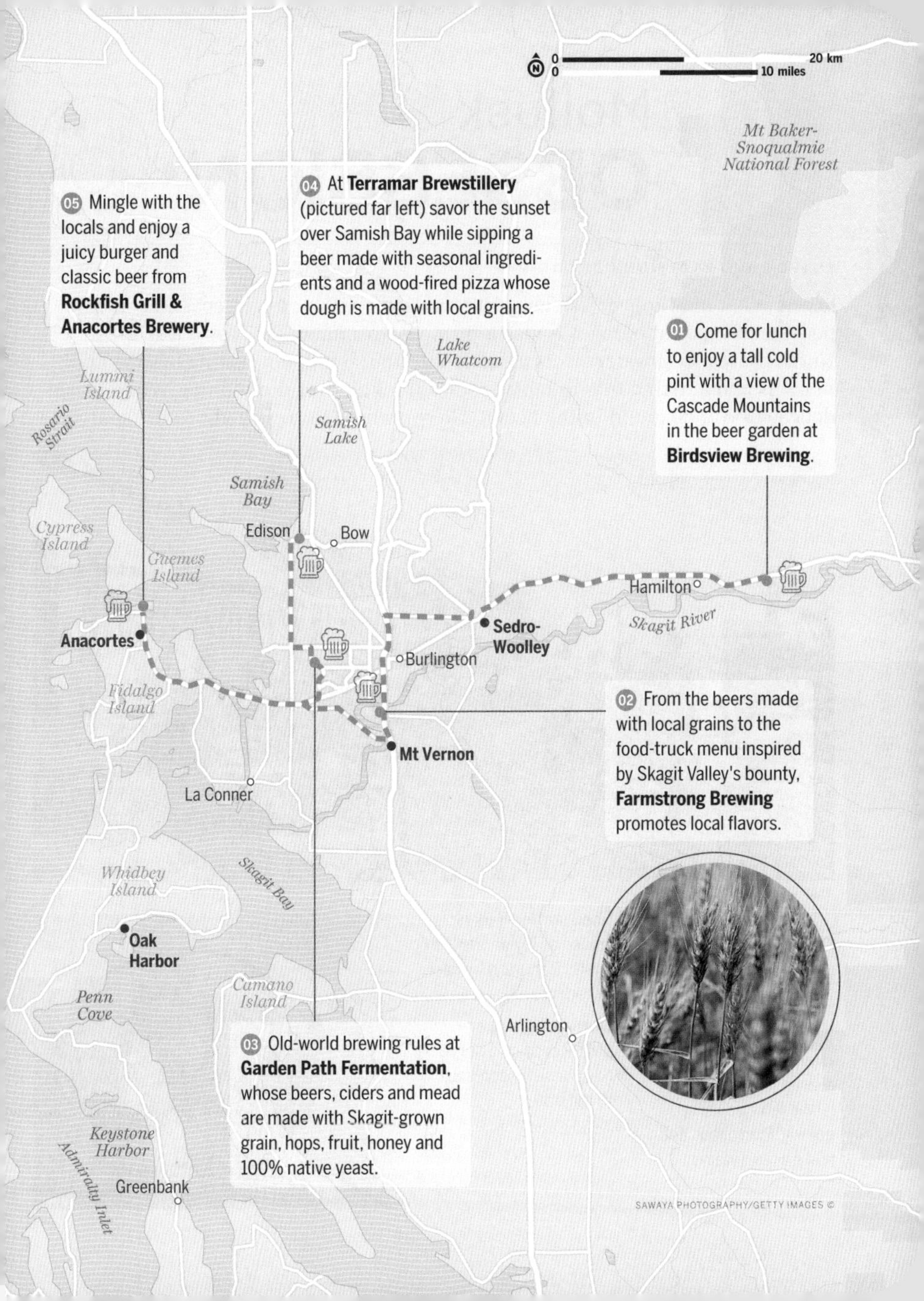

0 20 km
0 10 miles
Mt Baker-Snoqualmie National Forest
Lake Whatcom
Lummi Island
Rosario Strait
Samish Lake
Samish Bay
Cypress Island
Guemes Island
Edison
Bow
Hamilton
Skagit River
Sedro-Woolley
Anacortes
Burlington
Fidalgo Island
Mt Vernon
La Conner
Whidbey Island
Skagit Bay
Oak Harbor
Camano Island
Penn Cove
Arlington
Keystone Harbor
Admiralty Inlet
Greenbank

01 Come for lunch to enjoy a tall cold pint with a view of the Cascade Mountains in the beer garden at **Birdsview Brewing**.

02 From the beers made with local grains to the food-truck menu inspired by Skagit Valley's bounty, **Farmstrong Brewing** promotes local flavors.

03 Old-world brewing rules at **Garden Path Fermentation**, whose beers, ciders and mead are made with Skagit-grown grain, hops, fruit, honey and 100% native yeast.

04 At **Terramar Brewstillery** (pictured far left) savor the sunset over Samish Bay while sipping a beer made with seasonal ingredients and a wood-fired pizza whose dough is made with local grains.

05 Mingle with the locals and enjoy a juicy burger and classic beer from **Rockfish Grill & Anacortes Brewery**.

SAWAYA PHOTOGRAPHY/GETTY IMAGES ©

12 Mollusk OBSESSION

SEAFOOD I TRADITION I DAY TRIP

What may appear like an idyllic seascape with a rugged coastline and pockets of exposed beaches is also a prime environment for growing shellfish. Nutrient-rich freshwater rivers cascade into the sound, nourishing oysters and mussels and enticing tide-to-table foodies from all over the country. While these delicacies can be found in the big city, here's where to go straight to the source.

STEPHANIE BRACONNIER/SHUTTERSTOCK ©

How to

Getting around Shellfish farms are in remote locations, and the best way to reach them is by car.

Island time During peak season, the San Juan Island ferry books up quickly. Plan ahead and make a reservation.

Shell station Parking is limited at Taylor Shellfish Oyster Bar. You may have to park nearby and walk.

Clamouflage Wear layers, even on a sunny day; it can be cool next to the water.

DOUGLAS PEEBLES/GETTY IMAGES ©

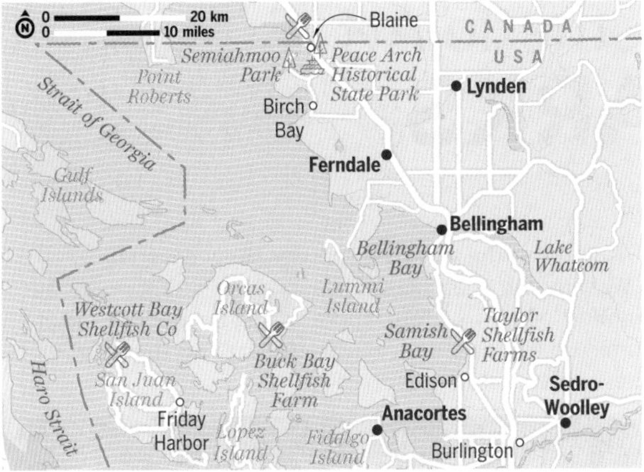
0 20 km
0 10 miles
Blaine
CANADA
USA
Semiahmoo Park
Peace Arch Historical State Park
Point Roberts
Lynden
Strait of Georgia
Birch Bay
Ferndale
Gulf Islands
Bellingham
Bellingham Bay
Lake Whatcom
Orcas Island
Lummi Island
Westcott Bay Shellfish Co
Taylor Shellfish Farms
Samish Bay
Buck Bay Shellfish Farm
Haro Strait
San Juan Island
Edison
Sedro-Woolley
Friday Harbor
Anacortes
Lopez Island
Fidalgo Island
Burlington

Far left top Taylor Shellfish, Chuckanut Dr **Far left bottom** Bucket of oysters, Taylor Shellfish Farms

Coastal eats While **Taylor Shellfish Farms** (taylorshellfish farms.com) has three oyster bars in Seattle, if you drive two-hours north to the Samish Oyster Bar along Chuckanut Dr (one of the most scenic roads in the state), you'll be at the heart of its operation. Hang out for a while, savoring an oyster tray with a local beer and admiring the gorgeous views.

Run by a father-and-son duo with a serious passion for oysters, **Drayton Harbor Oyster Bar** (draytonharboroysters.com) in Blaine serves up tide-tumbled oysters in a cozy rustic bar. Try the grilled Draytons with savory focaccia bread and plan to visit the 67ft grandeur of the peace arch at **Peace Arch Historical State Park** near Blaine (Day Pass or Discover Pass required).

Island eats Sip your favorite vino while indulging in oysters at **Buck Bay Shellfish Farm** (buckbayshellfishfarm.com) on Orcas Island. The farm is open seasonally. Pick a picnic table overlooking the farm and slip into island time.

Take a farm tour at **Westcott Bay Shellfish Co** (westcottbayshellfish.com) on San Juan Island. Armed with an appreciation of the seed to harvest process, relish those mollusk mouthfuls at lunch.

Join fellow mussel aficionados as they descend upon Coupeville to satiate their appetite at **Musselfest** (thepenncovemusselsfestival.com) in March. With Penn Cove Shellfish as the star, indulge in all things mussels: sample mussel creations, participate in the chowder tasting, and tour ($15) the farm.

A Day in Blaine

This undiscovered corner of Washington lets you walk among Salish Sea history. Head to the public pier to see local fishermen haul out Dungeness crab and oysters. In the summer, hop aboard the historic **Plover Ferry** to Semiahmoo Spit and explore the beaches and trails of **Semiahmoo Park**. Back in town, taste what makes our waters so unique at **Drayton Harbor Oyster Company**, where my father and I serve up a tide-to-table menu with fresh oysters 13 minutes from the water and within view of the farm. I suggest pairing your oysters alongside a hyper-local craft beer or wine, perhaps relishing the brine and silky notes of Blaine's own Atwood Ales Oyster Stout, made with, you guessed it, Drayton Harbor Oysters.

■ **Tips by Mark Seymour,** *owner/operator, Drayton Harbor Oyster Company @draytonharboroysterfarm*

13 Aesthetic Art PARKS

ART I NATURE I RELAXATION

From its windswept islands all the way to its craggy snow-covered mountains, Northwestern Washington is bathed in beauty. Maybe that's why the arts flourish in even the smallest of towns. Here, appreciating art doesn't mean a day stuck inside a museum. You can experience beautiful art and the glory of Mother Nature at one of these three outdoor art parks.

MICHAEL STADLER ©

How to

Getting around The art parks are near small towns or in remote locations, and the best way to get here is by car.

Art apparel Plan for outdoor weather, bring sturdy shoes, a hat and sunscreen.

Cash is king Have cash on hand for donations. For Earth Sanctuary, pay in advance and put the receipt on your car dashboard ($7 per person).

Doggie don'ts Dogs are not allowed at the parks.

SAN JUAN ISLANDS
Sculpture Park

THE IMAGE PARTY/SHUTTERSTOCK ©

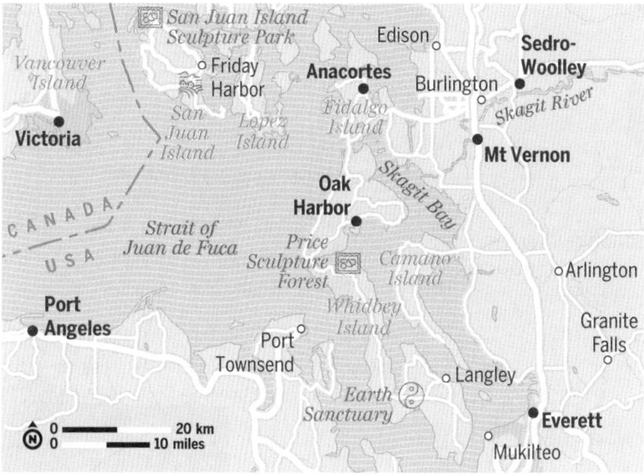
San Juan Island Sculpture Park
Edison
Sedro-Woolley
Vancouver Island
Friday Harbor
Anacortes
Burlington
Skagit River
Victoria
San Juan Island
Lopez Island
Fidalgo Island
Mt Vernon
Oak Harbor
Skagit Bay
CANADA
USA
Strait of Juan de Fuca
Price Sculpture Forest
Camano Island
Arlington
Port Angeles
Whidbey Island
Granite Falls
Port Townsend
Langley
Earth Sanctuary
Everett
Mukilteo
0 20 km
0 10 miles

Far left top Cottonwood Stone Circle, Earth Sanctuary **Far left bottom** San Juan Island Sculpture Park

Whidbey Island Built with multiple meditative spaces for personal reflection, **Earth Sanctuary** (earthsanctuary.org) on Whidbey Island is not a place to rush through. Let tranquility overtake you as you wander its 2 miles of paths through forests and marshes and past reflective ponds. Slip into a meditative mindset at its sacred sites, sculpture gardens, salal labyrinth, Buddhist stupa and Native American medicine wheel. Learn about the sanctuary's biodiversity on a naturalist-led tour, or relax on a meditative tour ($35 per hour, plus a $7 entry fee).

Also on Whidbey Island, the **Price Sculpture Forest** (sculptureforest.org) is an interactive display showcasing art and nature. Let curiosity be your guide as you meander through a 100-year-old forest investigating outdoor art. With the assistance of your phone, watch videos from the artists talking about the meaning of the sculptures and their creation process.

San Juan Island Take the ferry to San Juan Island to view more than 150 rotating sculptures at the **San Juan Island Sculpture Park** (sjisculpturepark.com). Spread across 20 acres, sculptures are tucked within meadowlands and forests. Spend the afternoon exploring its five trails, and before you leave, engrave your name on Friendship Totem. Close to the park is the trail to the John S McMillian Memorial Mausoleum. Built as a memorial, the columned and open-air rotunda gives off a peachy glow when hit by sunlight.

Islands & the Arts

Art flourishes on the islands. Along Friday Harbor's waterfront, you'll find a piece called *Interaction* by world-renowned Salish Coast artist Susan Point. In town are studios like the collective **Island Studios** and galleries like **Arctic Raven Gallery** featuring work from Arctic and Northwest Coast Native artists. Travelers can sign up for classes at **Alchemy Art Center**. Lovers of the written word will treasure Friday Harbor's poetry garden and the **Orcas Island Lit Fest** (June), which brings best-selling authors and readers together. Cinephiles won't be left wanting with the **Orcas Island Film Festival** (October), and if documentary films are your jam, the **Friday Harbor Film Festival** (October) is a must-attend.

■ **Amy Nesler,** *Stewardship & Communications Manager, San Juan Islands Visitor Bureau @visitsanjuans*

Listings

BEST OF THE REST

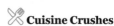

Cuisine Crushes

A'Town Bistro $$

Savor rustic food and cocktails inspired by the Prohibition era in a welcoming and unpretentious atmosphere. The made-to-order clam chowder is a signature dish.

Nell Thorn Waterfront Bistro & Bar $$

Enjoy farm-to-table Northwest fare and craft cocktails while taking in the views of the Swinomish Channel.

Oyster & Thistle $$

Grab a seat in this cozy English-style pub and order French-inspired cuisine with local ingredients from the Skagit Valley and Samish Bay.

Slough Foods $

Enjoy European favorites from this Italian-inspired cafe and delicatessen, including all-you-can-eat paella events in summer.

Duck Soup $$$

Dine at a cabin nestled in the woods and feast on the bounty of San Juan Island's produce and botanicals.

Whidbey Island Pies $

The place for the perfect slice; local marionberry is a must-try.

Roots Orcas Island $$

European-inspired wine bar with special tasting events where owners bring their island and worldly connections to you by the plate and glass.

Oystercatcher $$

The creative menu is a foodie lover's dream with hyper-local ingredients and delicious housemade bread.

Mijitas $$

The crab enchiladas are a must.

Dirty Dan Harris Steakhouse $$$

Named after a local legend, this place serves mouth-watering steaks and seafood.

Keenan's at the Pier $$$

Sip cocktails or dine on Northwest cuisine with Bellingham Bay and San Juan Islands views.

13moons $$$

On a sunny summer day, choose the patio and imbibe with views of the bay and Mt Baker.

Parks & Views

Cap Sante Park

Fantastic views east and west, including Mt Rainier on a clear day. A paved road to the top makes it easy for all to visit; free parking. Along the road on the north side is a trail that takes you to an old stone-built amphitheater.

Washington Park

Walk or drive the paved 2.3-mile loop or hike the trails for seaside vistas of the San Juan Islands and the Olympic Mountains. Free parking with several pull-out areas for cars.

Double Bluff Beach

A perfect beach escape, especially with your dog, as it's off-leash. You can see the Space Needle and the Olympic Mountains on a clear day. Free with limited parking.

Oyster Dome

Hike the 6.5-mile round trip trail to Samish Overlook for breathtaking views of the bay and islands. In ideal conditions, hang gliders and paragliders launch from here.

Fort Casey State Park

Explore a historic fort, tour Admiralty Lighthouse and watch huge tankers cruise through Admiralty Inlet.

Cattle Point Lighthouse

Hike the short trail through windswept grassy dunes to spectacular vistas and a lighthouse erected in 1935.

Unique Stays

Rosario Resort & Spa

Built by shipping magnate Robert Moran, the resort features a selection of accommodations and a family museum.

Leanto

Overnight in fully outfitted luxury glamping sites in Moran State Park on Orcas Island. No cell signal.

Comforts of Whidbey

Stay at this B&B, whose six opulent rooms are right above the winery tasting room and afford water or vineyard views.

Beer, Wine, Distilleries & Markets

Kulshan Brewing Company $

Kulshan's seasonal pop-up at Trackside is the place for summer fun with yard games and live performances.

Mutiny Bay Distillery $

The flavorful blueberry liqueur made with Mutiny Bay Blues is a local favorite.

Spoiled Dog Winery $

Pick up a bottle of the estate pinot noir, which has received many accolades.

Doe Bay Winery $$

While there are many wines to sample, try the 'Orcas Project' wines produced with acclaimed winemakers and vineyards.

Fort Casey State Park

3 Sisters Market

Discover all Whidbey Island offers, from artisan crafts and products to locally grown produce and meats.

Girl Meets Dirt

Taste Orcas Island's heritage fruit in the form of award-winning preserves, shrubs and jams.

Recharge

Chrysalis Inn & Spa

Experience the healing arts of Hawaiian *lomi lomi*, Japanese *ashiatsu* barefoot massage, reflexology, and craniosacral or other, more traditional, spa treatments.

Apothecary Wellness & Spa

Revitalize your body and mind with salt-room therapy, float-pod session, or more traditional spa treatments.

Flow Motion

Rejuvenate the mind and soul via a floor-to-ceiling Himalayan salt cave and sound baths, meditation, massage and therapeutic relaxation.

Scan to find more things to do in Northwest Washington & San Juan Islands online

WASHINGTON COAST

NATURE | HISTORY | CULINARY TRADITIONS

Experience Washington Coast online

WASHINGTON COAST
Trip Builder

Moss-laden rainforests and a rocky coastline strewn with pockets of sandy beaches, parks and remote trails beckon. Adding to the allure of Washington's Coast are its wild winter storms, culinary traditions, historic sites and welcoming small coastal towns.

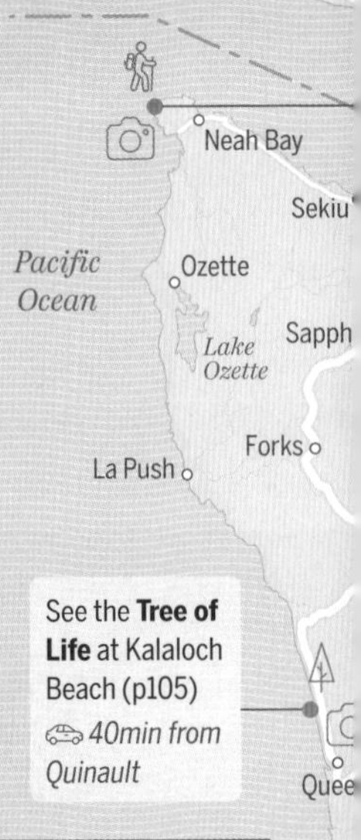
Neah Bay
Sekiu
Pacific Ocean
Ozette
Lake Ozette
Sapph
Forks
La Push
See the **Tree of Life** at Kalaloch Beach (p105)
40min from Quinault
Quee
Tahola

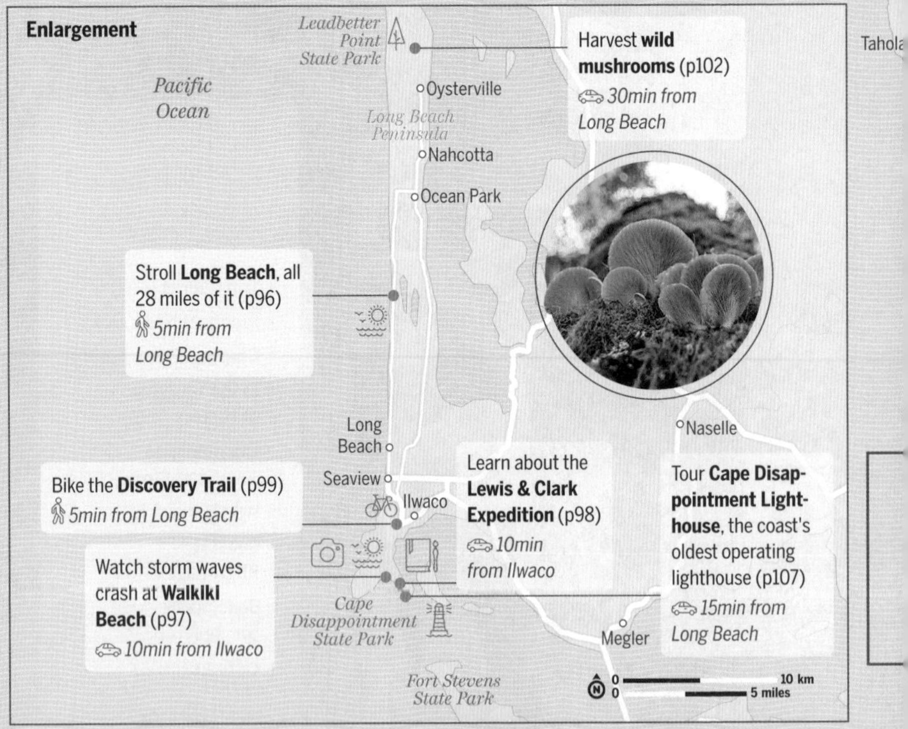
Enlargement
Leadbetter Point State Park
Pacific Ocean
Oysterville
Long Beach Peninsula
Nahcotta
Ocean Park
Harvest **wild mushrooms** (p102)
30min from Long Beach
Stroll **Long Beach**, all 28 miles of it (p96)
5min from Long Beach
Long Beach
Seaview
Ilwaco
Naselle
Bike the **Discovery Trail** (p99)
5min from Long Beach
Learn about the **Lewis & Clark Expedition** (p98)
10min from Ilwaco
Tour **Cape Disappointment Lighthouse**, the coast's oldest operating lighthouse (p107)
15min from Long Beach
Watch storm waves crash at **WaikIki Beach** (p97)
10min from Ilwaco
Cape Disappointment State Park
Megler
Fort Stevens State Park
0 10 km
0 5 miles

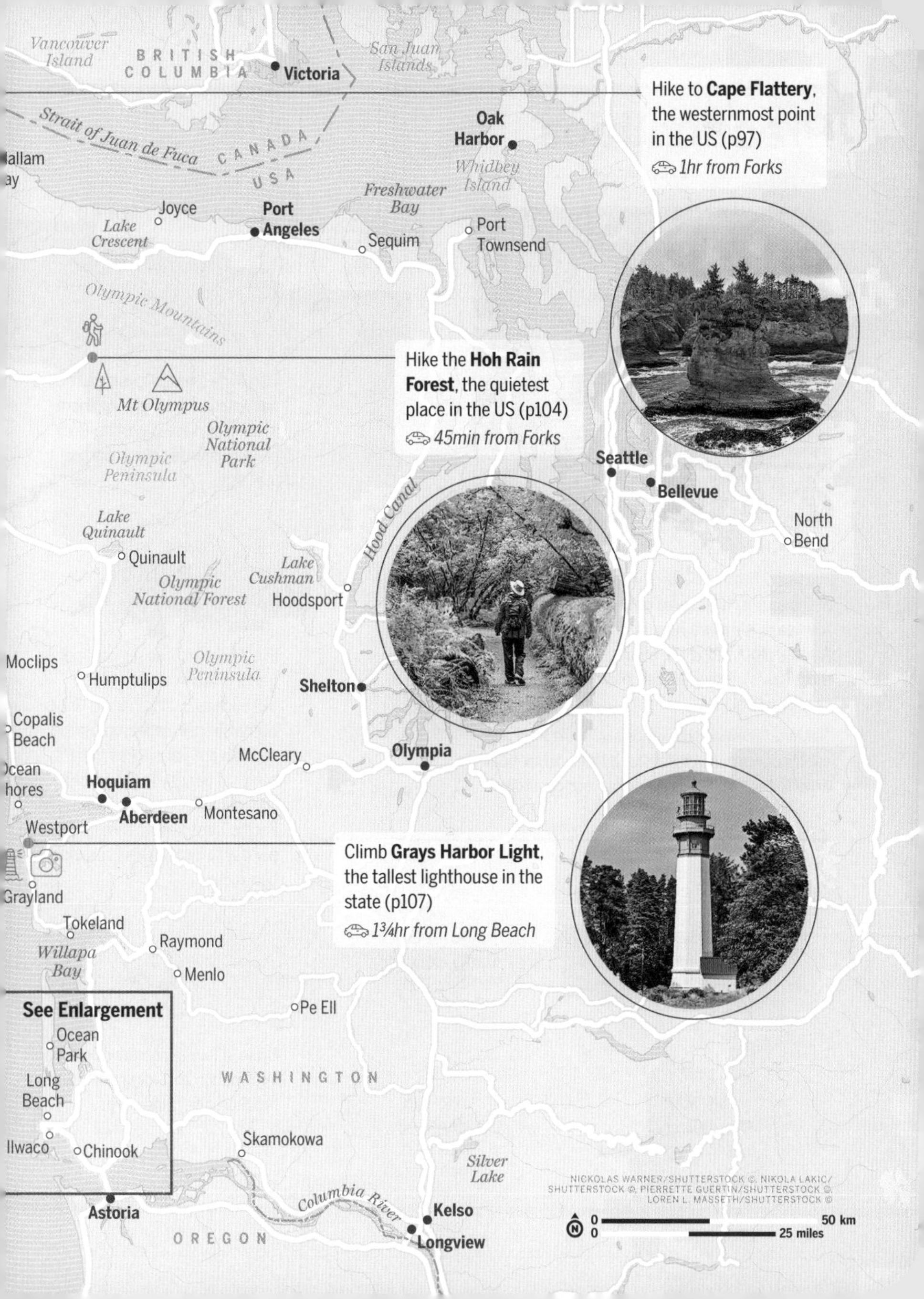
Vancouver Island
BRITISH COLUMBIA
Victoria
San Juan Islands
Strait of Juan de Fuca
CANADA
USA
Oak Harbor
Whidbey Island
Freshwater Bay
Joyce
Port Angeles
Lake Crescent
Sequim
Port Townsend
Olympic Mountains
Mt Olympus
Olympic National Park
Olympic Peninsula
Seattle
Bellevue
North Bend
Hood Canal
Lake Quinault
Quinault
Lake Cushman
Olympic National Forest
Hoodsport
Moclips
Humptulips
Olympic Peninsula
Shelton
Copalis Beach
McCleary
Olympia
Hoquiam
Aberdeen
Montesano
Westport
Grayland
Tokeland
Raymond
Willapa Bay
Menlo
Pe Ell
See Enlargement
Ocean Park
Long Beach
Ilwaco
Chinook
WASHINGTON
Skamokowa
Silver Lake
Columbia River
Astoria
Kelso
Longview
OREGON
0 50 km
0 25 miles

Hike to **Cape Flattery**, the westernmost point in the US (p97)
1hr from Forks

Hike the **Hoh Rain Forest**, the quietest place in the US (p104)
45min from Forks

Climb **Grays Harbor Light**, the tallest lighthouse in the state (p107)
1¾hr from Long Beach

NICKOLAS WARNER/SHUTTERSTOCK ©, NIKOLA LAKIC/SHUTTERSTOCK ©, PIERRETTE GUERTIN/SHUTTERSTOCK ©, LOREN L. MASSETH/SHUTTERSTOCK ©

Practicalities

VICTORIA DITKOVSKY/SHUTTERSTOCK ©

ARRIVING

Portland International Airport Renting a car at the airport is the best option for travel to the coast; it's a two-hour drive to Long Beach. Amtrak stops along the I-5 corridor; however, in most cases, getting to the coast via bus is not very practical.

Seattle-Tacoma International Airport Rent a car for onward travel. Plan for a three- to six-hour drive to the coast, depending on your destination.

HOW MUCH FOR A...

latte $5

craft cocktail $12

serve of fish & chips $10

WHEN TO GO

JUL–SEP
Warmest months of the year; high tourist season

OCT–DEC
Partly cloudy to rainy; cool

JAN–MAR
Overcast, cool and rainy

APR–JUN
Partly cloudy, with mild temperatures

GETTING AROUND

Car While smaller towns can be navigated on foot, getting there in the first place is best done by car, as distances along the coast are large.

Bus There are also regional public transportation options ($1 to $2) such as Pacific Transit, Grays Harbor Transit, Jefferson Transit and Clallam Transit. Point offers two trips per day to the Astoria Transfer Station ($18); from there Pacific Transit offers three trips per day to Ilwaco. Buses provide bike racks.

Bicycle Tourist centers offer useful information, including maps and brochures on things to do.

EATING & DRINKING

Seafood rules along the coast. Pacific razor clams (pictured top) are served in various ways – grilled, fried, steamed – and there's nothing quite like a hearty bowl of decadent West Coast–style chowder. Try oysters barbecued, smoked, fried or fresh on the half-shell with a dash of lemon and fresh herbs. Locally caught Dungeness crab also makes its way onto the menu. On a chilly day, warm up with a decadent Dungeness crab mac 'n' cheese.

Best flash-fried razor clams 42nd Street Cafe and Bistro (p103)

Must-try Leadbetter red Scottish ale North Jetty Brewing (p109)

WHERE TO STAY

From touristy beach towns to remote inland locations, you'll find a wide range of choices for every budget and desired accommodation style, including unique lodging choices.

Location	Pro/Con
Long Beach Peninsula	Motels, inns, hotels, vacation rentals. Some within walking distance of historic sites, shops, dining, beach. Pricey in season. Touristy.
Westport	Accommodations include water-side cottages, and a rustic surf camp. Some within walking distance of museums, parks, town, marina. Pricey in season.
Ocean Shores	Affordable. Most motels, inns, cottages within walking distance of shops, dining, beach. Touristy.
Forks	Affordable. Good overnight stop on northern region tours. Twilight attractions. Isolated. Few amenities.

CONNECT & FIND YOUR WAY

Wi-fi Along the more remote coastal areas and in Olympic National Park connecting to a signal can be difficult. Bring a portable phone charger and if possible download driving and trail maps to your phone.

Navigation Tourist centers offer useful information, including maps and brochures on things to do.

WEATHER-WISE

While the climate is typically mild year-round, and summers often reach 70°F (21°C), the weather can be unpredictable. Pack a raincoat, windbreaker, umbrella and layers.

MONEY

Most businesses take credit cards and towns have ATM machines. Have some cash on hand for day passes at parks and the occasional vendor who operates cash-only.

14 Chasing STORMS

NATURE I BEACHES I STORMS

Travelers searching for unforgettable experiences will go wild for Washington's storm-watching season. With the coast exposed to the open ocean, there are plentiful opportunities to witness Mother Nature's power first hand as the coast is bombarded with gale-force winds and massive waves that crash so high they seem to defy gravity.

How to

Getting around The coast is remote and rugged; it's best to explore by car.

Storm etiquette Heed the local saying, 'Never turn your back on the sea.' Bring a heavy and light rain jacket and waterproof boots. Stay away from driftwood and large logs.

Deals When the storms arrive, so do hotel deals.

Required You'll need passes for state parks (parks.wa.gov), the national park (nps.gov/olym) and the Makah Recreation Area (makah.com). Check ahead for closures.

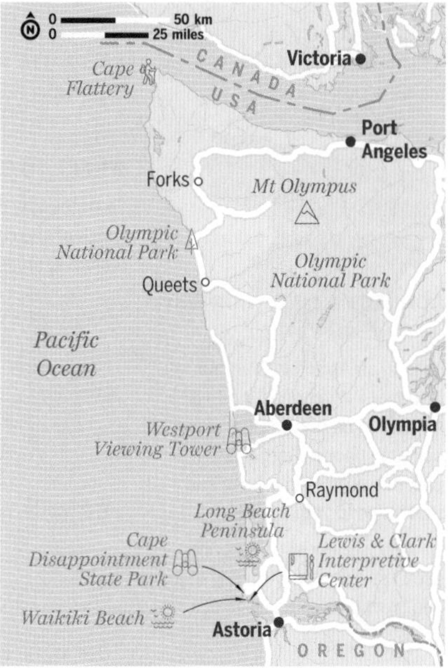
0 50 km
0 25 miles
CANADA
USA
Cape Flattery
Victoria
Port Angeles
Forks
Mt Olympus
Olympic National Park
Olympic National Park
Queets
Pacific Ocean
Aberdeen
Olympia
Westport Viewing Tower
Raymond
Long Beach Peninsula
Cape Disappointment State Park
Lewis & Clark Interpretive Center
Waikiki Beach
Astoria
OREGON

Every winter, storms pummel the coast from Cape Flattery all the way down to Cape Disappointment. It's a one-of-a-kind experience of huge winds, horizontal rain and magnificent crashing waves.

Long Beach Peninsula Bundle up and brace yourself for 28 miles of wind, sand and wave action. As you stroll the beach, let the full force of Mother Nature press against you, sometimes from all directions. At **Cape Disappointment State Park**, take in the scene from a height of 200ft in the comfort of the **Lewis & Clark Interpretive Center**. Afterwards, **Pickled Fish** (pickledfishrestaurant.com) is the only restaurant on the peninsula that overlooks the ocean; pick a table and enjoy the show.

Westport A safe enough distance away from waves pounding against the breakwall, but close enough to get kissed with salty surf, the **Westport Viewing Tower** doesn't disappoint. Wear a rain jacket and hear the roar

Storm Watching on the Peninsula

It's an exhilarating experience seeing 40ft waves, but it's also a dangerous one, so be cautious. Sneaker waves are real; they can overtop jetties, dunes and anything 50ft tall. The key is to stay alert and keep your distance. The 'holy grail' of storm watching is seeing an unusual wave phenomenon at Waikiki Beach at Cape Disappointment State Park. Massive waves hit the cliffs and bounce off, creating a wave that goes back to sea. A climatic splash occurs when this reflected wave meets an incoming wave at precisely the right time. To increase your odds, check the surf forecast for waves between 15ft and 20ft and visit in the hour before high tide. From the safety of the parking lot, watch the drama unfold.

■ Tips by Andi Day, *Andi Day Consulting, Destination Marketing & Management, Seaview*

of the storm on one of three open-air viewing platforms.

Olympic National Park To watch the storm surge against the coastline and crash against sea stacks, head to one of these beaches (some require a hike): **Second Beach**, **Ruby Beach**, **Rialto Beach**. Or enjoy the action while safely inside the **Creekside Restaurant at Kalaloch Lodge** (thekalalochlodge.com).

Neah Bay Don your boots and gators for the trek out to the cliffs overlooking **Cape Flattery**, whose rocky outcrops are slammed with impressive rushing waves.

Above Cape Disappointment State Park

15 In the Footsteps of HISTORY

HISTORY I NATURE I DAY TRIP

Washington's Columbia River and Pacific Coast are deeply tied to the Lewis and Clark Expedition. Travelers who love to explore historical spots will appreciate discovering their footsteps over a couple of leisurely days on Long Beach Peninsula.

SCULPTOR: JIM DEMETRO; IMAGE: SPRING IMAGES/ALAMY STOCK PHOTO ©

Lewis & Clark

On October 10, 1805, the Lewis and Clark Expedition paddled down the converging Snake and Clearwater Rivers. A month later, they'd gaze at the stormy waters of the Pacific Ocean at Cape Disappointment, marking the end of their 8000-mile journey. Eighty-four years later, Washington became a state.

Trip Notes

Getting around Long Beach's town center is easily explored on foot; you'll need a car to visit parks and remote attractions.

Two wheels Rent a bike, bring your own or stay at a hotel with complimentary beach cruisers.

Weatherwise Summers are cool, winters rainy; bring sweaters and rain gear.

Before arrival Download area maps to use offline (visitlongbeachpeninsula.com).

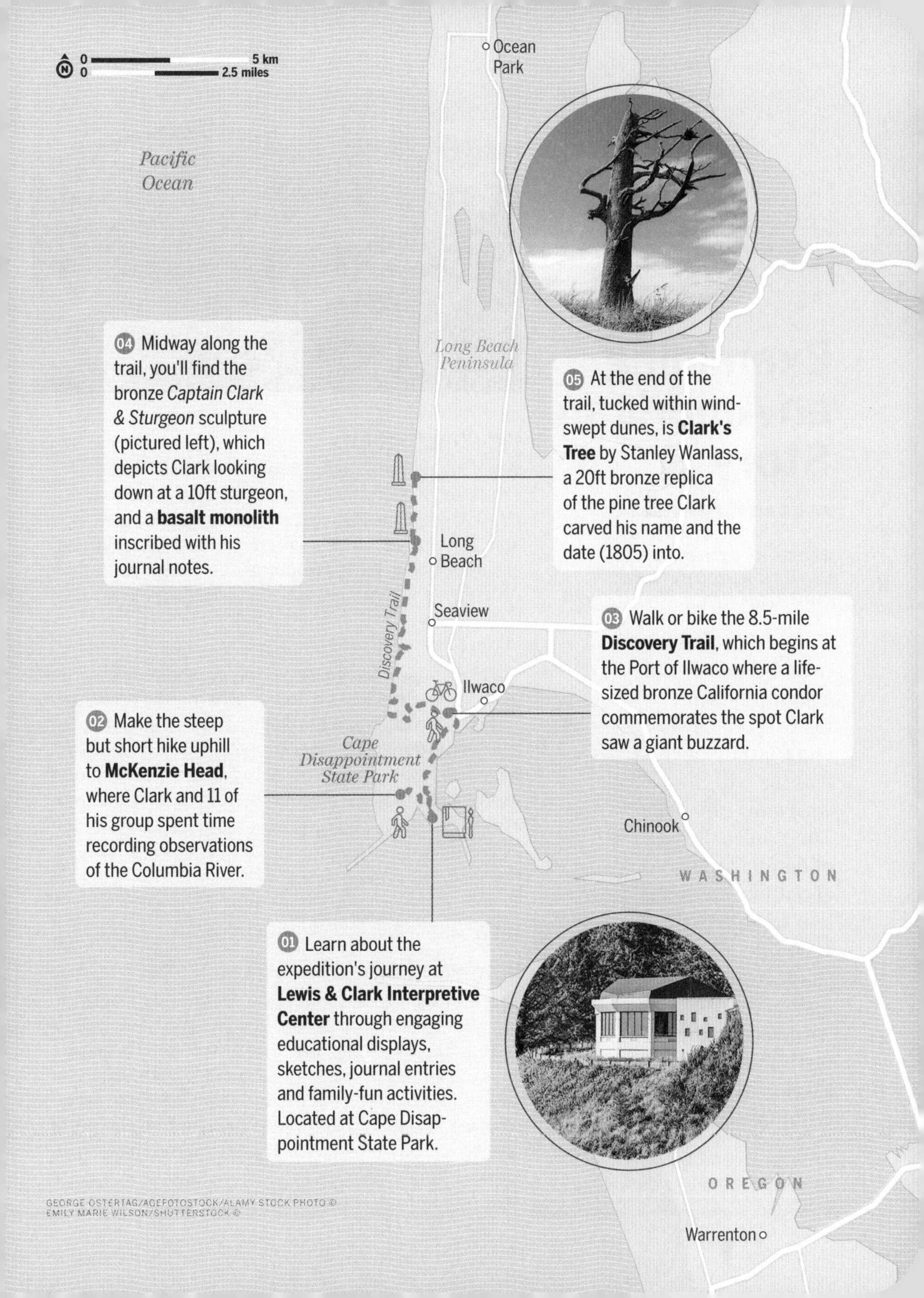
0 5 km
0 2.5 miles
Ocean Park
Pacific Ocean
Long Beach Peninsula
Long Beach
Seaview
Discovery Trail
Ilwaco
Cape Disappointment State Park
Chinook
WASHINGTON
OREGON
Warrenton

04 Midway along the trail, you'll find the bronze *Captain Clark & Sturgeon* sculpture (pictured left), which depicts Clark looking down at a 10ft sturgeon, and a **basalt monolith** inscribed with his journal notes.

05 At the end of the trail, tucked within wind-swept dunes, is **Clark's Tree** by Stanley Wanlass, a 20ft bronze replica of the pine tree Clark carved his name and the date (1805) into.

03 Walk or bike the 8.5-mile **Discovery Trail**, which begins at the Port of Ilwaco where a life-sized bronze California condor commemorates the spot Clark saw a giant buzzard.

02 Make the steep but short hike uphill to **McKenzie Head**, where Clark and 11 of his group spent time recording observations of the Columbia River.

01 Learn about the expedition's journey at **Lewis & Clark Interpretive Center** through engaging educational displays, sketches, journal entries and family-fun activities. Located at Cape Disappointment State Park.

Examining an American Story

RECONNECTING TO NATURE AND CULTURE THROUGH ART

Heralded as one of the most successful explorations in history, the Lewis and Clark Expedition laid the path for westward expansion. Their journals, full of detailed notes about plants, animals and tribes they encountered, helped shape American history. It also perpetuated the myth that Lewis and Clark 'discovered' the Columbia River.

Left Columbia River **Middle** Sacagawea statue, Fort Clatsop (p178) **Right** Vancouver Land Bridge art installation

EASTANDWEST/SHUTTERSTOCK ©

Retelling the Story

When the expedition's bicentennial approached, tribal elders and leaders, historians, and political and community leaders in the Pacific Northwest all agreed the Lewis and Clark Expedition story needed a more inclusive and accurate telling. While the journey laid the groundwork for America's economic growth and populating the west, for Native Americans, it brought a multitude of changes: loss of life, culture and land.

In 1999, by serendipitous coincidence, Antone Minthorn of the Confederated Tribes of the Umatilla Indian Reservation and Jane Jacobson came up with the same idea on the same day – enlist designer and sculptor Maya Lin, who designed the Vietnam Veterans Memorial, to build a series of outdoor art installations along the Columbia River and its tributaries.

Through these public art landscapes, people could explore another side of the Lewis and Clark story – one that included different voices and living cultures, and illustrated the resilience of the Indigenous peoples and the ecosystem of the Columbia River system.

Reconnecting to Tribal Voices

That melding of minds inspired the creation of Confluence, a nonprofit that 'connects people to the history, living cultures and ecology of the Columbia River system through Indigenous voices.' Developing the art installations was just the first step to accomplishing this mission. Confluence also delivers by collaborating with Northwest tribes and communities to offer educational programs and gatherings and have an extensive library that shares Indigenous stories, videos, audio and images on its website (confluenceproject.org).

SCULPTOR: JIM DEMETRO; IMAGE: K_Z/SHUTTERSTOCK ©

VAN ROSSEN/SHUTTERSTOCK ©

There are six art installations. Of the five completed ones, three are in Washington State and two in Oregon. Four of the five completed sites were designed by Lin; the fifth, the Vancouver Land Bridge, was designed by architect Johnpaul Jones with Lin consulting.

Confluence River Sites

The installation sites include the **Listening Circle** in Chief Timothy Park (Clarkston, WA); the **Story Circles** in Sacajawea State Park (Pasco, WA); the **Vancouver Land Bridge** (Vancouver, WA); a series of **art installations** in Cape Disappointment State Park (Ilwaco, WA); **Bird Blind** in the Sandy River Delta (Troutdale, OR); and **Celilo Park** (The Dalles, OR).

> While the expedition laid the groundwork for America's economic growth, for Native Americans, it brought a multitude of changes: loss of life, culture and land.

Lin selected these sites with great care, choosing locations that embody ecological, cultural, tribal and historical significance. Using the Expedition's extensive field notes as a guide, she researched well-documented meeting places between Expedition members and Indigenous tribes along the Columbia River.

Spread out over 438-miles along the Columbia River, the art installations are best explored over three or four days. Each river site is different yet similar in Lin's artistic approach in how it relates the environment to tribal memory, history, and culture. Find out more at confluenceproject.org and @confluencenw.

An American Legacy

In 1804, President Thomas Jefferson commissioned Meriwether Lewis and William Clark to explore the Louisiana Purchase, charting rivers, tracing boundaries and finding a navigable Northwest Passage across its 530 million acres. The expedition included an intrepid troupe of 45 members, including Clark's slave named York and a Native American woman named Sacagawea. They traveled from the Mississippi River to the Pacific Ocean and back home, an 8000-mile journey that took them more than two years to complete. Surprisingly, all but one survived. One of America's most famous expeditions, it provided detailed notes and invaluable scientific observations on the geography, flora, fauna and cultures encountered.

16 Wild HARVEST

CULINARY ARTS I CULTURE I TRADITION

The deep-rooted culinary traditions of foraging for wild mushrooms and digging for razor clams create a lot of delicious reasons to put the Long Beach Peninsula on your off-season travel itinerary. Bring a basket and a shovel and give it a go, or come to feast on these wild delicacies prepared by talented local chefs.

KNELSON20/SHUTTERSTOCK ©

How to

Getting around Driving is the best way to access remote locations.

Grab a shovel Razor clam digging is allowed a few days each month from October to April, set by the Washington Department of Fish and Wildlife.

Fall forage October 1 to November 15; varies. Download a mushroom guide (wildmushroom celebration.com). Foraging is not allowed at Cape Disappointment State Park.

Mushroom tip to live by When in doubt, throw it out.

BENOIT LEFEBVRE/SHUTTERSTOCK ©

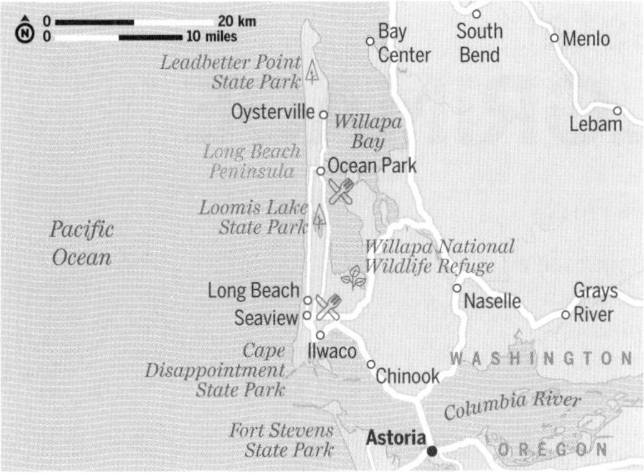
0 20 km
0 10 miles
Leadbetter Point State Park
Bay Center
South Bend
Menlo
Oysterville
Willapa Bay
Lebam
Long Beach Peninsula
Ocean Park
Loomis Lake State Park
Pacific Ocean
Willapa National Wildlife Refuge
Long Beach
Seaview
Naselle
Grays River
Cape Disappointment State Park
Ilwaco
Chinook
WASHINGTON
Columbia River
Fort Stevens State Park
Astoria
OREGON

Fall fungi When summer sunshine gives way to misty autumn mornings, Long Beach Peninsula's 43-sq-mile corner of the Pacific Northwest becomes a mushroom hunter's paradise. Foragers scour the forests at **Leadbetter Point State Park**, **Loomis Lake State Park** and **Willapa National Wildlife Refuge** searching for edible mushrooms like chanterelles, porcini, lobster, oyster and king boletes. Taste this bounty during the six-week culinary extravaganza at the **Wild Mushroom Celebration** (wildmushroomcelebration.com), where local restaurants feature savory mushroom masterpieces and events offer opportunities to forage with an expert hunter or to cook with a pro. Indulge in all things mushroom at the **Depot Restaurant**, whose wild mushroom and wine dinner is a local favorite; **42nd Street Cafe & Bistro** for an array of mushroom dishes from appetizers to entrees; and **MyCovio's** for mushroom-inspired creations with a modern twist.

Crazy about clams Razor clams are a Pacific Northwest delicacy and can grow up to 12in long and live up to 11 years. Digging dates are set by the Washington Department of Fish and Wildlife and the beach location (regions of Kalaloch, Mocrocks, Copalis, Twin Harbors, and Long Beach; permit required). Kitted out in rubber boots and rain gear, with a shovel, bucket, and clam 'gun,' digging is an unforgettable experience. Attend a razor-clam festival mid-April in Long Beach (longbeachrazorclamfestival.com) or mid-March in Ocean Shores (osrazorclamfestival.org). Sample clam fritters and clam chowder, learn how to dig, and more (olympic culinaryloop.com).

Far left top Clamming, Copalis Beach **Far left bottom** Cluster of wild mushrooms

Foodie Must-Dos

Pro hikes Join a ranger-led mushroom hike at Fort Stevens State Park in Oregon (stateparks.oregon.gov) or attend a two-hour foraging class in Seabrook (seabrookwa.com) in the fall.

Fritter love In Long Beach, grab a photo in front of 'World's Largest Fraying Pan' that commemorates the Razor Clam Festival making the 'World's Largest Clam Fritter' in 1940. Within squirting distance is the 'World's Largest Spitting Clam.'

Epicurean outing Drive and dine on the area's premier culinary food trail (olympicculinaryloop.com).

Learn to dig Take a clam digging lesson (longbeachrazorclamfestival.com).

Fungi love Learn how to identify, forage and cook mushrooms at the annual mushroom festival at Lake Quinalt Lodge each October.

17 Coastal PILGRIMAGE

NATURAL BEAUTY I BEACHES I HIKES

From a magical tree that seems to grow in mid-air to a moss-laden forest that is the quietest place in the United States, to spectacular beaches begging for a leisurely stroll, Washington's coast is a treasure trove of gems to explore. Take your time and visit them all over a long weekend.

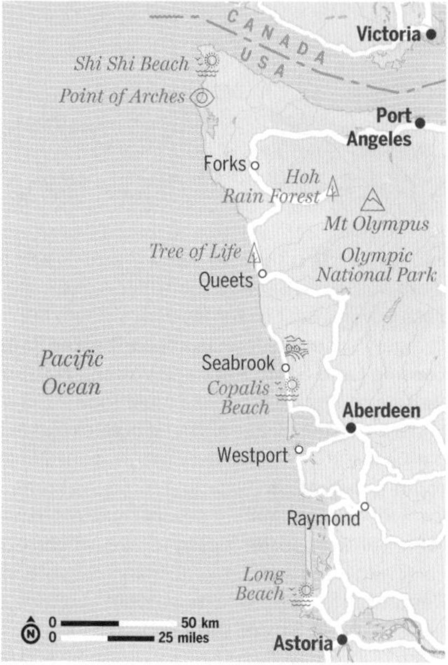

CANADA
USA
Victoria
Shi Shi Beach
Point of Arches
Port Angeles
Forks
Hoh Rain Forest
Mt Olympus
Tree of Life
Olympic National Park
Queets
Pacific Ocean
Seabrook
Copalis Beach
Aberdeen
Westport
Raymond
Long Beach
0 50 km
0 25 miles
Astoria

How to

Getting around Driving is the best way to experience the Olympic Peninsula.

The more you know Before you visit Olympic National Park, check operating hours (reduced in winter) and for weather-related closures.

Weather gear Bring a rain jacket, waterproof hiking boots, and pants. Stash dry socks in your car/pack. Bring a power bank.

Map tips Download the National Park Service maps to use offline.

Beaches Stretching for a glorious 28 miles, **Long Beach** is a sight to behold. As the world's longest beach on a peninsula, it is easily accessed but somehow never feels crowded. Go for a long walk. Bike or drive a car onto the hard-packed sand. Cozy up next to a beach bonfire. Let Fido run off-leash. Riptides are dangerous, so don't swim.

The 8-mile round-trip hike to **Shi Shi Beach** and the **Point of Arches** discourages the faint of heart. Once there, admire the seascape and investigate the tide pools. Bring food, plenty of water and know the tides. Park fees, plus a Makah Recreation Pass ($10) required.

Silence & spruce Break up the drive between Long Beach and Shi Shi Beach with these two Olympic National Park attractions. Relish the silence at the **Hoh Rain Forest**, the quietest

Exploring Seabrook

Perfect for families and pups, this coastal town is not to be missed. You may think it's a beach getaway, but there are plenty of outdoor activities, so bring your bikes and tennis rackets, and plan to rent clamming guns or skimboards, or take a surfing or kayak lesson. A cinnamon bun or cruffin at the **Vista Bakeshop** is a must-try; you might end up there every day. If you visit on a Saturday, learn about the town's new urbanism design with its founder on a **Seabrook Town Tour**. Make the 15-minute drive south to **Copalis Beach**, and drive your car right onto the sand. We bring our Nespresso machine and plug it in the back of our SUV to sip on lattes and watch the waves.

Tips by Terumi Pong, *travel writer,* An Emerald City Life *@helloterumi*

place in the US. Make the two-hour trek from the visitor center to this serene spot. Once you see a red stone on a moss-covered log, you've arrived. Next, drive west to the **Tree of Life**. Storm after storm, it continues to cling to the bluff's edge with its massive belly of exposed roots dangling in mid-air. Take the trail from Kalaloch Campground to the beach, and walk a short distance to the right. Bring snacks, and watch the sunset. Plan for an early start to conquer both.

Above Tree of Life

18 Beacons by THE SEA

ADVENTURE | HISTORY | DAY TRIP

Spend an unforgettable weekend exploring four stunning lighthouses along the Washington Coast. Join a guided tour to learn about their fascinating history and the keepers who made their living guiding sailors to safety, and savor the incredible seascape views.

POEMNIST/SHUTTERSTOCK ©

Trip Notes

Getting around Car is the best transportation. Some lighthouses require a hike.

Tours Some lighthouses offer tours; check ahead. In summer, Grays Harbor Light tours are by reservation only.

Unique stay Stay in a former lighthouse keeper's residency turned vacation rental (parks.wa.gov).

Required permits A Day or Discover Pass at state parks. At Cape Flattery, a Makah Recreation Pass (makah.com).

Graveyard of the Pacific

Navigating the dangerous waters at the convergence of the Columbia River and the Pacific Ocean has been a nightmare since 1792, claiming more than 2000 vessels and 700 lives. Discover the region's rich maritime history and stories at the **Columbia Pacific Heritage Museum** (columbiapacific heritagemuseum.org) in Ilwaco.

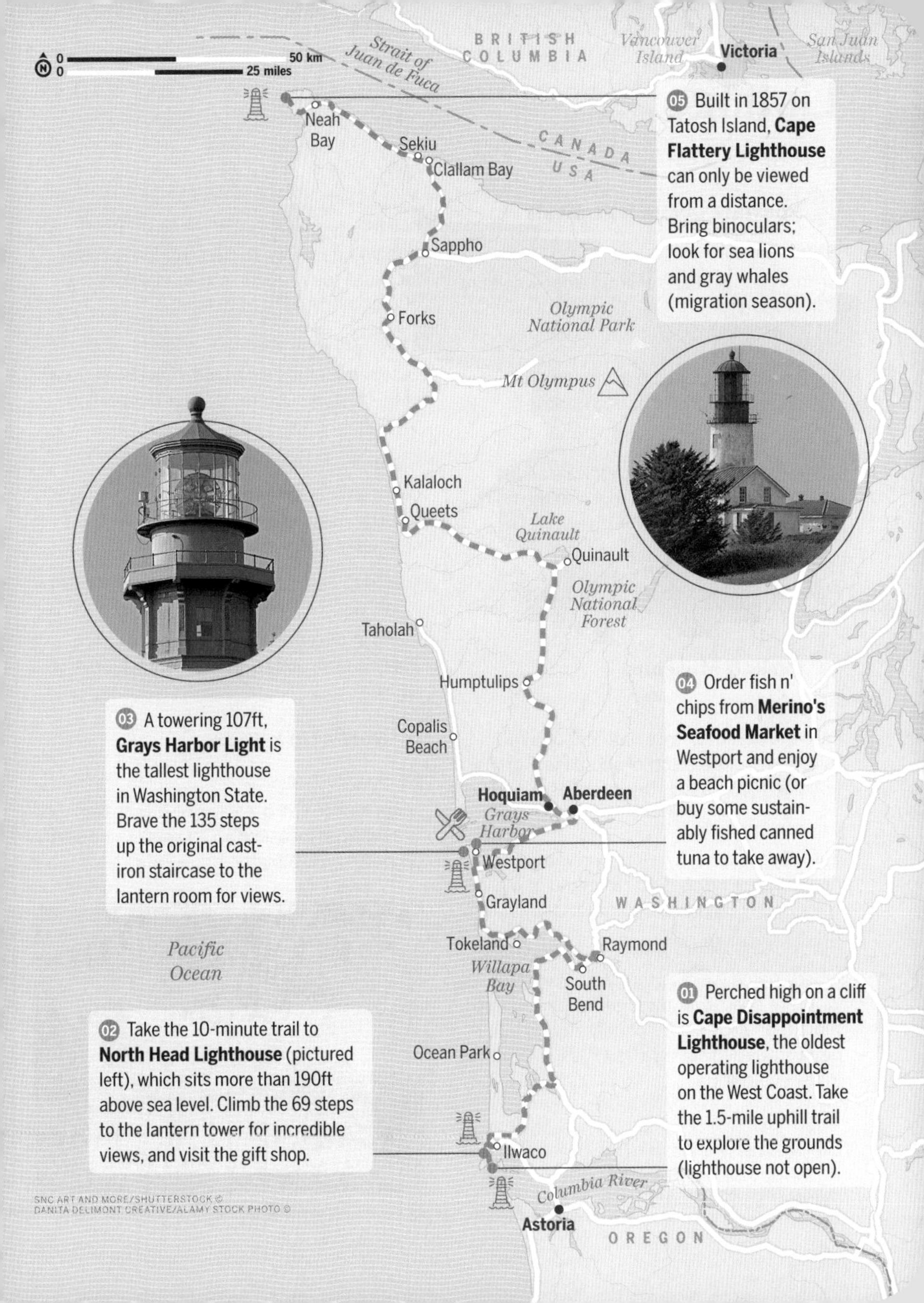
0 50 km
0 25 miles
BRITISH COLUMBIA
Vancouver Island
Victoria
San Juan Islands
Strait of Juan de Fuca
CANADA
USA
Neah Bay
Sekiu
Clallam Bay
Sappho
Forks
Olympic National Park
Mt Olympus
Kalaloch
Queets
Lake Quinault
Quinault
Olympic National Forest
Taholah
Humptulips
Copalis Beach
Hoquiam
Aberdeen
Grays Harbor
Westport
Grayland
WASHINGTON
Tokeland
Raymond
Willapa Bay
South Bend
Pacific Ocean
Ocean Park
Ilwaco
Columbia River
Astoria
OREGON

01 Perched high on a cliff is **Cape Disappointment Lighthouse**, the oldest operating lighthouse on the West Coast. Take the 1.5-mile uphill trail to explore the grounds (lighthouse not open).

02 Take the 10-minute trail to **North Head Lighthouse** (pictured left), which sits more than 190ft above sea level. Climb the 69 steps to the lantern tower for incredible views, and visit the gift shop.

03 A towering 107ft, **Grays Harbor Light** is the tallest lighthouse in Washington State. Brave the 135 steps up the original cast-iron staircase to the lantern room for views.

04 Order fish n' chips from **Merino's Seafood Market** in Westport and enjoy a beach picnic (or buy some sustainably fished canned tuna to take away).

05 Built in 1857 on Tatosh Island, **Cape Flattery Lighthouse** can only be viewed from a distance. Bring binoculars; look for sea lions and gray whales (migration season).

Listings

BEST OF THE REST

Coastal Cuisine & Festivals

Salmon House Restaurant $$

Salmon slow smoked over an alder-wood fire is its specialty.

Salt Hotel & Pub $

Try the salmon cioppino or smoked tuna melt and enjoy the views of Ilwaco Harbor.

Bigfoot Brewfest

Attend one of the biggest festivals on the coast; beer, food and live music in the first weekend of October.

International Kite Festival

Hundreds of kites soar in mid-August in Long Beach.

Parks & Museums

Westport Light State Park

Take the paved 1.3-mile path through the dunes to explore 1215ft of shoreline. Surfing hotspot. (Day Pass or Discover Pass required.)

Grayland State Park

Enjoy beach bliss: fly a kite, run with your dog, surf the waves, stroll the sand or dig for clams. (Day Pass or Discover Pass required.)

Bottle Beach State Park

A designated Washington State Birding Trail. Walk the boardwalk through the park where more than 130 species of migratory shorebirds stop each spring. (Day Pass or Discover Pass required.)

Twin Harbors State Park

Explore grassy dunes and the beach, fly kites, dig for clams or stroll the beach. (Day Pass or Discover Pass required.)

Kurt Cobain Memorial Park

Pay tribute to the soul of grunge at the bridge Cobain was known to sleep under. Features include a metal guitar, a granite slab of his quotes, and graffiti from fans.

Knappton Cove Heritage Center

Learn about the Ellis Island of the West Coast at this historic Columbia River Quarantine Station.

Cranberry Museum & Gift Shop

Learn about cranberry bog preparation and farming. Take a self-guided bog tour. Try cranberry ice cream.

Makah Cultural & Research Center

Learn about the Makah Tribe and the artifacts found at the Ozette Archaeological Site, where a slide buried six pre-contact longhouses.

Surf's Up & Tours

Big Foot Surf School

Learn how to catch a wave; all levels, beginner to advanced (seasonal). Only permitted surf school in a Washington State Park.

Kurt Cobain Memorial Park

Skookum Surf Co

Learn how to eFoil or surf. Rent equipment and spend an enjoyable day at the water's edge.

Tidepooling

Kalaloch Beach 4 and Ruby Beach offer ranger-led programs during the summer months. Arrive at least 30 minutes before the lowest tide: zero tide is best. (Olympic National Park day or annual pass required.)

Experience Olympic

Learn all about the Olympic NP's biodiversity with these naturalist-led ecotours. Kid-friendly with a wide range of tour options; by reservation only.

Long Beach Horse Rides

Head out with the entire family on horseback to explore the World's Longest Beach.

West Coast Rides

Saddle up and tick that beach horseback ride off your bucket list.

Twilight

Satiate your appetite for all things vampire by visiting points of interest in Forks, where the film was set.

Hiking Boots On

Hole-in-the-Wall

Hike the 4-mile beach trail to explore tide-pools and unique rock formations. At low tide, walk through the hole created by waves. No dogs allowed. (Olympic National Park fee or annual pass.)

Copalis River Spit

A 4-mile round-trip walk through the dunes and beach at Griffiths-Priday State Park leads to a quiet spit where the Copalis River meets the Pacific Ocean. (Day pass or Discover Pass required.)

Damon Point Hike

Located at the southern end of Point Brown Peninsula, the 4-mile round-trip trail leads you through Protection Island, a migratory nesting area for snowy owls in January and February.

Wedding Rocks

Make the 8.7-mile roundtrip moderately challenging hike to see carved petroglyphs. (Olympic National Park fee or annual pass required.)

Hall of Mosses

Experience a world draped in mosses on this easy, well-trafficked trail. (Olympic National Park fees or annual pass.)

Quinalt Rain Forest Nature Trail

Walk through an old-growth forest with 500-year-old Douglas fir trees; easy half-mile interpretive trail, well-trafficked. (Northwest Forest Recreation Pass required.)

Beer, Wine & Distilleries

North Jetty Brewing $

Beloved by locals and tourists. Grab a pint of the Honorable Mention IPA and strike up a conversation.

Adrift Distillers $

Made with local cranberries and Washington wheat, the cranberry liqueur has a tart kick that won *Sip Magazine*'s Best of the North-west Award.

Westport Winery Garden Resort $$

Sample wines and dine at a winery restaurant that twice made *USA Today*'s top-five list. Explore 15 acres of display gardens and a mermaid mythology museum.

Scan to find more things to do on the Washington Coast online

19 The Washington CASCADES

ROAD TRIPS | NATURE | OUTDOORS

The mesmerizing beauty of the Cascades lures adventure-seekers of all kinds. Ride a gondola to the top of a mountain for a breathtaking view of Mt Rainier, search for the legendary Sasquatch, or immerse yourself in nature while forest bathing. In these mountains on Seattle's doorstep, the choices are endless.

THINAIR28/GETTY IMAGES ©

How to

Getting around The best option is to explore by car as most places and parks are not serviced by regular public transportation.

When to go Mid-summer to mid-fall; the latter has fewer crowds.

White stuff At high elevations, snow lasts well into June, closing roads and hiking trails. Check ahead.

Passes The Cascade Mountains consist of national parks, state parks, national forests, national recreational areas and national monuments. Passes are required and can be obtained at some park entrances, visitor centers and online.

Bellingham
Newhalem
Diablo Lake
Burlington
Winthrop
Darrington
Glacier Peak
Granite Falls
Everett
Wenatchee National Forest
Leavenworth
Seattle
Burien
Wenatchee
Tacoma
Olympia
Mt Rainer
Ellensburg
Northwest Trek Wildlife Park
Ashford
Yakima
Toppenish
Mt Adams
Mt St Helens
0 50 km
0 25 miles

Iconic mountains As the most prominent Cascade peak, **Mt Rainier** is a much-loved icon throughout the state. Every year, more than two million people visit the park. At the visitor center in Paradise, take in the park's awe-inspiring beauty along the favored nature trail through the wildflower-laden meadows. Outdoor activities abound for all ages and skill levels (nps.gov). If you have your sights on **Mt St Helens**, head to **Johnston Ridge Observatory** to view the blast zone and learn about the 1980 eruption and human stories from that day.

Scenic loops Looking for the ultimate multi-day road trip? Drive the 440-mile **Cascade Loop** through two breathtaking mountain passes, past dozens of small towns, along pine-treed foothills and glacier-carved valleys, and loop back to Puget Sound. En route stop at the Bavarian-themed village of Leavenworth, the wild west town of Winthrop, and the company town of Newhalem. For full-on off-the-grid adventure, choose the **Mountain**

Left Cascade Loop
Above left Hikers, Mt Rainier

Loop Scenic Byway. Pioneered by miners in 1891, this 55-mile loop links the towns of Granite Falls and Darrington. But, there's a catch – due to snow, it's only fully open from late spring to early fall, and the middle portion is a 14-mile single-lane gravel road.

Unique experiences Search for the most elusive creature in the Pacific Northwest – Sasquatch – with the **Bigfoot Adventures**. With several tour options, including a thrilling night-time tour, put your sleuthing skills to the test and discover the mysteries of this legendary creature. Learn all about the hydro resources in the North Cascades on a **Seattle City Light Tour**. On the **Diablo Lake Boat Tour** cruise in a glass-roofed boat next to the dam, tour the powerplant, and lunch at the North Cascades Institute. Tours in summer only. At Crystal Mountain, ride the Mt Rainer Gondola to **Summit House Restaurant**, Washington's highest elevation restaurant. Sitting at 6872ft, it offers spectacular views of Mt Rainer. Open

Forest Bathing, Step-by-Step

1 Pause/stop your body.

2 Acknowledge the space around you.

3 Pay attention to the sensation and needs of yourself in this space.

4 Breathe deeply, slow your movements and note the ways you're being supported by the Earth.

5 Tune into your senses. What are you hearing? Feeling? Smelling?

6 Let your surroundings draw your focus. Give it your attention and gratitude.

7 Continue and move around slowly with intention and awareness.

8 Forest bathing is communal. Share in a way that feels authentic.

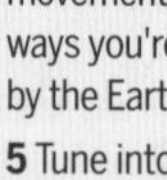

■ **By Jules Hepp,** *certified Nature and Forest Therapy Guide, Cascadia Forest Therapy @cascadia.forest.therapy*

DANITA DELIMONT/GETTY IMAGES ©

Restoring a Name

Long before Captain George Vancouver named Mt Rainier in 1792 after his friend Rear Admiral Peter Rainier, the mountain already had a name – Mt Tacoma or Mt Tahoma (depending on the tribe), meaning 'the mother of all waters.' The Puyallup Tribe is leading the appeal to restore the rightful name.

CAVAN IMAGES/GETTY IMAGES ©

year-round. Join the two-hour guided Elk Bugling tour at **Northwest Trek Wildlife Park**. See sparring elks and hear their distinctive high-pitched call during rutting season.

Outdoor adventures Relax your body and mind and discover a more mindful connection through **forest bathing**. This clothes-on activity is all about meandering slowing, letting yourself linger in the sensory invitations the forest presents. Go solo or learn the craft with **Cascadia Forest Therapy**. Cool off on a float trip down the Wenatchee River. **Leavenworth Outdoor Center** is family- and dog-friendly and routes have few rapids. **River Rider Leavenworth** is one of the most affordable (starts at $25 per person) operators. Multiple operators offer different packages.

Gear & Eats For 50 years, **BaseCamp** in Ashford has been the home of Rainier Mountaineering Inc and Whittaker Mountaineering. Rent or buy gear and meet mountain-minded souls (maybe even mountaineers Jim and Lou Whittaker) at the **outdoor bar and grill**. Nearby, **Wildberry Restaurant** serves up authentic Sherpa-Himalayan cuisine. Owner Lhakpa Gelu Sherpa holds the world speed record of summiting Everest. (Both restaurants are seasonal.)

KATIE COTTERILL/NORTHWEST TREK WILDLIFE PARK ©

Left Hiker among the trees, Washington Cascades **Above top** Diablo Lake **Above** Elk, Northwest Trek Wildlife Park

20 Washington Wine COUNTRY

WINE | TOURS | NATURE

Boasting perfect conditions for growing fruit-forward wines and 20 diverse and unique growing areas, known as American Viticultural Areas or AVAs, Washington Wine Country shows, with each sip, why the state is the second-largest producer of wines in the US.

NICHOLAS LAMONTANARO/SHUTTERSTOCK ©

How to

Getting around With the majority of wine country located in Eastern Washington and stretching all the way to the Idaho/Oregon border, it's best to explore the region by car.

When to go Year-round or join the excitement during April's Spring Barrel or September and October's Fall Crush (winecountrywashington.com).

Taste & tote On Alaska Airlines, mileage plan members can fly back home with their first case of Washington wine checked in for free and enjoy waived car rental and tasting fees (tasteandtote.com).

WWW.JBELLCELLARS.COM ©

Wine blending & music Discover the art of wine blending at **Chateau Ste Michelle**, the state's oldest winery. Led by expert guides, get hands-on by learning, tasting and refining your palate. The summer concert series held outdoors on the estate grounds is a local favorite. Concertgoers arrive early to get in line with their coolers, wine and snacks. Bring blankets and low chairs (available for rent), and have a jacket or sweater for the evening. Located in **Woodinville Wine Country**, there are more than 130 wineries and four wine districts to explore, as well as cideries, breweries and distilleries. Time-conscious travelers will appreciate the ability to sample so many different Washington wines in one location and the 30-minute drive from Seattle or Seattle-Tacoma International Airport. Purchase a digital tasting pass for extra savings at multiple locations in Woodinville.

KEVIN J SALISBURY/GETTY IMAGES ©

Wine Legacy

In 1937, Dr Walter Clore became passionate about vinifera grapes and determining where they would grow best and in what types of soil. His research paved the way for more than 1000 wineries, 400 grape growers and 80 grape varietals, earning him the title the 'Father of Washington Wine.'

Left Vineyard, Prosser
Above left Chateau Ste Michelle
Above right J Bell Cellars (p116)

Balloons & vino In Prosser (tourprosser.com) stroll from tasting room to tasting room in **Vintner's Village**, sampling products from top wineries, like Milbrandt Vineyards, Airfield Estates, and Thurston Wolfe Winery, whose avant-garde blends have received prestigious accolades. Visit on the last weekend of September to see dozens of balloons take to the skies at sunrise in the **Great Prosser Balloon Rally**. For an evening encore, anchored balloons are illuminated against the dark sky for the 'Glow Show.'

Bubbles & Pinzgauer Make your own bottle of sparkling wine on the **Treveri Cellars Premium Tour & Tasting**. Offered in the summer only, the tour dives into the sparkling-wine process and then lets you prepare your own bottle to take home. The day wraps up with an intimate wine tasting with the winemakers. Visit the neighboring winery, **Owen Roe**, and book a reservation for a ride through the vineyard in their Swiss Pinzgauer (army vehicle) that stops at an exposed hilltop showing off the soil layers from the Missoula Floods.

SEAHAWKS

On Cloud Wine

Zillah's Rattlesnake Hills are home to 16 world-class wineries. Touring on an eBike lets you sip and taste at a leisurely pace while thoroughly enjoying the views of vineyards, hop fields and fruit orchards. Begin at **Two Mountain Winery**. If its aromatic rose is available, consider yourself lucky! Red lovers will want to stop at **Cultura Wine**. Lively stories always ensue when Tad mans the tasting room. When hunger hits, order seasonal fare and a bright and crisp chardonnay at **Tin Roof Grill** in VanArnam Vineyards. Continue on to **J Bell Cellars** and **Dineen Vineyards**. Wrap up the evening with a wood-fired pizza topped with hops at everyone's favorite, **Hoptown Pizza**.

■ **Tips by Andy Zissermann,** *owner, Kickstand Tours*

@kickstandtours

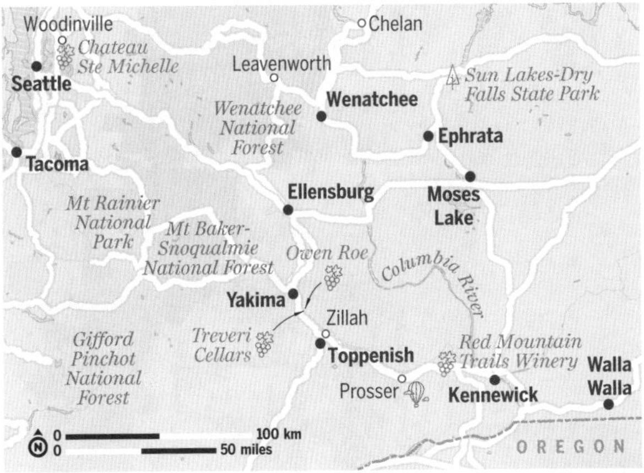
Woodinville
Chelan
Chateau Ste Michelle
Seattle
Leavenworth
Sun Lakes-Dry Falls State Park
Wenatchee National Forest
Wenatchee
Ephrata
Tacoma
Ellensburg
Moses Lake
Mt Rainier National Park
Mt Baker-Snoqualmie National Forest
Owen Roe
Columbia River
Yakima
Zillah
Gifford Pinchot National Forest
Treveri Cellars
Toppenish
Red Mountain Trails Winery
Walla Walla
Prosser
Kennewick
0 100 km
0 50 miles
OREGON

MICHELLE BAUMBACH/SHUTTERSTOCK ©

Far left Great Prosser Balloon Rally
Below Owen Roe winery

Two wheels or four hooves Hop on an electric bike and spend the day touring (kickstandtours.com) some of the region's most beautiful landscapes and tasting fabulous wines with knowledgeable guides. With three eBike routes in the **Yakima Valley** (Prosser, Rattlesnake Hills and Red Mountain) and one in **Walla Walla**, tours cover two major wine regions. Saddle up and go for a peaceful one-hour horseback ride through the vineyards of Red Mountain, Washington's smallest AVA, known for its prized red-grape varietals. End the tour next to a cozy campfire and enjoy a wine flight from **Red Mountain Trails Winery**.

Making the terroir The Missoula Floods occurred 15,000 years ago when an ice dam holding back Glacial Lake Missoula repeatedly broke. Water with waves 400ft high rushed into Washington and careened down the Columbia River at 60mph, leaving behind gravel, silt and sand layers. These well-drained soils paired with the region's arid climate make the ideal terroir for growing grapes. One of the state's most impressive flood features is Dry Falls at **Sun Lakes-Dry Falls State Park**. Its cliff is 3.5 miles wide and 400ft high, and the waterfall was four times the size of Niagara Falls.

TEGRA STONE NUESS/GETTY IMAGES ©

PORTLAND

CUISINE | NATURE | COFFEE

BARISTA
ESPRESSO
DRAUGHT
BOTTLES
WONDERS
COFFEE SHOP.
CHAMBORD
Cafetière
bonaVITA

Experience Portland online

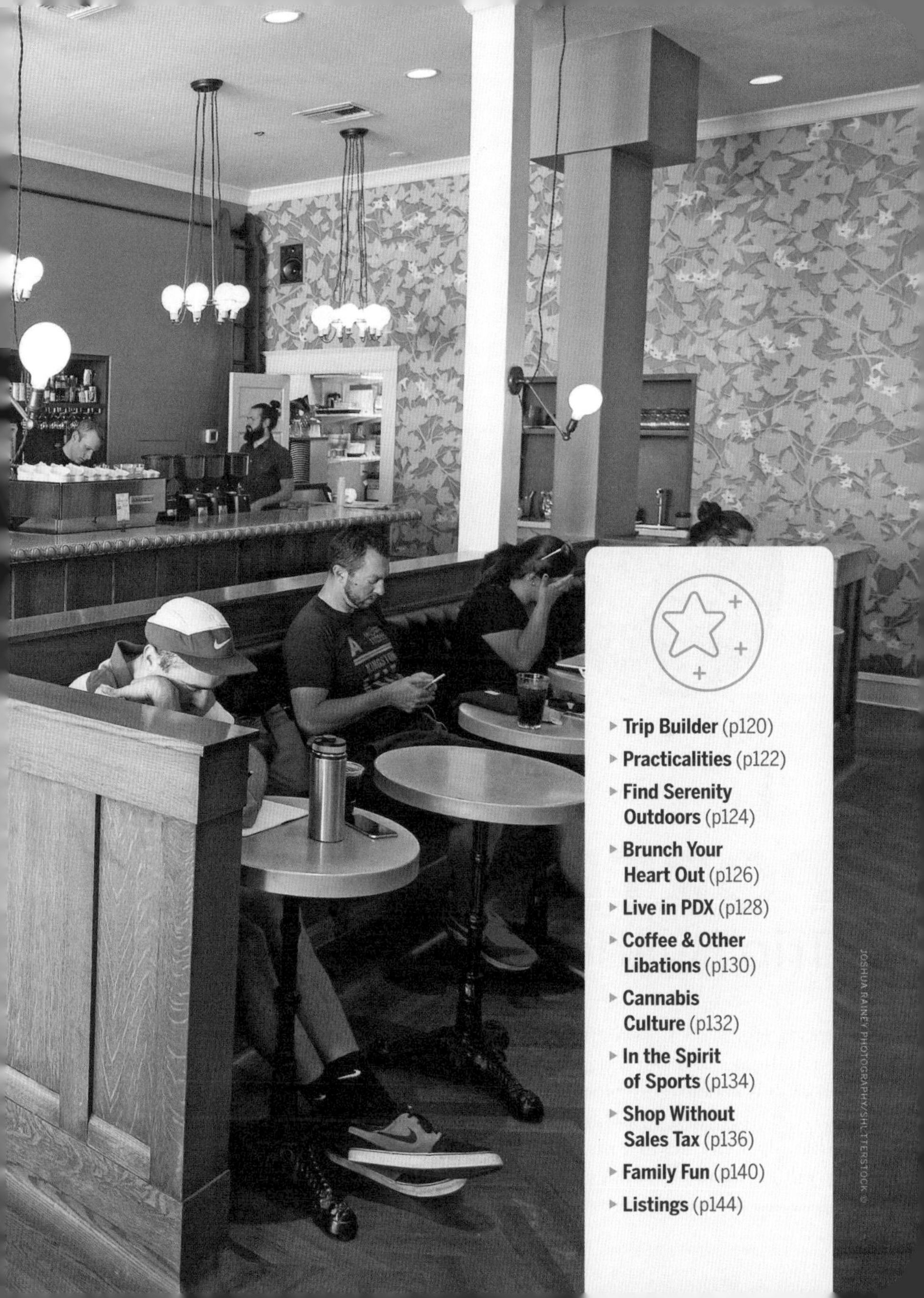

JOSHUA RAINEY PHOTOGRAPHY/SHUTTERSTOCK ©

PORTLAND
Trip Builder

Home of hipster culture, stellar libations and incredible eats from food carts to upscale dining, Portland is beloved by locals and tourists alike for its myriad trees and unparalleled natural beauty. Quite literally a city nestled inside a forest (Forest Park), fresh air abounds and a creative culture thrives.

Spend a day on **Sauvie Island** at Collins Beach, walking through natural areas, or stopping at a produce farm (p125)

40min from Downtown

Clear your mind and catch some shade at the colossal **Forest Park** via Lower Macleay Park's NW Upshur entrance (p125)

12min from Downtown

Pedal through an Eastside brewpub crawl on a **Brew-Cycle** (p131)

15min from Downtown

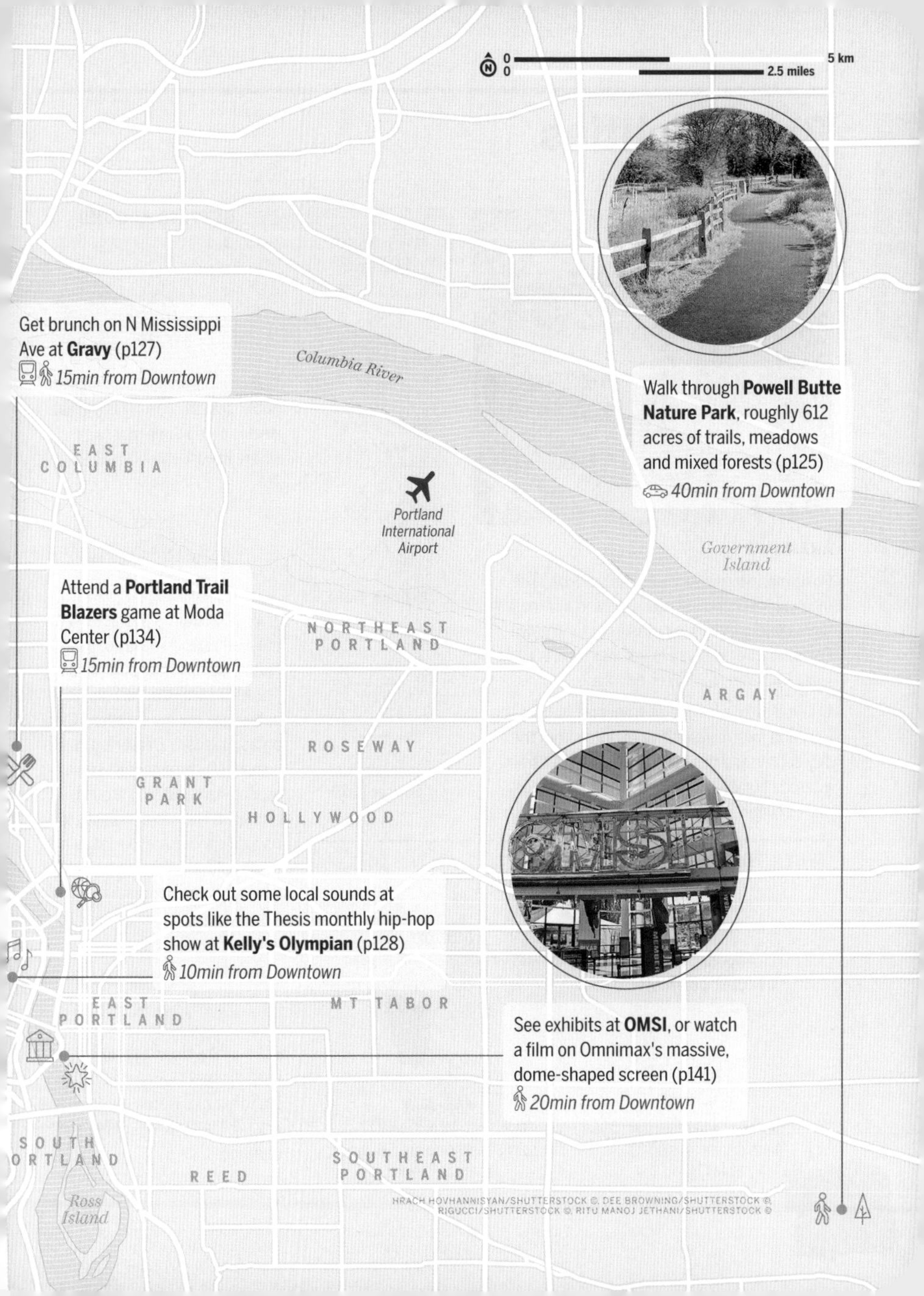

0 5 km
0 2.5 miles
Columbia River
EAST COLUMBIA
Portland International Airport
Government Island
NORTHEAST PORTLAND
ARGAY
ROSEWAY
GRANT PARK
HOLLYWOOD
EAST PORTLAND
MT TABOR
SOUTH ORTLAND
REED
SOUTHEAST PORTLAND
Ross Island

Get brunch on N Mississippi Ave at **Gravy** (p127)
15min from Downtown

Attend a **Portland Trail Blazers** game at Moda Center (p134)
15min from Downtown

Check out some local sounds at spots like the Thesis monthly hip-hop show at **Kelly's Olympian** (p128)
10min from Downtown

Walk through **Powell Butte Nature Park**, roughly 612 acres of trails, meadows and mixed forests (p125)
40min from Downtown

See exhibits at **OMSI**, or watch a film on Omnimax's massive, dome-shaped screen (p141)
20min from Downtown

HRACH HOVHANNISYAN/SHUTTERSTOCK ©, DEE BROWNING/SHUTTERSTOCK ©, RIGUCCI/SHUTTERSTOCK ©, RITU MANOJ JETHANI/SHUTTERSTOCK ©

Practicalities

PORTLAND INTERNATIONAL AIRPORT
ECHOVISUALS/SHUTTERSTOCK ©

ARRIVING

Portland International Portland (PDX) The main airport handling domestic and international flights is located 30 minutes from Downtown Portland. The best way to get into town is via MAX Light Rail train ($2.50) or rideshare.

Union Station The major transport hub for the Portland metro area is five minutes from the city center, and has connections to MAX train, intercity bus ($2.50 for 2½ hours, $5 per day) and Portland Streetcar ($2).

HOW MUCH FOR A...

happy-hour beer $5

brunch plate $14

local music concert $15

WHEN TO GO

JUN–SEP
Gorgeous warm weather; perfect for water sports

OCT–DEC
Cool fall weather; great for produce farms and farmers markets

JAN–FEB
Cold weather; slow event season; snow sports at Mt Hood

MAR–MAY
Beautiful spring weather; cherry blossoms and flowers start to bloom

GETTING AROUND

Walking Combined with excellent public transit, walking is a great means of reaching most anywhere in Portland.

Train MAX train is the fastest and most affordable means of travel ($2.50 per 2½ hours, $5 per day). The MAX connects Portland to outlying areas like Gresham, Clackamas, Hillsboro, Beaverton and the airport. Most trains start service around 4am and stop around midnight. The system is easy to navigate and use, especially when paired with the Trimet phone app, which lets you purchase fares right from your phone.

Ride-share Uber/Lyft-ing is useful, especially since Portland isn't that big. Watch out for surge pricing during times of high demand.

EATING & DRINKING

With locations inside the airport and in the Pearl District, the excellent Deschutes Brewery (pictured top) offers 26 mainstay beers on tap alongside seasonal experimental brews. It's best known for its Mirror Pond pale ale and its flagship Black Butte Porter. For those with a sweet tooth, Blue Star Donuts (pictured bottom), a gourmet donut shop with several locations, is mandatory. Offerings range from Lemon Poppy Buttermilk Old Fashioned to an ultra-moist powdered Orange Olive Oil donut.

Must-try Swiss cuisine
Swiss Hibiscus (p144)

Best noodles
Stretch the Noodle (p144)

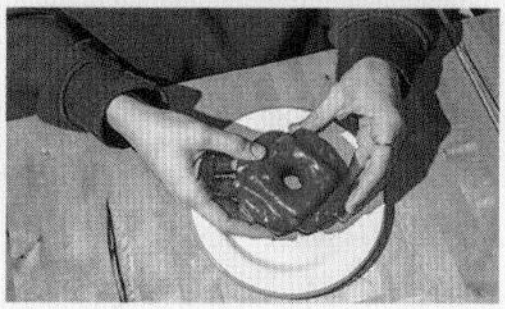

TOP: JOSHUA RAINEY PHOTOGRAPHY/SHUTTERSTOCK © BOTTOM: AGAVE PHOTO STUDIO/SHUTTERSTOCK ©

CONNECT & FIND YOUR WAY

Wi-fi Most businesses provide wi-fi, posting passwords for customers inside the location.

Navigation Willamette River splits the city into a West Side and an East Side. Portland is dubbed 'Bridge City' for its 12 unique bridges, among them is Burnside Bridge, which divides the city even further, into North and West quadrants.

DISCOUNT DAYS

Portland Art Museum offers free admission days several times a year. Check its website for schedule. OMSI offers admission for $2 the first Sunday of every month.

WHERE TO STAY

Portland has a slew of unique accommodations that span all budgets, although stays near the city center cost more, and more affordable options lie further east.

Neighborhood	Pro/Con
Downtown	Lots of hotels. Close to event venues, attractions and lots of good eating options. Easy access to all modes of public transit. Pricey. Noisy. Gets pretty sleepy at night; the only nightlife to speak of happens inside hotel bars.
Southeast Buckman/ Belmont	Live like a local in a house or apartment. Within walking distance of nearby shopping, food, bars. Close to downtown. Congested. Relatively gritty street scene, particularly at night.
North Kenton or St Johns	Tranquil neighborhood vibe. Close to parks and Sauvie Island. Less walkable. Further (15 to 20 minutes) from attractions.

MONEY

Due to COVID-19, the overwhelming majority of places prefer card payment. Cash is not necessary, since all restaurants and vendors have a card reader, with easy built-in tipping.

21 Find Serenity OUTDOORS

EXERCISE | OUTDOORS | NATURE

Portland boasts a multitude of green spaces, offering everything from water views to river banks, beaches, forests and mountain peaks. Visitors can choose to explore these varying landscapes in an array of different ways: walking, cycling, kayaking, stand-up paddleboarding, hiking or driving.

XIAO ZHOU/SHUTTERSTOCK ©

How to

When to go Barring inclement weather, Oregon's outdoor season is enjoyable year-round. Spring through fall is particularly optimal.

Hidden gem Located at the top of North Portland, across the Columbia River from Vancouver, **Broughton Beach** offers stunning water and mountain views. Walk, bike or skate on a paved upper trail, take the rugged path along the beach, or hang out on the bank where swimming, BBQ and games are ideal.

TUSHARKOLEY/SHUTTERSTOCK ©

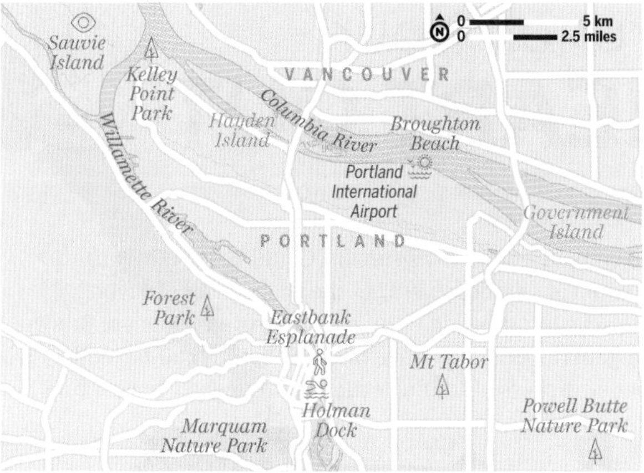
0 5 km
0 2.5 miles
Sauvie Island
Kelley Point Park
VANCOUVER
Columbia River
Hayden Island
Broughton Beach
Willamette River
Portland International Airport
Government Island
PORTLAND
Forest Park
Eastbank Esplanade
Mt Tabor
Holman Dock
Powell Butte Nature Park
Marquam Nature Park

Far left top Wildwood Trail, Forest Park **Far left bottom** Kelley Point Park

Sweet retreats The Pacific Northwest is home to many outdoorsy folks. No matter what neighborhood you're in, there's always a nearby park where you can touch some grass and take a break from screen time. West Portland's massive **Forest Park**, for example, has more walking and hiking trails than you could explore in a day. Take its Wildwood Trail up to the Pittock Mansion historical landmark. Alternatively, visit the summer oasis that is **Sauvie Island**. Locals adore the island's clothing-optional Collins Beach, and it also has a family-friendly beach, natural wildlife areas, and opportunities for fishing, canoeing and kayaking.

Splash time Seldom unbearably hot, Oregon summers are generally fantastic. While the coast is a couple of hours away, there are plenty of swimming opportunities and sandy river beaches right in town, from Sauvie Island to Poet's Beach, Sellwood Riverfront Park, Broughton Beach, and beyond.

Urban paths Want to get outside and enjoy city views without getting muddy? One central option is walking the **Eastbank Esplanade**, a pedestrian and bicycle path on the east bank of the Willamette River running all the way from the Steel Bridge to SE Caruthers St on the south end. On warm days, locals can often be found hanging out and swimming on the Esplanade-accessible **Holman Dock** near the Hawthorne Bridge. Alternately, walk the paved trail at **Kelley Point Park** and enjoy the water views – and see where the Columbia and Willamette Rivers merge – from the riverside forest.

Choose Your Own Adventure

The expansive **Powell Butte Nature Park**, on a peak in Southeast, has excellent mountain views, lots of sun and everything from hilly forested paths to grass-covered meadows and orchard trees. There are opportunities for horseback riding, mountain biking or a nice stroll.

Come to **Kelley Point Park** for biking, bird-watching, beachside picnics and romantic strolls under a tree canopy. You might spot animals like deer, rabbits, hawks and even a rare bald eagle.

Mt Tabor offers forested trails on an incline, and is also popular for its spectacular 360-degree view of Portland backed by the West Hills.

22 Brunch Your HEART OUT

BRUNCH | PEOPLE-WATCHING | QUEUES

Portland's favorite meal is undoubtedly brunch. (Could that be because Portlanders also love them some alcoholic beverages the night prior? Maybe!) While many places serve breakfast and brunch, the most admired spots are known for having a line – and, as a general rule, if a place has a line, the food is good. And at peak times, you'll be hard-pressed to find a place that doesn't have a line.

Alberta

JAY JUNO/SHUTTERSTOCK ©

How to

When to go Weekday brunches can drastically cut wait times. There are typically more seating options in summer, when lots of restaurants open up their patios. In almost all cases, beating the crowd – arriving at 9am not 11am – means minimal wait times.

Hidden gem On N Mississippi Ave, **Fried Egg I'm In Love** is a walk-up window serving delicious breakfast sandwiches in a fully covered food-cart pod.

LISA123456/STOCKIMO/ALAMY STOCK PHOTO ©

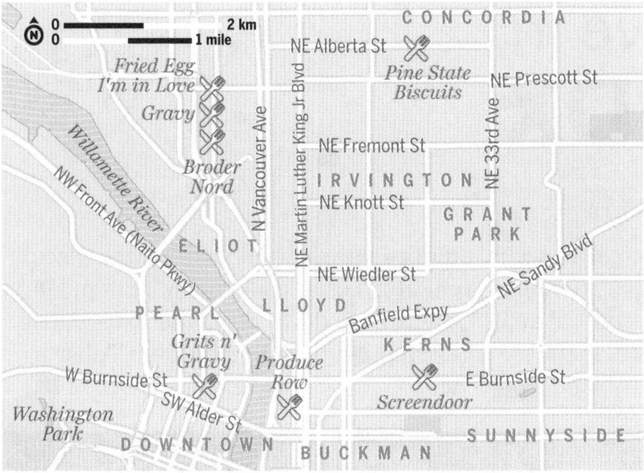

0 2 km
0 1 mile
CONCORDIA
NE Alberta St
Pine State Biscuits
NE Prescott St
Fried Egg I'm in Love
Gravy
Broder Nord
Willamette River
NW Front Ave (Naito Pkwy)
N Vancouver Ave
NE Martin Luther King Jr Blvd
NE Fremont St
NE 33rd Ave
IRVINGTON
NE Knott St
GRANT PARK
ELIOT
NE Wiedler St
NE Sandy Blvd
PEARL
LLOYD
Banfield Expy
KERNS
Grits n' Gravy
Produce Row
W Burnside St
E Burnside St
Screendoor
SW Alder St
Washington Park
DOWNTOWN
BUCKMAN
SUNNYSIDE

Brunch is more than just a meal; to Portlanders, it's an activity. There is perhaps no better introduction to Portland than going to one of the city's most iconic brunch spots, and yes, waiting in line. Portlanders pride themselves on finding the best brunch establishments, particularly under-the-radar spots that don't require a long line (yet). There are also more and more brunches popping up at restaurants that didn't initially serve the morning-to-afternoon meal.

Grits n' Gravy One new-ish breakfast place that opened in 2021 is the Black-owned Grits n' Gravy located in SW Portland and serving Southern-inspired fare such as fried catfish, chicken and waffles, andouille sausage and eggs, shrimp and grits, four-egg omelets, and more.

Produce Row Head to this stalwart Southeast bar for a low-key and modest brunch that can be enjoyed on its covered patio, which is arguably the best in Portland. During brunch you can still order its beer-battered fries – among the best in town – and mains like a breakfast sandwich, French toast with cardamom custard butter, or a *migas* plate (crunchy tortillas scrambled together with eggs and salsa) that can be made with either pork or vegetarian chipotle sausage, and served with homestyle potatoes.

Far left top Pine State Biscuits
Far left bottom *Aebelskivers*, Broder

Fine Brunch Fare

Gravy Massive comfort-food portions of biscuits and gravy, challah French toast, smoked-salmon hash, chicken-fried steak, build-your-own breakfast sandwiches, omelets, and scrambles.

Screendoor Southern plates like chicken and waffles, crispy fried oysters, shrimp and grits, and bananas Foster French toast. Go early or order takeout to avoid the two-hour wait.

Broder Nord Traditional Nordic fare. Try the *aebelskivers,* spherical Danish pancakes served with lingonberry jam and lemon curd for dipping.

Pine State Biscuits The go-to spot for biscuits, biscuit sandwiches and other Southern-inspired favorites like fried green tomatoes, hush puppies, shrimp and grits, blueberry cornmeal pancakes and collard greens.

23 Live in PDX

MUSIC | NIGHTLIFE | CONCERTS

In Portland's lively creative scene, there's always a local show taking place on any given night. In fact, a live-music event at a bar is easily the more popular form of nightlife. Shows with local artists typically go down at smaller bar-centric venues like Kelly's Olympian, Fixin To, Mississippi Studios, Kenton Club, Alberta Street Pub, Turn! Turn! Turn!, and Holocene.

GARAGE
AUTHORIZED SERVICE

CHRIS OWENS/SHUTTERSTOCK ©

How to

Getting here Order an Uber or Lyft to spare yourself the search for a parking spot.

Tip Many venues require vaccination cards, and some don't allow bags of a certain size. Check venue websites for up-to-date info.

Hidden gem The small room inside **Kelly's Olympian** biker bar is dedicated to local talent of all genres from rock to hip-hop, as well as comedy. It's the home of monthly local hip-hop showcase the **Thesis**, which happens every first Thursday of the month for the last several years.

JOSHUA RAINEY/ALAMY STOCK PHOTO ©

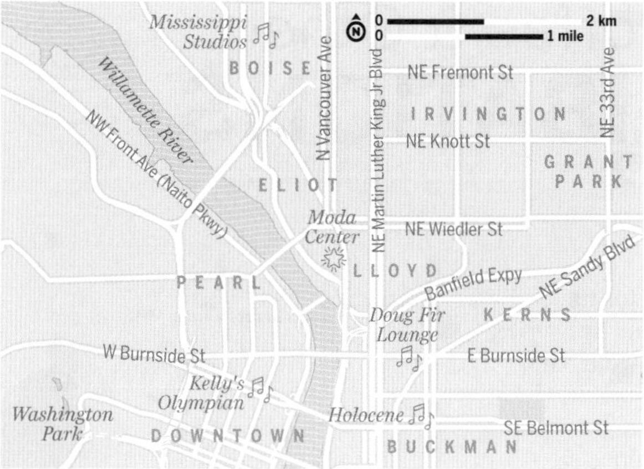
Mississippi Studios
0 2 km
0 1 mile
BOISE
N Vancouver Ave
NE Martin Luther King Jr Blvd
NE Fremont St
IRVINGTON
NE 33rd Ave
Willamette River
NW Front Ave (Naito Pkwy)
NE Knott St
GRANT PARK
ELIOT
Moda Center
NE Wiedler St
LLOYD
Banfield Expy
NE Sandy Blvd
PEARL
Doug Fir Lounge
KERNS
W Burnside St
E Burnside St
Kelly's Olympian
Washington Park
DOWNTOWN
Holocene
SE Belmont St
BUCKMAN

Local scene The music scene in Portland has been known for its jazz and indie-rock scene, but in recent years genres like hip-hop and R&B have been thriving, too. Portland's hip-hop scene has been gaining prevalence again since the decades-earlier '90s boom that birthed scene vets like Illmaculate, Cool Nutz, Mic Crenshaw, Vursatyl and Libretto. Today it's led by emcees like Mic Capes, Wynne, Rasheed Jamal producer/rapper/singer Fountaine, and R&B singer Blossom. Some artists with Portland roots have even been making major moves into the mainstream, like The Last Artful, Dodgr, who has collaborated with Anderson .Paak, Alicia Keys and Dr Dre; and viral rapper Aminé, who has leveled-up to playing arena shows. Portland Trail Blazers starting point guard Damian Lillard has even lent his own rap talents to the scene by recording music in the off-season. He's collaborated with local artists like Mic Capes and Wynne on several occasions, helping them gain exposure.

Check it out Peruse local shows of all genres by skimming the events calendar on the websites of the *Portland Mercury* or *Willamette Week*. It's worth checking the calendars of individual venues for particular acts. Also scan the calendar at the **Moda Center** arena to see if one of your favorite mainstream acts is coming to town; major artists like Justin Bieber, Jay-Z, Olivia Rodrigo and Travis Scott have played there in the past.

Far left top Kelly's Olympian **Far left bottom** Novo Amor, Doug Fir Lounge

Venues Galore

Owned and operated by musicians, **Mississippi Studios** has superior acoustics and quality curation. Never genre-specific, Mississippi's known to book local shows and acclaimed national and international acts.

A tree-themed basement venue with log cabin walls, the **Doug Fir Lounge** is many Portlanders' favorite venue for its hip vibe, impeccable sound quality, and coveted calendar – everything from local up-and-comers to major-label touring acts, and from indie rock to neo soul.

With open floor plan and stellar lighting and sound, **Holocene** is a dance-night stalwart. Local shows and up-and-coming touring acts. It books music of every genre, including hip-hop, R&B, indie rock and electronic.

24 Coffee & Other LIBATIONS

BEER | WINE | COCKTAILS

Portland is famous for its abundance of craft beer and breweries, and for the number of its wine bars, cideries and cocktail bars too. But it's not just alcoholic beverages that Portland does well: coffee is undoubtedly Portland's favorite beverage, and who can forget the reign of the kombucha craze?

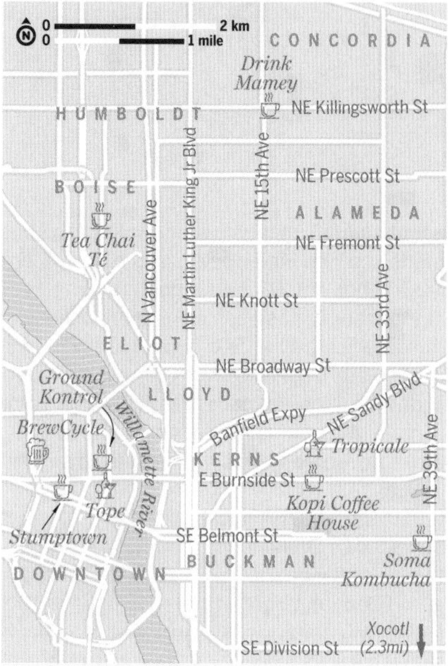

0 2 km
0 1 mile
CONCORDIA
Drink Mamey
NE Killingsworth St
HUMBOLDT
NE 15th Ave
NE Prescott St
BOISE
ALAMEDA
Tea Chai Té
N Vancouver Ave
NE Martin Luther King Jr Blvd
NE Fremont St
NE 33rd Ave
NE Knott St
ELIOT
NE Broadway St
Ground Kontrol
LLOYD
Willamette River
Banfield Expy
NE Sandy Blvd
BrewCycle
Tropicale
KERNS
NE 39th Ave
E Burnside St
Kopi Coffee House
Tope
Stumptown
SE Belmont St
BUCKMAN
Soma Kombucha
DOWNTOWN
Xocotl (2.3mi)
SE Division St

How To

Getting around Take Uber or Lyft, then walk from place to place. It's good for you, and the safest option.

When to go To avoid crowds, go brewery crawling on a weekday.

Highlight In Old Town, **Ground Kontrol** is a futuristic two-story barcade that serves beer and light snacks. Patrons come for the 100 classic arcade games. Cupholders sit next to consoles such as Ms Pac-Man, Tekken, Soulcalibur, Teenage Mutant Ninja Turtles and Donkey Kong.

Caffeine & co Serving South Asian coffee drinks and Indonesian food items, **Kopi Coffee House** has mastered some unique concoctions: ube blossom lattes, cereal toast cold brew, and Kedai Susu made with lime leaf and lemongrass, espresso and sweetened condensed milk. For a different coffee experience, visit the sneaker-themed cafe of **Deadstock Coffee Roasters**, round the corner from Ground Kontrol. Or try brew-at-home beans from **Stumptown**. Tea drinkers will prefer **Tea Chai Té**, which offers every tea imaginable:

Right top Stumptown **Right bottom** Portland latte

STUMPTOWN
open
STUMPTOWN
COFFEE ROASTERS

MICHAEL GORDON/SHUTTERSTOCK ©

TIFA UNIVERSE/SHUTTERSTOCK ©

Kombucha

Visit a **Soma Kombucha** taproom for samples, and to see what the kombucha craze is all about. The locally made **Brew Dr** kombucha can be purchased in any flavor from a local grocery.

hot or bubble, chai, matcha and loose leaf.

Juice Try **Drink Mamey** for bottled juices in flavors like watermelon-lemon-apple, and a 'majikal' concoction made with mint, pineapple and blue spirulina. Alternatively, sip on a juice or smoothie from **Xocotl**, located in Portland Mercado.

Boozy options If you prefer to work up a thirst before slaking it, hop aboard the **BrewCycle** ($30 to $35 per person). It seats up to 14 people, who all pedal while the driver steers on a two-hour, three-stop brewery crawl. After that, if you have any energy left, you can walk to as many other breweries as you please!

Atop the Hoxton Hotel, cocktail bar **Tope** offers phenomenal city views at sunset, award-winning drinks and stellar squash tacos. **Tropicale** is home to the best piña coladas in town, which can be served out of a hollowed-out pineapple.

25 Cannabis CULTURE

MARIJUANA | DISPENSARIES | CBD

Portland's cannabis industry is a wonderland for weed connoisseurs, and anyone who's curious about trying recreational weed now that it's legal. Don't be shy: walk right into a nearby dispensary, whip out that ID card, and ask the budtender any questions you might have about choosing a strain or method of consumption.

ELECTRIC LETTUCE
ELECTRIC LETTUCE
NOW OPEN

TADA IMAGES/SHUTTERSTOCK ©

How to

How much Saturation of the market means weed is ultra-cheap and dispensaries are always doing deals. An eighth of bottom-shelf weed costs as little as $4 to $6, and an eighth of top-shelf weed as little as $16.

Need to know To avoid legal issues, do not smoke cannabis or consume cannabis edibles in a public place or in public view; do not drive or bike under the influence; and make sure you finish your stash before heading to the airport or crossing state lines.

HEATH KORVOLA/GETTY IMAGES ©

Left Corazon strain plant **Far left top** Electric Lettuce **Far left bottom** Golden Pineapple buds

Legalization

Since recreational cannabis was legalized in 2016, the number of dispensaries has exploded in Portland. Even before legalization, Oregon had been known for its robust medical-cannabis industry, and had long boasted the best (and most) weed in the country. Even though it's not technically legal to smoke in public, don't be surprised if you see people openly partaking in cannabis at a local beach or even on the street. To get around the legality issue of smoking in public, do edibles instead! Take cannabis-infused gummies or chocolate with you on day trips to the river beach, music festival or even to Forest Park. Just make sure that wherever you go, you have a designated driver.

CBD

Another big thing right now in Portland is the prevalence of CBD; that is, the non-psychoactive ingredient in cannabis. It doesn't get you high, but it does help you feel good and may help alleviate aches and pains, as well as anxiety, allergies, inflammation, insomnia and more. Ask for it at any given coffee shop or bar; they'll probably have CBD-infused soda or kombucha, or CBD shots that can be added to your beverage for an extra charge.

Pot Shops

Green Muse One of Portland's only Black-owned dispensaries, and located in the historically Black neighborhood of Woodlawn. Specializing in top-shelf strains, its stock is themed by pop-culture and hip-hop references.

Electric Lettuce Known for carrying top-tier bud from brands like LOWD.

Nectar Like the Starbucks of pot shops; it might not be the most esteemed dispensary, but it sure is accessible, and often the most convenient option.

High 5 Tours A party bus and mobile smoking lounge that takes passengers on tours to cannabis-related destinations followed by lunch stops at food carts.

26 In the Spirit of SPORTS

BASKETBALL | FOOTBALL | SPORTS BARS

Dress in red and black, and cheer on Damian Lillard and the Trail Blazers at the remodeled Moda Center arena. For vaguely Quidditch vibes, score tickets to a soccer game to see the Thorns (women) or Timbers (men). Portland also has its own collegiate wood-bat baseball club, the Portland Pickles, who play in Lents Park.

WE'RE ALL MENTAL HERE

KEETON GALE/SHUTTERSTOCK ©

How to

Getting here Take the MAX or a bus to Providence Park to save yourself a massive parking-related headache. Park at the SmartPark downtown on NW Naito Pkwy, and take the MAX train across the river to the arena.

When to go Basketball is December through April, and play-offs go into summer. Soccer goes from March through October.

Tickets Check out the Trail Blazers app or Stubhub to find basketball tickets. Head to timbers.com for Timbers and Thorns tickets.

moda

ARTYOORAN/SHUTTERSTOCK ©

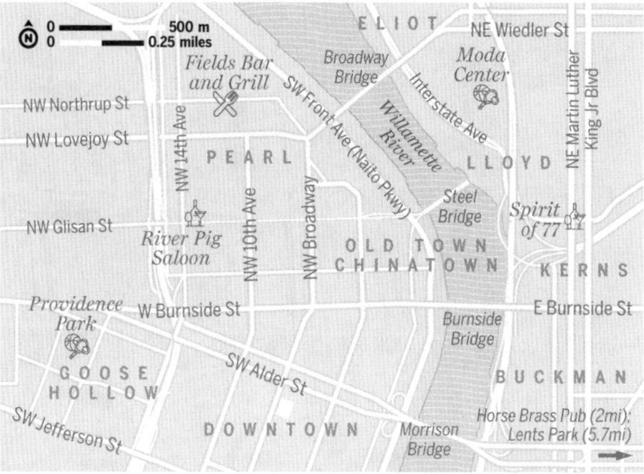
0 500 m
0 0.25 miles
ELIOT
NE Wiedler St
Broadway Bridge
Moda Center
Fields Bar and Grill
Interstate Ave
NW Northrup St
SW Front Ave (Naito Pkwy)
Willamette River
NW Lovejoy St
NW 14th Ave
PEARL
LLOYD
NE Martin Luther King Jr Blvd
Steel Bridge
Spirit of 77
NW Glisan St
NW 10th Ave
NW Broadway
River Pig Saloon
OLD TOWN CHINATOWN
KERNS
Providence Park
W Burnside St
E Burnside St
Burnside Bridge
GOOSE HOLLOW
SW Alder St
BUCKMAN
SW Jefferson St
DOWNTOWN
Morrison Bridge
Horse Brass Pub (2mi); Lents Park (5.7mi)

Far left top Timbers supporters, Providence Park **Far left bottom** Moda Center

Fan(tastic) colors Portlanders are a passionate bunch, and that definitely applies to our sports team fandoms, which are often a uniting force. You might notice lights cast under Morrison Bridge near the water, which take on different colors every day; that's because individuals and organizations pay to light the bridge with the colors of their choosing. That means Blazers, Timbers, Thorns or Oregon Ducks colors embody game-day spirit on an almost daily basis. On days when the Timbers are playing, NW Portland can become gridlocked, with few places to park and swarms of pedestrians in green-and-white scarves and garb. So get into the spirit and see what all the fuss is about.

Struggle & glory Even if you're not typically a soccer watcher, the euphoric vibe and camaraderie is contagious at **Providence Park**, home ground of the Timbers and Thorns. When the Blazers are playing, the same applies. While the 'Zers have only won one NBA championship in 1977, the fan-fare at Blazers games is always wildly fun, even if they don't end up winning. In fact, the years when the teams aren't at their best often mean cheaper tickets – and you never know, they might just win! The Portland Thorns FC are currently the most successful of all Portland-based professional sports teams, since the ladies have won two NWSL Championships in recent years.

Portland's Best Sports Bars

Spirit of 77 is a spirited Blazers-themed sports bar offering arcade games, darts, various large screens, and an even more massive projector screen for a theater-like sports experience.

The **Fields Bar and Grill** is beloved for its potato wedges, burgers, tacos and avocado fries, and for its big comfy booths in view of large-screen TVs.

To watch Timbers games, go to the English-style **Horse Brass Pub** – and don't forget to order its incredible fish-and-chips.

The acclaimed bar and restaurant **River Pig Saloon** is pretty much guaranteed to play the Timbers and Thorns for soccer-fan regulars.

27 Shop Without SALES TAX

MARKETS | MUSIC | BOOKS

Oregonians pay a higher income and property tax, so shoppers get to enjoy a lack of sales tax within the state. In condensed areas around Portland – strips like NW 23rd Ave, SE Division St, NE Alberta St, and downtown – tourists and locals take advantage of the shopping mecca, often choosing to shop local.

MICHAEL GORDON/SHUTTERSTOCK ©

How to

Getting here To avoid congestion and parking, take public transit (the MAX is super close on 2nd Ave) for downtown shopping. Take the bus or rideshare to Eastside shopping districts.

When to go Go shopping on a weekday to avoid crowds. Many shops have later hours in the summer and holiday season.

Hidden gem Located in Pioneer Place Mall, **N'Kossi Boutique** offers custom couture African fashions designed by Togo native Jean Pierre Nugloze.

No Grit, No Pearl

TADA IMAGES/SHUTTERSTOCK ©

Downtown

Powell's City of Books This world-famous bookstore with color-coded rooms is an absolute labyrinth of books. There are computers that customers can access throughout the store, allowing you to browse the store inventory and identify the room in which your title is located. Be sure to check out the Rare Books room, with titles like a first-edition *Lord of the Rings*, a signed copy of *The Haunting of Hill House* and a first-edition of *Huckleberry Finn*.

Pearl District Retailers range from Posh Baby to Anthropologie, and Columbia to Lululemon. There's also MadeHere, across the street from Powell's Books, stocking locally made goods like Shwood wood-framed sunglasses to jewelry, to One Stripe Chai.

MUSIC MILLENNIUM

ROBERT K. CHIN - STOREFRONTS/ALAMY STOCK PHOTO ©

Crate Digging

The vinyl trend doesn't seem to be stopping any time soon, and Portland has an impressive bunch of record shops to peruse. Ones to check out: **Jackpot Records** on SE Hawthorne Blvd, long-standing music mega-store **Music Millennium** and the thoughtfully curated **Tomorrow Records**, as well as **Everyday Music**.

Left Music Millennium **Above left** Powell's City of Books **Above right** Lululemon

NW 23rd Ave This street – along with NW 21st Ave a couple blocks up – is the definition of bustling. Pedestrians cover the sidewalks, grabbing beverages at Barista or Smith Teamaker on their way to places like Portland Leather Goods, stationary store Paper Source, thrift shop Crossroads Trading Co, and local record label Tender Loving Empire, which also sells locally handmade goods and gifts.

Saturday Market The largest open-air market in the country, with all booths staffed by local artists, selling their handmade items. You'll find everything from pottery to catnip pillows to artwork, floral bouquets and elephant ears. The market has got a distinctly Oregon hippie vibe, and you'll also encounter street performers, and a glass shop specializing in pipes. Around the corner from the market on Naito Pkwy, Duck Store sells University of Oregon merchandise and athletic wear, but also stocks reasonably priced soft drinks, bakery items and snacks.

SATURDAYS & SUNDAYS

Market Madness

Now appearing weekly on Sundays, **Portland Flea** brings together a plethora of vintage clothing, home goods and jewelry, along with local food vendors like Fried Egg I'm In Love and Bella Luna Coffee.

Encompassing more than 175 of Portland's most exciting vendors, **Portland Night Market** is open three weekends a year – in September, April and December – and merges retail, culture, food, music and drinks in a fun atmosphere.

The free, all-ages **Last Thursday** cultural event and market happens on NE Alberta St between NE 15th Ave to NE 30th Ave. May through September around 4pm, galleries and businesses located on Alberta will typically host live music and events inside, while outside the street is filled with arts and craft vendors, food and performers.

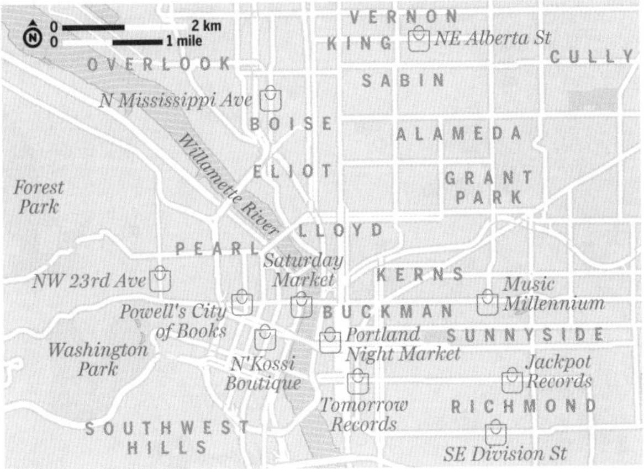
0 2 km
0 1 mile
VERNON
KING
NE Alberta St
CULLY
OVERLOOK
SABIN
N Mississippi Ave
BOISE
ALAMEDA
Willamette River
ELIOT
GRANT PARK
Forest Park
LLOYD
PEARL
Saturday Market
NW 23rd Ave
KERNS
Music Millennium
Powell's City of Books
BUCKMAN
Portland Night Market
SUNNYSIDE
Washington Park
N'Kossi Boutique
Jackpot Records
Tomorrow Records
RICHMOND
SOUTHWEST HILLS
SE Division St

Left Saturday Market **Below** Barista, NW 23rd Ave

Shopping Strips

Support small businesses by frequenting one of Portland's bustling shopping strips:

NE Alberta St Also a great place to grab food and drinks, Alberta Ave is loaded with shopping opportunities. Head to Collage for anything and everything craft and DIY, while spots like Cord have lots of survival, convenience and camping gadgets. There's also Ecovibe, a fantastic home-decor store, and the Pencil Test, a bra store for the busty.

SE Division St Here you can shop everything from ceramics to bath and body products, candles and wall planters at Carter & Rose, before sampling all the gourmet ice cream flavors at Salt & Straw. This street also boasts stellar thrift shop Artifact PDX: Creative Upcycle, stocking lots of vintage clothing, furniture and home goods.

N Mississippi Ave In addition to lots of great bars and restaurants, N Mississippi also boasts shops like the unique quality-focused Black Wagon Kids Boutique, and the Herb Shoppe, selling everything from tinctures and immune support to bath salts and essential oils. You can also find trendy women's clothing boutique Sloan, browse rare and new comics at Bridge City Comics, and play around at electronic instrument store Control Voltage.

BARISTA

28 Family FUN

ZOO | MUSEUM | OUTDOORS

With its plethora of outdoors parks, many of which include stellar playgrounds and splash pads, Portland is family-friendly by nature. During the rainy season, there are also plenty of kid-friendly activities – Play Date PDX! OMSI! – when staying indoors is a must.

PNG STUDIO PHOTOGRAPHY/SHUTTERSTOCK ©

How to

Getting here Drive and pay to park at the zoo using the Parking Kitty app. Alternatively, take the MAX red- or blue-line train or bus line 63 to the Washington Park stop.

When to go Year-round. OMSI and Oaks Amusement Park's roller rink are both ideal on rainy days. The zoo is optimal from spring through fall – keep in mind that crowds peak during summer.

GAGLIARDIPHOTOGRAPHY/SHUTTERSTOCK ©

Oregon Zoo (adult/child $24/19) Lions, tigers and bears – *oh my!* Located just west of Portland in Beaverton, the Oregon Zoo is a lovely respite from the city, and offers kids an exciting place in which to run around and see a plethora of animals, such as polar bears, elephants, mountain lions, giraffes, flamingos, owls and reptiles – not to mention an indoor tropical rainforest.

OMSI (Oregon Museum of Science and Industry; adult/child $21/14) There are rotating exhibits, some of which – like Body Worlds – might not be appropriate for kids. But the museum does have a Science Playground for kids under six and their families. This includes an infant and toddler space, a frequently changing water area, a discovery lab with weekly experiments, and a climbing area. Also check out the schedule for its

JABÓN

ALEXANDER OGANEZOV/SHUTTERSTOCK ©

Splash Pads

On warm days, take the kids to a park with a splash pad (a water-play area with minimal standing water). They're safe and keep kids cool and entertained. Try fountain-adjacent water-play areas at North Portland parks like Kenton, Columbia, and Peninsula, as well as West Side parks Jamison Square, Director Park, and Waterfront Park (on Salmon St).

Left OMSI **Above left** Oregon Zoo **Above right** Waterfront Park

OmniMax – a massive dome-shaped theater and screen that makes for an immersive experience – for upcoming educational and movie programming.

Oaks Amusement Park This skating rink ($10) and amusement park (ride bracelets $22 to $48) boasts one of the country's oldest trolley parks. Food options include ICEEs, popcorn, cheeseburgers, chicken strips and nachos.

Slappy Cakes Kids love this pancake restaurant. It has griddles right at the dining tables, so families can make their own pancake recipes using batter from squeeze bottles, and bowls of assorted fixings like blueberries, nuts and chocolate chips. For adults who don't want to make their own pancakes, Slappy Cakes also has a menu of entrees like a breakfast burrito, *huevos rancheros,* and avocado pesto Benedict.

Bullwinkles Family Fun Center

Located in Wilsonville, just south of Portland, Bullwinkles offers an almost overwhelming number of kid-friendly activities that extend far beyond the massive play structure and arcade games. There are also plenty of fun activities fit for adults, including bowling, bumper boats, go-karts, mini-golf and laser tag. If you work up an appetite, try the Bullwinkles pizza restaurant inside (it's actually good pizza). It makes for a somewhat quiet place to hang out while the kids continue to burn off energy – that is, if you don't mind electronic Rocky-and-Bullwinkle figures playing songs and doing sketches.

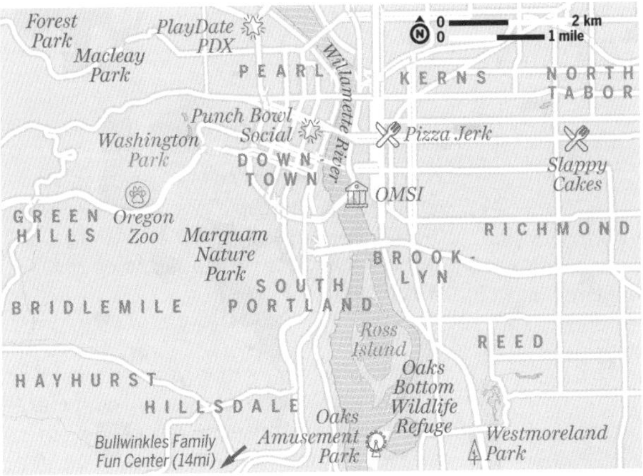
Forest Park
PlayDate PDX
Macleay Park
PEARL
Willamette River
KERNS
NORTH TABOR
0 2 km
0 1 mile
Punch Bowl Social
Washington Park
DOWNTOWN
Pizza Jerk
Slappy Cakes
OMSI
GREEN HILLS
Oregon Zoo
Marquam Nature Park
RICHMOND
BROOKLYN
SOUTH PORTLAND
BRIDLEMILE
Ross Island
REED
HAYHURST
Oaks Bottom Wildlife Refuge
HILLSDALE
Oaks Amusement Park
Westmoreland Park
Bullwinkles Family Fun Center (14mi)

Pizza Jerk As the rule goes, all kids love pizza and soft serve. The good news is that Pizza Jerk also has some of the best pizza pies in town – try the margherita and the white pie made with ricotta, fresh mozzarella, garlic, chili flake and black pepper. Pizza Jerk also has a big backyard with a neat play structure, and room for kids to run around.

Punch Bowl Social Open to all ages until 10pm, Punch Bowl Social has everything from karaoke and bowling to table games and an arcade.

PlayDate PDX Kids love this spot offering an indoor, three-story playground, two dance floors and a ball cannon area. It's also got a cafe and dining area geared toward adults (beer and wine!), who can also play for free.

Westmoreland Park Westmoreland Park's nature-based playground is a real beauty. Located next to a pretty pond inside a nature park, the playground has awesome logs and boulders to climb, a sandpit with digging tools, a water pump that's on in the warmer months, and even opportunities to build forts from tree limbs.

Left Oaks Amusement Park
Below Westmoreland Park

Listings

BEST OF THE REST

Gourmands' Guide

Swiss Hibiscus $$

Swiss Hibiscus serves worship-worthy Swiss dishes like *spätzli* (pan-fried noodle dumplings), rosti (hashbrowns), *älpler* (a mac and cheese with potatoes and onion), cheese fondue, *jägerschnitzel* (pork medallions with white wine) and so much more. Don't leave without a bottle of its famous Martin's Swiss Dressing.

Tin Shed Garden Cafe $$

Tin Shed allows dogs in its heated, cozy, fully covered patio with a fireplace. It even offers a couple of dishes for pooches, and some great eats for humans such as the Big Hit Burrito, stacked scrambles four ways, and sides like and cheese grits.

Pambiche $$

Longstanding outpost for Cuban Creole food and rum flights. Highlights include maduros (cigars), avocado salad, *pescado con coco* (fish in coconut sauce), and *tres leches* (milk cake) for dessert.

Miss Delta $$

Come to Southern-inspired Miss Delta for soul-food classics such as griddle cakes, biscuits and gravy, country fried steak, cheesy grits and smoked brisket. Miss Delta keeps it moving, often with short or no wait time.

Jam on Hawthorne $

Extremely vegan- and vegetarian-friendly, Jam is beloved for biscuits served with, yes, jam that comes in a squeeze bottle. Offers a wide array of mimosas. Juice and flavor options include strawberry, blood orange and lavender.

La Piñata Takos $

This small family-owned Mexican cart serves up authentic, affordable food. Its no-lard beans mean it's vegan- and vegetarian-friendly. Don't sleep on the fish or carnitas tacos, churros, or horchata.

Mama Bird $$

A chicken restaurant that caters to those with gluten allergies and dietary allergies. It makes melt-in-your-mouth grilled chicken, where you pick how much of the bird you want, and which sides and sauces.

Ate Oh Ate $

A Hawaiian BBQ joint, Ate Oh Ate primarily makes teriyaki chicken and pork. Its teriyaki tofu plate is excellent, especially when made spicy Korean-style. Don't leave without some mac salad.

Stretch the Noodle $

One of the best food carts in Portland features monstrous portions of hand-stretched Chinese noodles made fresh right in front of you, and stir fried with chili oil, and a bevy of colorful veggies.

KATRINAMARIE/SHUTTERSTOCK ©

Salt & Straw

Matt's BBQ $

Voted Best Food Cart, Matt's BBQ serves incredibly tender meats like brisket, pork spare ribs, beef rib and turkey on a tray with butcher paper, as the BBQ gods intended.

Matt's BBQ Tacos $

The equally esteemed Matt's BBQ Tacos adds the same quality meats to a tortilla with breakfast or regular fixings. It also offers all-day breakfast tacos, pork-belly or ground-beef tacos, and some excellent meat-free options.

Gado Gado $$-$$$

Switching up its family-style menu frequently, Gado Gado makes a blend of pan-Asian and Dutch-Indonesian cuisine.

Salt & Straw $

The artisanal ice cream comes in flavors you can't find anywhere else: honey lavender, pear and blue cheese, strawberry honey balsamic and Arbequina olive oil.

Mama Dut $

Serving authentic vegan versions of Vietnamese classics, Mama Dut offers chicken-fried oyster mushroom banh mis, garlic phish sauce 'rybs' in bao buns, and passionfruit limeade.

Bullard $$

Latin American–inspired eats are served all day, but the brunch is noteworthy for its shrimp and grits, apple-cake donuts, and fried chicken or sweet-potato tacos.

¿Por Que No? $

This wildly popular street taco spot almost always has a line. If you're going to wait, may as well wait for its weekend brunch, which offers breakfast tacos and *chilaquiles verdes*.

Blossoming Lotus $$

Bring a skeptic here for fancy vegan brunch, with options like pancakes topped with berries and toasted nuts, and a Lotus Benedict made with spinach and lemon hollandaise sauce.

RITU MANOJ JETHANI/SHUTTERSTOCK ©

Pioneer Place

Ruby Jewel $

Come for customizable (or pre-made) ice cream sandwiches, in flavors like lemon cookies with lavender ice cream, chocolate with mint, oatmeal with butterscotch, and brown-sugar cookies with strawberry ice cream.

Portland for Shopaholics

Pioneer Place

A downtown mall featuring high-end designer brands like Coach and Gucci, along with more accessible outlets like H&M, J Crew and Zara.

Woodburn Outlets Mall

Located 31 miles south of Portland, the Wood-burn Outlets is the place to shop for lower prices of every major fashion brand imaginable, from GAP to Kate Spade, Guess and Nike.

Washington Square Mall

Located in Beaverton, this is one of the Portland area's best malls. It's home to a Cheesecake Factory and a Tesla store and is near Benihana Sushi and Japanese Steakhouse.

Jantzen Beach

In a massive outdoor mall in the northernmost part of Portland, find megastores like Target, Ulta, Best Buy, Home Depot, Lowes, TJ Maxx, Petco and more.

Green Spaces

Tryon Creek State Natural Area

Located in deep SW Portland and away from the city center, Tryon Creek sees fewer crowds than other natural areas in Portland, making it a great choice for peace and quiet.

Sellwood Riverfront Park

Below the Sellwood Bridge and neighboring Oaks Bottom Wildlife Refuge and Oaks Amusement Park, this spot has great views and plenty of shade trees. Lots of dogs and kids swimming and splashing.

Laurelhurst Park

This 26-acre city park has a serene duck pond (that's gorgeous in snowy weather), paved paths, a playground and a wide variety of trees.

Pier Park

Comprising a large forest with paved and unpaved trails, Pier Park has a lot going on. Locals visit for disc golf, basketball, baseball, tennis and, over the bridge, Chimney Dog Park.

Poet's Beach

Family-friendly spot for river swimming just south of downtown, under the Marquam Bridge. Accessible via a path lined with rocks with children's poems carved into them.

Bars, Brews & Cocktails

Rum Club $

A tiki bar without excessive kitsch, Rum Club serves tropical drinks from its U-shaped bar, and offers patio seating.

Psychic Bar $

Drink a craft cocktail or tropical Scooby Snack slushy, and eat tots and jalapeño queso (dipping sauce) on Psychic Bar's sprawling covered patio.

BrewBarge $$

On this 1½-hour cruise ($35 to $40 per person), you can bring your own beer aboard or grab some at the check-in spot.

Moloko $

Ultra-vibey coral-reef cocktail lounge Moloko is unique for its eight saltwater tanks filled with coral, fish and invertebrates.

10 Barrel Brewery $$

Drink brews on the rooftop patio while enjoying the city views. The brewery's kitchen makes excellent food to pair with your beer flight.

Breakside Brewery $

This appealing brewery offers extra-long patio tables, waffle fries, mac 'n' cheese, jalapeño poppers and beer flights, as well as beers to-go.

M Bar $

This hole-in-the-wall wine bar on NW 21st Ave offers NW beers, Japanese sake, and thoughtfully curated old-world wines from all over the globe. It stocks light snacks, but also allows guests to bring their own food.

Bar Bar $

Come for the enormous patio – where movies are sometimes played – solid beer and cider on draft, and bites like deep-fried ravioli.

MICHAEL STRAND/SHUTTERSTOCK ©

Laurelhurst Park

ENSO Winery $$

This winery is close to the city center. The urban winery is a spacious, modern space that also includes patio seating. Here you can sip on old-world-style wines made with grapes sourced from up and down the West Coast.

Victoria Bar $

Locals love Victoria Bar – a mostly vegan bar on N Albina Ave – for its sprawling patio and incredible drinks like the 'Fire Swamp,' a spicy, effervescent gin-based cocktail.

Pink Rabbit $

Locals love Pink Rabbit for its excellent drinks, hip design, Asian-fusion food, and friendly service. Cocktails include banana daiquiris, frosé slushies, palomas, or a 'Make It Snap Pea' – a concoction of gin, fino sherry, bay leaf, snap pea and egg white.

Bible Club $

A speakeasy-style bar filled with antiques. It files a slew of classic cocktails under 'The Old Testament,' and more adventurous, inventive libations under 'The New Testament.'

For Fun

McMenamins Crystal Ballroom

A large historic venue known for its iconic bouncy floor and regal aesthetic, and for bringing major artists to a unique space that's more intimate than an arena.

Arlene Schnitzer Concert Hall

Locals lovingly refer to this grand venue as 'The Schnitz.' It's the kind of venue you dress up for, since its ornate Rococo Revival architecture seems to demand it. Acts like Solange, Miguel and HAIM have played here in the past. It often hosts the Oregon Symphony, and other classical-music ensembles.

Arlene Schnitzer Concert Hall

Keller Auditorium

Portland's home for touring Broadway musicals and ballet, the Keller Auditorium is a fancy venue for high-caliber artists like Lauryn Hill, Avril Lavigne, Regina Spektor, and the Indigo Girls with the Oregon Symphony.

Roseland

Longstanding venue, the Roseland, with its capacity of 1400 people, is a must-stop for a variety of major hip-hop, R&B, rock and electronic-music acts.

Wonder Ballroom

With its original Mission and Spanish Revival architecture, the Wonder has been many things. Since 2004, it's been a music venue and has hosted acts from NAO to Dinosaur Jr, and Death Cab for Cutie to the Black Pumas.

McMenamins Edgefield

An outdoor music venue located east of Portland in Troutdale, on the 74-acre McMenamins' property, which also hosts a brewery, winery, distillery, spa, movie theater and more.

Scan to find more things to do in Portland online

WILLAMETTE VALLEY

WINE | SCENERY | SPORTS

Experience Willamette Valley online

WILLAMETTE VALLEY
Trip Builder

Taking a drive in the largely rural and suburban Willamette Valley region means getting acquainted with Oregon's stunning natural variety. Once outside Portland and in the valley, luxuriate in the small-town vibes and slower pace, savoring the produce stands, myriad farms, vineyards and other remote destinations nestled in nature.

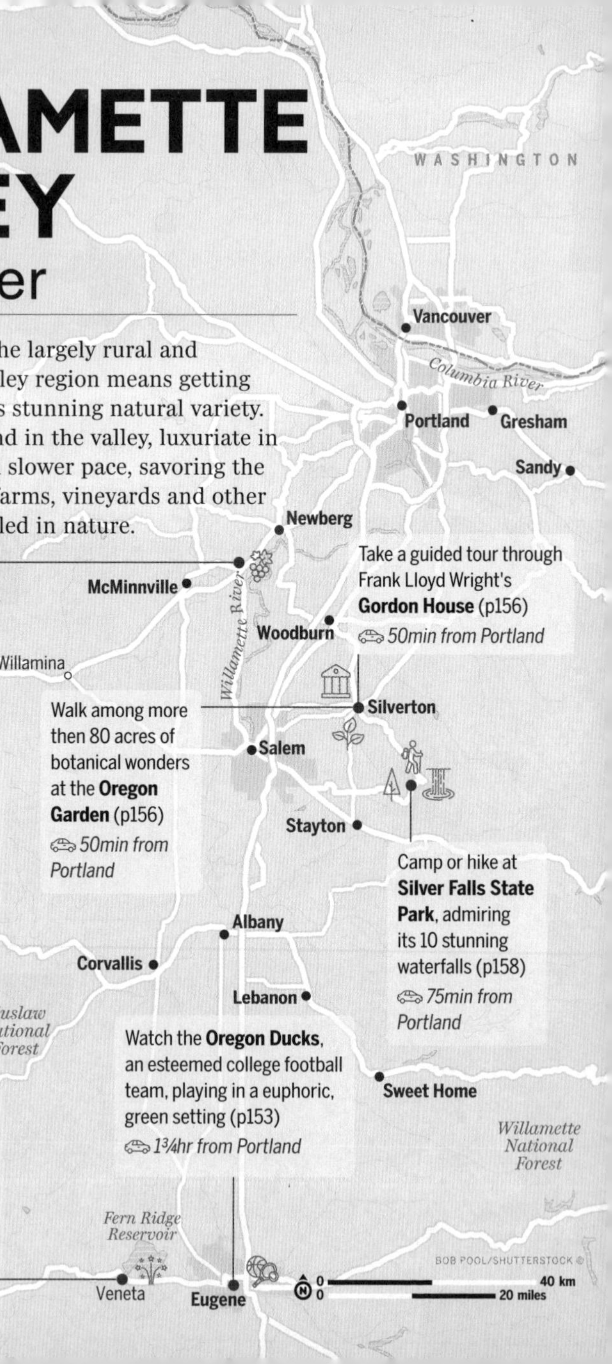
WASHINGTON
Vancouver
Columbia River
Portland
Gresham
Sandy
Newberg
McMinnville
Siuslaw National Forest
Willamette River
Woodburn
Willamina
Silverton
Salem
Pacific Ocean
Stayton
Albany
Corvallis
Lebanon
Siuslaw National Forest
Sweet Home
Willamette National Forest
Fern Ridge Reservoir
Veneta
Eugene
0 40 km
0 20 miles

Sip Willamette Valley wine amid vast fields at **Stoller Family Estate** in Dayton (p155)
45min from Portland

Take a guided tour through Frank Lloyd Wright's **Gordon House** (p156)
50min from Portland

Walk among more then 80 acres of botanical wonders at the **Oregon Garden** (p156)
50min from Portland

Camp or hike at **Silver Falls State Park**, admiring its 10 stunning waterfalls (p158)
75min from Portland

Watch the **Oregon Ducks**, an esteemed college football team, playing in a euphoric, green setting (p153)
1¾hr from Portland

Immerse yourself in the **Oregon Country Fair**, a celebration of all things arty, crafty and bohemian (p153)
75min from Portland

Practicalities

ARRIVING

Eugene Amtrak Station Centrally located; from here take a rideshare or public transit around town.

Eugene Airport The best and fastest way into town is by car (20 minutes).

FIND YOUR WAY

Visit *traveloregon.com* for guides and travel tips on different parts of the Willamette Valley.

MONEY

Bring your credit/debit card to pay at most places, but carry cash for Eugene's Saturday Market.

WHERE TO STAY

Location	Pro/Con
Eugene	Lots of attractions and nightlife. Two-hour drive from Portland. Prices can rise sharply during key football games (September to November) and at graduation (mid-June).
Dundee	Slower pace of life. Easy access to wineries. Limited public transit.
Salem	Close to the 27-stop Marion Farm Loop, with various farm tours and opportunities for tastings. Little nightlife.

GETTING AROUND

Car Drive throughout the whole Willamette Valley, including Silverton, Nerberg and Dundee.

Bus FlixBus goes from Portland to Salem, Corvallis or Eugene.

Train Amtrak travels from Portland to Salem or Eugene. The Emerald Express serves the Eugene-Springfield region.

PRINCE PUCKLERS

TOP: EMMA EDDY/CORNUCOPIA, EUGENE © BOTTOM: WWW.PRINCEPUCKLERS.COM ©

EATING & DRINKING

Cornucopia makes what has been voted Eugene's favorite burger (pictured top) for multiple years in a row. It also offers craft cocktails and rotating microbrews. Also in Eugene, Marché serves up French cuisine with a focus on locally grown, seasonal and sustainable ingredients.

Best for lunch in Silverton
Los Girasoles (p160)

Must-try ice cream
Prince Pucklers (pictured bottom; p160)

JUN–SEP
Gorgeous warm weather; perfect for water sports and river floats

OCT–DEC
Cool fall weather; great for produce farms and farmers markets

JAN–FEB
Cold weather; slow event season; ideal for basketball games

MAR–MAY
Beautiful spring weather; cherry blossoms and flowers start to bloom

29 Falling for EUGENE

FOOTBALL | RUNNING | BREW PUBS

Located a couple of hours south of Portland, the town of Eugene is made up of equal parts college spirit and hippie vibes. Along with sports tourism, brewery hopping and the arts, there's also plenty of nature and trails to explore, such as Pre's Trail (ideal for runners) and peaks like Spencer Butte, which offers a complete view of Eugene.

DIANEBENTLEYRAYMOND/GETTY IMAGES ©

How to

Getting here If driving isn't an option, take a FlixBus to get here in 2½ to three hours, and be dropped off at the historic Hayward Field, AKA the longstanding home of Tracktown USA.

When to go Visit in fall to experience the electricity of college football. However, anytime from spring through fall is great. Winter brings less traffic, and fun opportunities like Oregon Ducks Basketball games at the impressive Matthew Knight Arena.

JOSHUA RAINEY PHOTOGRAPHY/SHUTTERSTOCK ©

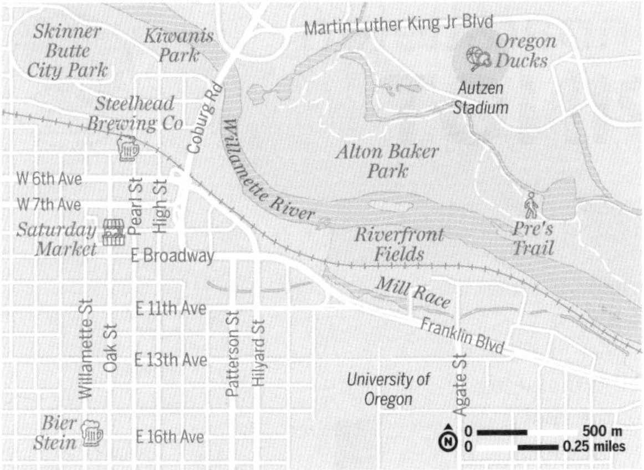
Skinner Butte City Park
Kiwanis Park
Martin Luther King Jr Blvd
Oregon Ducks
Autzen Stadium
Steelhead Brewing Co
Coburg Rd
Willamette River
Alton Baker Park
W 6th Ave
W 7th Ave
Pearl St
High St
Saturday Market
E Broadway
Riverfront Fields
Pre's Trail
Mill Race
E 11th Ave
Franklin Blvd
Willamette St
Oak St
E 13th Ave
Patterson St
Hilyard St
University of Oregon
Agate St
Bier Stein
E 16th Ave
0 500 m
0 0.25 miles

Oregon Ducks football 'Game Day' in Eugene is unlike any other. For the full experience, park near the University of Oregon then walk through the campus, across Franklin Blvd, over the river and through the woods to Autzen Stadium. The moment fans see the Oregon 'O' peering through the trees is magical. On the other side of the forest, people line up for photo ops with Autzen in the background.

TrackTown USA Immerse yourself in the concept of Track-Town USA, the name with which Eugene was dubbed for its long history of track running. The Track & Field Olympic Trials have gone on here for decades. Runners should explore running trails like **Pre's Trail** – named after Steve Prefontaine, the late long-distance runner and University of Oregon legend who competed in the 1972 summer Olympics. Pre's Trail winds through Alton Baker Park and follows trails he used to run. (There are also two feature films about the legend: *Prefontaine,* starring Jared Leto as Prefontaine, and *Without Limits*, as well as a documentary film, *Fire on the Track*.) Also worth visiting is the sports-themed joint Track Town Pizza.

Brew pubs For delicious upscale brewery dining, try **Steelhead Brewing Co** in downtown Eugene. The **Bier Stein** has 27 brews on tap, largely from around Oregon and the West Coast. The menu is solid, with excellent options like a turkey 'Up In the Club,' mac 'n' cheese cooked in the restaurant's bier soup, and a plate of chicken strips and doughnut holes.

Events Check out lively events like the Saturday Market and the Whiteaker Block Party. See the calendar at the Hult Center.

Far left top Willamette River, Eugene
Far left bottom Oregon Ducks mascot, Autzen Stadium

Fun at the Oregon Country Fair

Every July this three-day festival epitomizes the hippie culture of Oregon. Nestled in a wooded setting in Veneta, just 15 miles west of Eugene along the Long Tom River, the OCF hosts roughly 45,000 people, celebrates all things artsy and feels like a massive outdoor party. The event offers entertainment such as acrobatics and music, handmade art and crafts, and food. The OCF often donates proceeds to local arts programs, as well as summer and after-school programs in underfunded schools. You'll find everything from textiles to clothing and gemstones to leatherwork. Bringing cash is recommended, as many vendors do not accept credit/debit cards.

30 Unparalleled PINOT

WINE | FOOD | TOURS

In terms of wine, Oregon is most famous for its pinot noir, which is thought by many to be the best in the country. Pinot noir from the Willamette Valley is so good because of the cool climate and prolonged grape-growing season. The wine boasts an earthy taste, with notes of cranberries and lovely high acidity.

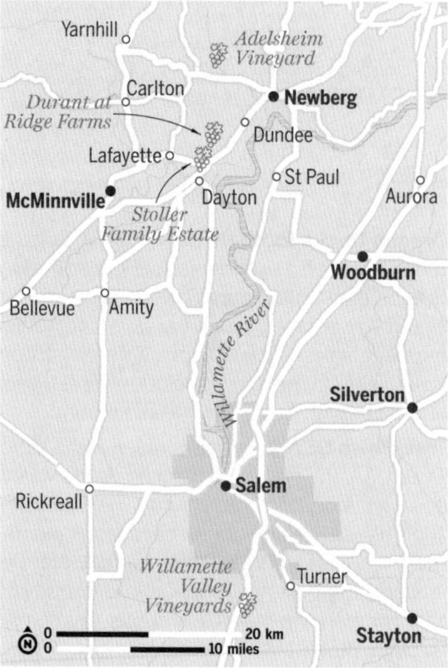

Yarnhill
Adelsheim Vineyard
Carlton
Newberg
Durant at Ridge Farms
Dundee
Lafayette
St Paul
McMinnville
Dayton
Aurora
Stoller Family Estate
Woodburn
Bellevue
Amity
Willamette River
Silverton
Salem
Rickreall
Willamette Valley Vineyards
Turner
Stayton
0
20 km
0
10 miles

How to

Getting here From Portland, winery-packed Dundee is 25 miles and 40 minutes away by car, while Turner is 55 miles and an hour. Hop-on, hop-off winery tour shuttles are available (nwwine shuttle.com).

When to go Although Willamette is a year-round destination, harvest season, between September and October, is best for both wines and tours – and offers the fall bonus of gorgeous golden leaves. Summer means nice weather, but more crowds.

Willamette Valley Vineyards Basic tastings for just $15 to $20, plus dinner-pairing options, as well as private winery tours (with tastings). It also provides the opportunity to customize your own wine blends with the Pinot Noir Clonal Blending Experience. For a food-and-beverage minimum, the vineyard also offers private wine pods: lit-up domed structures for guests to sit in on the outdoor patio or courtyard.

Adelsheim Vineyard This Newberg's vineyard has been around for more than 50 years, specializing in pinot noir and wines from the Chehalem Mountains. In 1978, it became the first-ever winery in that

Right top Stoller Family Estate **Right bottom** Adelsheim Vineyard

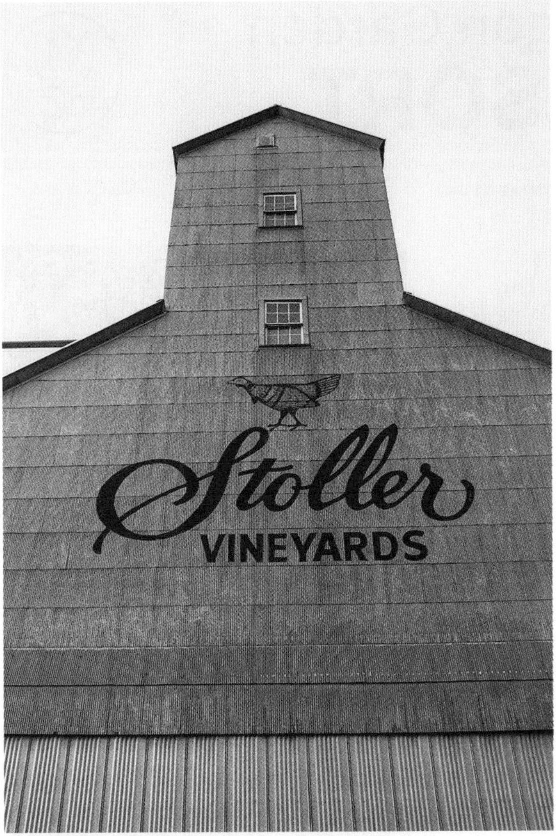
Stoller
VINEYARDS

GEORGE ROSE/GETTY IMAGES ©

JORGE GARRIDO/ALAMY STOCK PHOTO ©

Winery Picnics

In pre-pandemic times, many Willamette Valley wineries and vineyards allowed guests to bring their own picnics, as long as they ate them outside. Since times and protocols are constantly changing, it's advisable to call ahead to confirm whether your chosen winery is currently allowing guests to bring their own food.

region. Go for the Estate Tasting ($55), which comes with a market box, filled with some of the winery's favorite locally made bites.

Stoller Family Estate With a vineyard that spans over 400 acres in the cool climate beneath the Dundee Hills, Stoller Family Estate dedicates 158 acres to growing pinot noir varieties, and 55 acres to chardonnay. The farm has a strong focus on sustainability, and the wines are chosen for their elegance.

Durant at Ridge Farms At this Dayton winery, customers can reserve one of its private vineyard cabanas for up to four people ($350). The property also boasts a 1-mile nature trail that takes you through vineyards, sheep pastures, lavender fields, an old-growth forest and more, and hosts a Lavender Festival each July.

31 Oregon Garden RESORT

GARDENS | RELAXATION | ARCHITECTURE

The Oregon Garden has established itself as a destination since 1999. Those who love plants and architecture will enjoy visiting this resort for a quiet getaway that includes pool lounging, fireside chats, strolling through botanical gardens, and architectural wonders.

How to

Getting here The gardens are in Silverton, about an hour from Portland by car.

When to go Spring, summer and fall are particularly beautiful for garden viewing. Going during December has its perks, too – after Thanksgiving the garden puts up an enchanting Christmas-lights display. Firepits are scattered throughout the venue.

Tip The Oregon Garden has pet-friendly rooms, and lots of areas to take your pup.

How much Admission is free for kids under four, $2 to $6 for kids aged five to 11, $5 to $9 for students, and $8 to $12 for adults.

Gordon House Architect Frank Lloyd Wright's Gordon House is one of the main attractions. Visitors can schedule a 45-minute guided tour of the interior of Lloyd Wright's only design built in Oregon and learn about his vision and how the project ended up in Silverton.

Botanical marvels The garden itself – over 80 acres and encompassing more than 20 gardens – creates a beautiful getaway setting. The property has a garden for every botanical interest: a water garden that's reminiscent of Claude Monet, a tropical house, wetlands, a rediscovery forest,

Above Water feature **Far right top** Christmas lights **Far right bottom** Gordon House

Food with a View

Sourcing local ingredients for Northwest-inspired fare, the dinner menu includes lemon pepper salmon, crab cakes, breaded pork chop and sundry pastas. The views of the gardens and the Willamette Valley are incredible. Pets are welcome on the restaurant patio.

a children's garden and even a pet-friendly garden.

Moonstone Spa Is a vacation *really* a vacation without some sort of spa treatment? The garden-themed spa at Oregon Garden offers various ways to achieve relaxation, offering a slew of massages, holistic or clinical facials, body treatments, just-for-men specials and more.

Winter wonderland As part of its Silverton Christmas Market, the Oregon Garden puts on a fantastic lights display every December. You can stroll along the garden's lit paths while basking in the enchantment of more than a million lights. Other winter festivities at the authentically German market typically include an ice-skating rink, sledding, visits with Santa, various vendors offering food and artisan goods, and a Biergarten serving local brews.

BOB POOL/SHUTTERSTOCK ©

DAN CAMPBELL/SHUTTERSTOCK ©

32 Waterfall WONDERS

WATERFALLS | HIKING | NATURE

Spend a few hours in Silver Falls State Park hiking dense forested trails and basking in the beauty of 10 waterfalls of varying height and size, one of which you can see from behind its 177ft curtain fall. Walk along the rocky canyon that slopes down to a creek and, finally, the forest floor.

BOB POOL/SHUTTERSTOCK ©

How to

Getting here By car, Portland to the park takes a little over an hour.

When to go May through October offer swimming opportunities at Silver Falls. If only hiking and sightseeing, any time of the year is lovely, with wildflowers at their best from late March to May.

Tips Pack lunch, bring water and wear practical shoes. If you want to swim at the base of a waterfall, don't forget a towel, waterproof sandals, and dry clothes for after.

Fruit stop If visiting Silver Falls from Portland, stop en route at **EZ Orchards Farm Market**, right off the I-5, to grab produce and snacks for your long day of hiking.

Hiking trail The **Trail of Ten Falls** is a 7.2-mile loop of 10 waterfalls at Silver Falls. It's a moderate hike with an overall elevation of 800ft, and sturdy shoes are encouraged. (Several connecting trails can make the route shorter, and since pets are not allowed on the canyon trail, these other trails are safe routes for hikers with pooches to take.) The first waterfall that hikers encounter is the famous

Above South Falls **Far right top** Trail of Ten Falls, Silver Falls State Park **Far right bottom** Mt Angel Oktoberfest

September Brews

An added bonus of a September visit to the park is the nearby **Mt Angel Oktoberfest**, during which celebrations take over the town, and participants imbibe a wide variety of craft and German beer.

South Falls, a 177ft curtain fall you can view from behind while walking underneath a massive rock overhang. The route passes through Douglas fir trees and ferny undergrowth and follows a winding creek. From the **Silver Falls State Park Scenic Viewpoint** take in the rolling hills, trees and far-off mountain sides. You'll definitely want to bring a camera.

Overnighting Visitors can choose to make Silver Falls a day trip or an overnight visit by staying in a nearby hotel or the park's main campground. The day-use area has sizable lawns, BBQ stands, picnic areas with shelters and tables, horseshoe pits, a playground and an off-leash area for dogs. For staying overnight, there are cabins and an area for RVs and tents. There's also a horse campground with horse stalls for those riding horses through the backcountry trails. Campsites can be booked six months in advance (oregonstateparks.reserveamerica.com).

JOSHUA RAINEY PHOTOGRAPHY/SHUTTERSTOCK ©

JANIS MIGLAVS/DANITA DELIMONT/ALAMY STOCK PHOTO ©

Listings

BEST OF THE REST

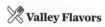

Valley Flavors

Mike's Drive-In $

This old-school Oregon drive-in chain boasts some of the best fish-and-chips in town, as well as darn good chicken strip baskets, burgers and shakes.

Super Torta $

When in Oregon City, getting a burrito from authentic Mexican joint Super Torta is a must.

Cheesecake Factory $$

The Cheesecake Factory at Washington Square Mall in Tigard has an enormous menu with options for everyone.

Benihana $$$

Famed Hibachi spot Benihana in Beaverton is an obvious go-to for celebrities, as evidenced by the wall of photos depicting celeb guests. Reservations advisable.

Mazzi's $$

This South Eugene Italian restaurant is fitted with cozy fireplaces, and serves delectable pasta dishes like pesto ravioli and fettuccini.

Beppe & Gianni's Trattoria $$$

This Italian spot is arguably the best restaurant in all of Eugene, with dishes like the *lasagna della casa*, and pasta options that let guests pick and choose their sauce and noodles.

Off the Waffle $

Mouthwatering Liége waffles in Eugene. The waffles are savory (goat cheese, avocado, and sunnyside-up eggs), sweet (strawberries and cream) and everything in between (bacon, havarti and maple syrup).

Little Big Burger $

This excellent burger chain was born in Portland, but has opened a Eugene location. If nothing else, order the always-perfectly hot, fresh and salty truffle fries.

Agate Alley Bistro $$

One of the Eugene campus area's better restaurants and bars, casual haunt Agate Alley does taco Tuesday, burgers, a great mac 'n' cheese, and weekend brunch.

Prince Pucklers $

The go-to spot for ice cream in Eugene, Prince Pucklers has even had President Barack Obama as a visitor.

Sweet Life $

Vegans and non-vegans alike love this 100% plant-based patisserie serving cheesecakes, tortes, pies, cupcakes, wedding cakes and morning pastries.

Los Girasoles $

This no-frills joint offers tasty burritos in Silverton. Notable for its fresh tortillas, attention to detail and superb baked goods.

Thai Dish Cuisine $

Quality Thai food in Silverton. Pad Thai or one of the curries will not disappoint.

Green Spaces

Skinner's Butte

Named after the city's founder, Eugene Skinner, a name you may recognize from *The Simpsons*, which was created by Portland-born Matt Groening. The park includes 100 acres of play area and natural area, with fishing, ball fields, community gardens, rock climbing and hiking trails.

Spencer Butte Trail

Hiking this 1.7-mile loop up to the summit is a moderately challenging hike that lets hikers see the whole city of Eugene from the top.

Alton Baker Park

Located along the Willamette River, this wooded area features wetlands, biking trails, Pre's running trails and a dog park.

Hendrix Park

Eugene's oldest city park covers 80 acres and features 200-year-old Douglas fir trees, a 12-acre rhododendron garden, hiking paths, looped trails, wildflowers and more.

Like the Nightlife

barTini bistro $

Loved by Eugene locals for its fun vibe, inventive cupcake flavors and firepits, as well as great drinks and service.

Ex Novo Brewing Co $$

This historic downtown Beaverton location slings hop-forward, malt-forward light and fresh beers alongside some wine, cocktails and cider. Detroit-style pizza with dollops of red sauce on top.

Tigard Taphouse $

Offering a wide drink selection such as Japanese lager from pFriem and blackberry habanero cider from Oregon Cider Company, Tigard also has a big patio and outstanding panini, chicken wings, and mac 'n' cheese.

Silver Falls Brewery Alehouse $$

Perfect sunny-day spot for a post–Silver Falls drink and meal. Offerings include burgers and a hazy NE IPA or cider. Sit on the patio to enjoy the twinkle lights and firepit.

Sam Bond's Garage $

Serving local beer and organic food, this Eugene bar often doubles as a music venue.

MARK KIVER/ALAMY STOCK PHOTO ©

Black Rabbit House, McMenamin's Edgefield

Rennie's Landing $

This iconic college hangout bar in Eugene is ideal for anyone wanting to catch a Ducks or Blazers game – along with a good drink and good food – in a spirited environment.

Venues

McMenamin's Edgefield

McMenamin's 74-acre property in Troutdale encompasses a brewery, distillery and winery, as well as a spa, hotel and most notably, a large outdoor music venue.

Hult Center

This grand performing-arts center is where you'll find everything from dance and theater to classical music and comedy in downtown Eugene.

Cuthbert

Open seasonally for outdoor shows and events, the Cuthbert typically features food and drink vendors, with people setting up outside the venue selling glass pipes and handmade items.

Scan to find more things to do in Willamette Valley online

33 Columbia River GORGE

WATERFALLS | HIKES | WINERIES

A short drive from Portland is the mighty Columbia River, guide to westward pioneers, and today's dividing line between Washington and Oregon. World-class windsurfing and kiteboarding are popular activities on the river, and on land, there are great hikes and cycling opportunities.

STEVE TERRILL/GETTY IMAGES ©

How to

Getting here & around The gorge is most easily explored by car. The Columbia Gorge Express (ridecatbus.org) is a convenient way to see the sights. This shuttle bus leaves four times a day to Hood River, stopping at Multnomah Falls and Cascade Locks.

Permits Starting in 2022, timed entry permits along the 'waterfall corridor' of the Columbia River Gorge Hwy will be required from late May to early September for those traveling by private car. Permits available online through ODOT (oregon.gov/odot/waterfall-corridor-permits).

RIGUCCI/SHUTTERSTOCK ©

The 74-mile-long **Historic Columbia River Hwy** (US Rte 30), which runs from Troutdale to The Dalles was the first planned scenic roadway in the US, built between 1913 and 1922. The more modern I-84 covers a portion of the original route, but you can take a leisurely drive on sections of the historic highway. From Troutdale, the road meanders past farms to the first main stop at **Vista House**, an art nouveau–style gift shop and welcome center, which offers sweeping views of the Columbia River.

Hwy 30 continues to loop through the hills, passing a series of waterfalls and trailheads: **Latourell Falls** (249ft), **Bridal Veil Falls** (140ft) and **Wahkeena Falls** (242ft) are all photogenic, but the granddaddy of them all is **Multnomah Falls**, a 620ft waterfall with a 1-mile trail to the top. For longer hikes,

RYBARMAREKK/SHUTTERSTOCK ©

Dam Big Sturgeon

Bonneville Dam (exit 40), built during the Great Depression, offers tours of its powerhouse from June to September. Note the giant fish ladders that help fish swim past the dams. The Bonneville Fish Hatchery is home to ponds full of trout and an 11ft-long, 70-year-old sturgeon named Herman. The nearby Eagle Creek Trail offers terrific hiking past waterfalls.

Left Multnomah Falls **Top left** Columbia River Gorge **Top right** Bonneville Dam

a 5-mile trail connects Multnomah and Wahkeena Falls. Visit early or on weekdays to beat the crowds.

East of **Bonneville Dam** is the small town of **Cascade Locks** (exit 44), perhaps best known for its **Bridge of the Gods**, which marks the end of the Oregon portion of the Pacific Crest Trail. The town gets its name from a series of locks and a 3000ft canal that allowed boats to bypass rapids in the early 1900s.

The town of **Hood River** is a popular place to overnight in the gorge and serves as a logical base. Mountain biking is a popular activity; road cyclists can ride car-free on a 7-mile bike path from Hood River to Mosier.

Hood River is best known for its world-class windsurfing and kiteboarding on the Columbia. You can watch the action on the beach at the **Hood River Water Front Park**, then stop by **pFriem Family Brewers** for a beer. **Full Sail** is another popular brewery in Hood River;

Offbeat Options

Schreiner Exotic Animal Farm, near Dallesport, WA, this cattle ranch also has around 20 exotic animals roaming in open areas, including zebra, camel, giraffe and antelope. Entry is free.

Western Antique Aircraft & Auto Museum, in Hood River, has a large collection of rare automobiles and planes.

Horsethief Lake State Park View Native American pictographs and petroglyphs in this park, 6 miles east of Dallesport.

Pacific Crest Trail Hike a section of the famed route, perhaps the 2-mile stretch from Cascade Locks to Dry Creek Falls. Upon return, enjoy beverages and bites at Thunder Island Brewing or Gorges Beer on Hwy 30.

■ **Martin Hecht,** *guide and owner of Martin's Gorge Tours*

@MartinsGorgeTours

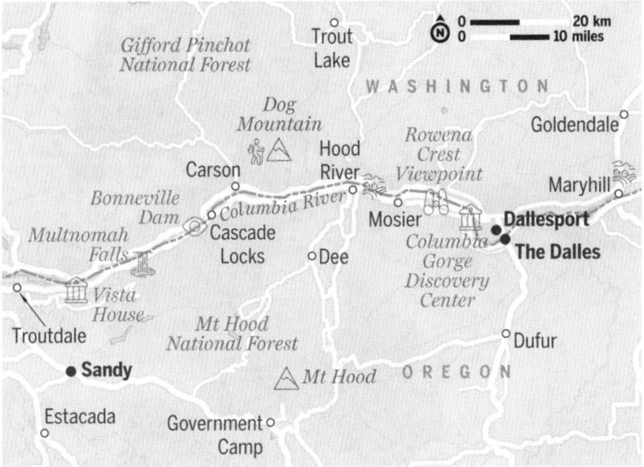
Gifford Pinchot National Forest
Trout Lake
20 km
10 miles
WASHINGTON
Dog Mountain
Hood River
Rowena Crest Viewpoint
Goldendale
Carson
Maryhill
Bonneville Dam
Columbia River
Mosier
Dallesport
Multnomah Falls
Cascade Locks
Dee
Columbia Gorge Discovery Center
The Dalles
Vista House
Troutdale
Mt Hood National Forest
Dufur
Sandy
Mt Hood
OREGON
Estacada
Government Camp

Left Dry Creek Falls, Pacific Crest Trail
Below Mountain biker, Hood River

it offers free tours of its facility. There are several wineries in the area too; ask the local Chamber of Commerce for a map.

In summer, tour the Hood River Valley's **Fruit Loop**, a splendid 35-mile driving (or cycling) tour of fruit stands, wineries, brewpubs, cider houses, craft shops, bakeries and farms. It's good family fun; there are places the kids can stop and pick berries, buy antiques and see farm animals.

Hwy 30 becomes rural again east of Hood River, and the drive becomes particularly stunning at the **Rowena Crest Viewpoint**. Further east, the **Columbia Gorge Discovery Center** is an excellent museum covering the geological and human history of the gorge.

On the Washington side of the river, don't miss the **Stonehenge** replica on a windswept promontory near **Maryhill**. Sam Hill, who built the monument as a WWI memorial, is buried nearby. Hill was also behind the impressive **Maryhill Museum of Art**, which contains a collection of sculptures and drawings from Auguste Rodin. The nearby **Maryhill Winery** has tours.

Another Washington side highlight is **Dog Mountain**, a strenuous but rewarding hike with awesome views of the Cascade volcanoes from the top. Spring is a great time to go when wildflowers are in bloom.

OREGON COAST

BEACHES | SEAFOOD | WILDLIFE

Experience the Oregon Coast online

OREGON COAST
Trip Builder

From Astoria to Brookings, Oregon offers up 363 miles of stunning sea views, wide sandy beaches and pounding surf. Peaceful seaside communities dot the coast and there are great hikes, excellent seafood, and activities to keep families busy.

0 50 km
0 25 miles

Savor crab cakes, chowder and fish at a seafood restaurant in **Seaside** (p182)
1½hr from Portland

Gaze out at iconic Haystack Rock and browse the boutiques at **Cannon Beach** (p175)
1½hr from Portland

Visit the kid-friendly **Tillamook Creamery** to watch dairy products go from field to table (p175)
1½hr from Portland

Pacific Ocean

Enjoy the sea views from the iconic **Yaquina Head Lighthouse** (p175)
10min from Newport

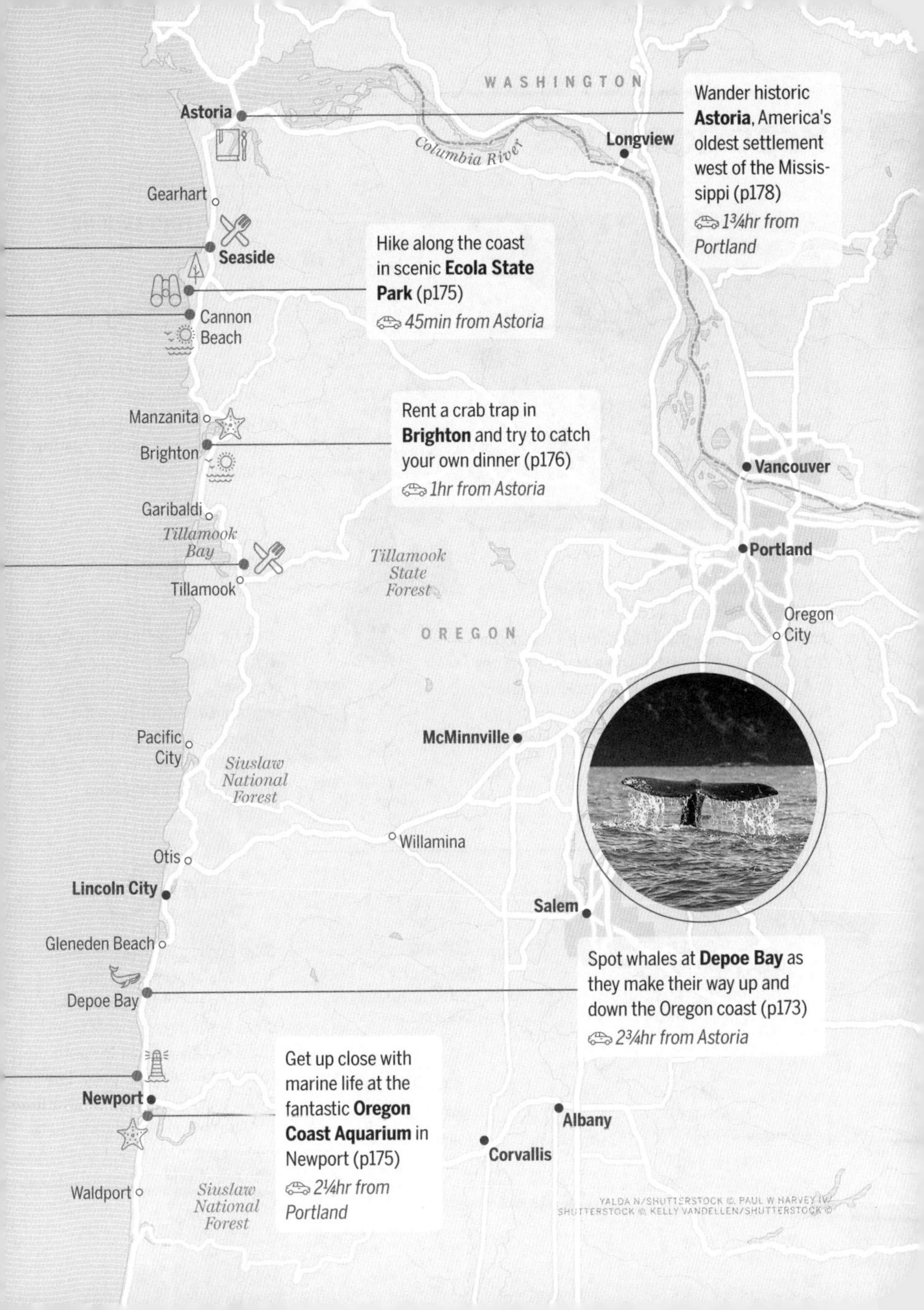

WASHINGTON
Astoria
Columbia River
Longview
Wander historic **Astoria**, America's oldest settlement west of the Mississippi (p178)
1¾hr from Portland
Gearhart
Seaside
Hike along the coast in scenic **Ecola State Park** (p175)
45min from Astoria
Cannon Beach
Manzanita
Brighton
Rent a crab trap in **Brighton** and try to catch your own dinner (p176)
1hr from Astoria
Vancouver
Garibaldi
Tillamook Bay
Tillamook
Tillamook State Forest
Portland
Oregon City
OREGON
McMinnville
Pacific City
Siuslaw National Forest
Willamina
Otis
Lincoln City
Salem
Gleneden Beach
Spot whales at **Depoe Bay** as they make their way up and down the Oregon coast (p173)
2¾hr from Astoria
Depoe Bay
Get up close with marine life at the fantastic **Oregon Coast Aquarium** in Newport (p175)
2¼hr from Portland
Newport
Albany
Corvallis
Waldport
Siuslaw National Forest

Practicalities

Portland

SKORZEWIAK/SHUTTERSTOCK ©

ARRIVING

Portland International Airport (PDX)
Portland's main gateway is also the best way to access the coast. Upon landing, hire a rental car and drive out to the coast. There are a few routes to Astoria; Hwy 26 is the most scenic. In winter, Hwy 30 to Astoria is safer as it avoids mountain snow. For the south coast, take I-5 to Albany then Hwy 20 to Newport.

HOW MUCH FOR A...

crab trap rental $30

3hr cruiser bike rental $25

whale-watching tour $38

GETTING AROUND

Car Driving is the most popular way to reach the coast. Expect lots of traffic during summer and on sunny weekends. Timing your trip at irregular hours can save hours.

Bus For travel on the North Coast between Astoria and Yachats, you can buy a three- or seven-day all-you-can-ride pass on the NW Connector (nworegontransit.org). The pass is a partnership across five different bus agencies.

Bike Cycling the Oregon coast is a popular summer activity. Covering the entire coast takes six to eight days. From May to October, travel north to south to take advantage of prevailing winds from the northwest. North to south travel also allows you to ride on the more scenic ocean-side (west side) of Hwy 101.

WHEN TO GO

JUL–SEP
Warm days for beach or camping trips, but expect crowds

OCT–DEC
Rain returns but crowds disappear; low-season prices

JAN–MAR
Rainy season; good time for crabbing, storm-watching

APR–JUN
Rainy but warmer; good for whale-watching

EATING & DRINKING

Seafood is plentiful along the coast; you'll find it in many restaurants, but takeaway-style seafood shacks are also recommended. The wharf in Newport has one of the largest concentrations of seafood restaurants. Beer is also plentiful, with a brewery in almost every town and Astoria particularly well-endowed. Breweries are also good spots when you're craving a good burger or sandwich.

Best dining with ocean views
Tidal Raves (p182)

Must-try fish-and-chips
South Beach Fish Market (p183)

Mo's ANNEX
World Famous Clam Chowder

ASTORIA BREWING

CONNECT & FIND YOUR WAY

Wi-fi For free wi-fi along the coast, local libraries and coffee shops are good spots to get online. The coast is well-covered by cellular networks.

Navigation Most towns along the coast have a chamber of commerce or visitor information center where you can pick up brochures for local attractions and get area information.

WHERE TO STAY

Accommodation varies from campgrounds and low-cost motels to high-end digs. Book well ahead in summer as places book out weeks in advance.

Location	Pro/Con
Camping	Some campgrounds have yurts so you don't always need a tent. Crowded in summer.
Seaside	Walking distance to the beach and amenities. Packed on weekends; book ahead in July and August and expect two-night minimum stays.
Canon Beach	Quiet, intimate beach experience. Expect to pay more as the available accommodations are generally quite exclusive.
Newport	Good base to explore up and down the coast, with plenty of economy hotels on Hwy 101. Busier than most towns on the coast.

HANDY WEBSITES

tides.net/oregon Check tides before heading to the tidepools.

visittheoregoncoast.com Lots of general info about activities, events, dining and lodging

MONEY

Hotel prices double or triple in summer compared to off-season rates. You can save money by bringing a tent and staying at campsites.

34 Whale of A TIME

WHALE-WATCHING | WILDLIFE | TOURS

An estimated 25,000 gray whales make their way along the Oregon coast each year, migrating between Mexico and Alaska. From a boat or from the beach you can spot a few of these majestic creatures as they swim past. Humpbacks, orcas and blue whales can also be seen along the route. California sea lions are another awesome sight, and these are easily spotted on the wharf in Newport.

ADRIAN GEORGE STEWART/SHUTTERSTOCK ©

How to

When to go Migration occurs between mid-December through January and then again from mid-March and into June. Some whales can still be seen in late summer and fall. July to September has calmer water and whales move closer to shore.

Volunteer Oregon has a program just for whale lovers. During migrations, trained volunteers are dispatched to overlooks along the coast to help visitors spot gray whales. To sign up, go to orwhalewatch.org/volunteer.

Info See individuwhale.com to better understand these amazing creatures.

BOB POOL/SHUTTERSTOCK ©

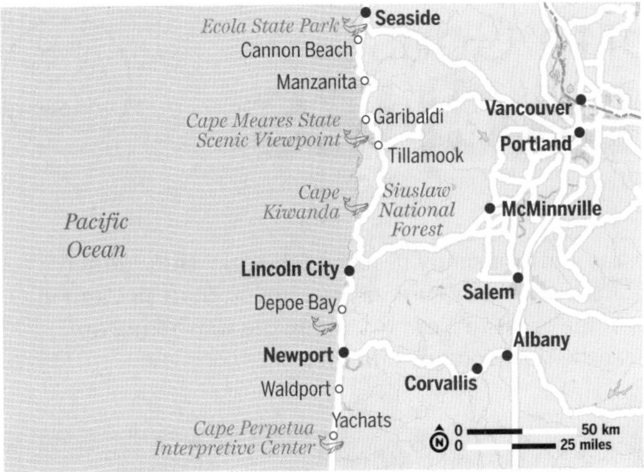
Ecola State Park
Seaside
Cannon Beach
Manzanita
Cape Meares State Scenic Viewpoint
Garibaldi
Tillamook
Vancouver
Portland
Cape Kiwanda
Siuslaw National Forest
McMinnville
Pacific Ocean
Lincoln City
Salem
Depoe Bay
Albany
Newport
Corvallis
Waldport
Yachats
Cape Perpetua Interpretive Center
0 50 km
0 25 miles

Cetacean information Stand on a beach almost anywhere on the Oregon coast and you might catch a glimpse of a whale cruising past. Oregon marks the halfway point on their annual migration from Alaska, where they feed in summer, to Mexico where they breed and calve in winter. The whales travel about 100 miles a day, and their round-trip journey is some 10,000 miles, one of the longest annual migrations for any species.

Whales consume food as they migrate, gobbling up mysid shrimp from the kelp beds near the bottom of the ocean. The 'wave' of their massive tail is a sign that they are about to dive to the bottom in search of a meal.

Viewing opportunities Recommended spots to look for whales include **Ecola State Park**, **Cape Meares State Scenic Viewpoint**, **Cape Kiwanda** and **Cape Perpetua Interpretive Center**. The Whale Watching Center at **Depoe Bay** is another obvious choice; staff and volunteers here can answer questions and help you spot whales.

For a more intimate experience, board a whale-watching tour and view these marine mammals up close. Operators run trips from various sites, including Marine Discovery Tours in Newport, Whale's Tail Charters in Depoe Bay, and South Coast Tours in Port Orford. Biologists are often on-board to provide a comprehensive lecture. They will also point out other wildlife, including California sea lions.

Far left top Grey whale tail **Far left bottom** Whale-watching boat, Depoe Bay

Close Encounters

I'm not sure how many places there are in the world where you can look a 40ft whale in the eye while you sit on a park bench, but that's the case in Depoe Bay, Oregon. In the summer months, there are gray whales all along our coastline, but I've had my best shore-based whale-watching on the central coast. You can take charters out of Newport and Depoe Bay to get out on the water with them, but there are also dozens of viewpoints where you can stand on shore and literally be 10ft away from a whale. My favorite spots to look for whales include Boiler Bay, Cape Foulweather, Otter Rock and Yaquina Head.

■ **Tips by Erik Urdahl,** *wildlife photographer documenting gray whales and marine life for two decades urdahlphoto.com*

35 North Coast BEACHES

BEACHES | HIKING | SCENIC DRIVES

Oregon's North Coast is a mix of sandy beaches and rocky cliffs, dotted with coastal communities offering low-key cottages and hotels. Start in Cannon Beach and slowly head down the coast to Newport, along the way hiking on scenic trails and enjoying excellent seafood restaurants.

CHRIS ANSON/SHUTTERSTOCK ©

Trip Notes

When to go June to August is wall-to-wall with tourists and getting a hotel during the weekend on short notice is difficult. Travel in the shoulder seasons (April to May and September to October) if possible for good weather and smaller crowds. In winter the hiking trails are muddy but fun!

Kid-friendly If you have kids, extend this tour a little north to the town of Seaside, where the main street is lined with boardwalk-style fun games, arcades and ice-cream parlors.

Oysters Ahoy!

Yaquina Bay is famed for its oysters, which were once harvested and shipped to San Francisco and the California goldfields in the mid-1800s, as miners developed a taste for them. On a kayak tour of the bay and the Newport Bayfront, you can see where the oysters were harvested. Trips are run by the **Oregon Boating Foundation**.

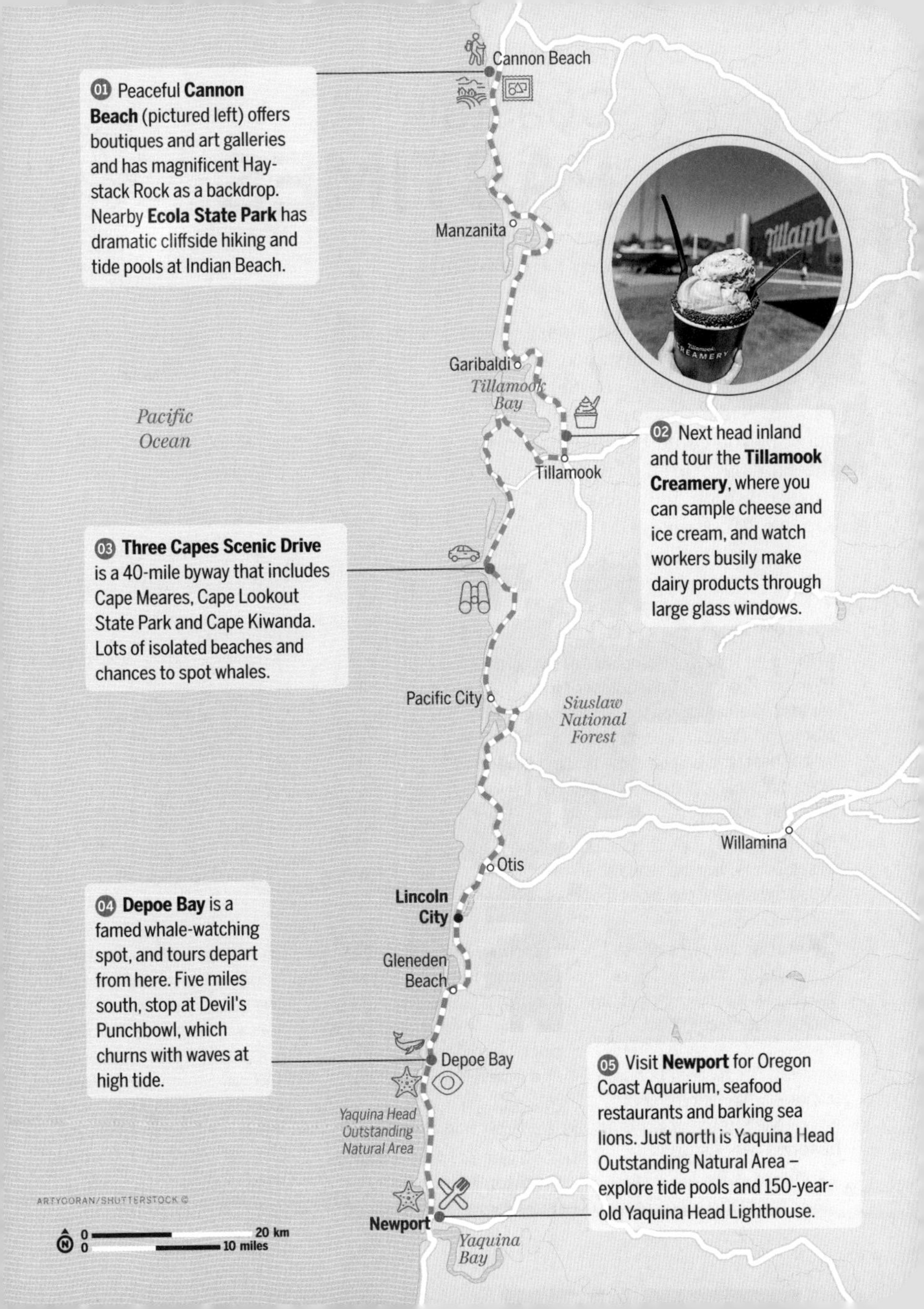

Cannon Beach
Manzanita
Garibaldi
Tillamook Bay
Tillamook
Pacific Ocean
Pacific City
Siuslaw National Forest
Willamina
Otis
Lincoln City
Gleneden Beach
Depoe Bay
Yaquina Head Outstanding Natural Area
Newport
Yaquina Bay
0 20 km
0 10 miles
N
ARTYOORAN/SHUTTERSTOCK ©

01 Peaceful **Cannon Beach** (pictured left) offers boutiques and art galleries and has magnificent Haystack Rock as a backdrop. Nearby **Ecola State Park** has dramatic cliffside hiking and tide pools at Indian Beach.

02 Next head inland and tour the **Tillamook Creamery**, where you can sample cheese and ice cream, and watch workers busily make dairy products through large glass windows.

03 **Three Capes Scenic Drive** is a 40-mile byway that includes Cape Meares, Cape Lookout State Park and Cape Kiwanda. Lots of isolated beaches and chances to spot whales.

04 **Depoe Bay** is a famed whale-watching spot, and tours depart from here. Five miles south, stop at Devil's Punchbowl, which churns with waves at high tide.

05 Visit **Newport** for Oregon Coast Aquarium, seafood restaurants and barking sea lions. Just north is Yaquina Head Outstanding Natural Area – explore tide pools and 150-year-old Yaquina Head Lighthouse.

36 Coastal PASTIMES

DIY ADVENTURE | WILDLIFE | KID-FRIENDLY

The Oregon coastline is spectacular from a distance, but get up close and there is another world to explore. Tidepools are a great place to start, or you could beachcomb across the sands in search of items that have washed ashore, including debris from Japan's 2011 tsunami. When hunger strikes, grab a clam gun or crab trap and catch yourself a meal.

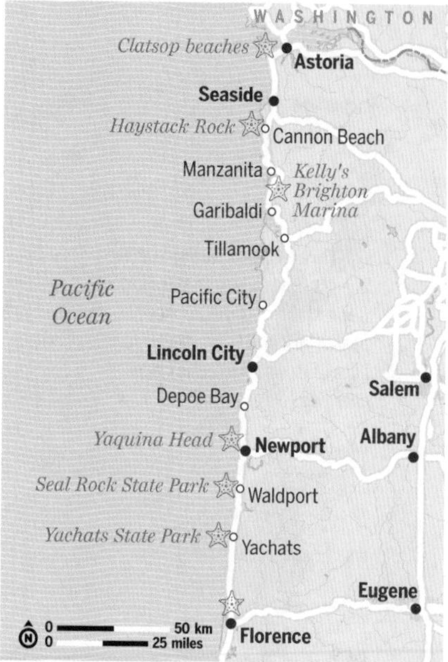
WASHINGTON
Clatsop beaches
Astoria
Seaside
Haystack Rock
Cannon Beach
Manzanita
Kelly's Brighton Marina
Garibaldi
Tillamook
Pacific Ocean
Pacific City
Lincoln City
Salem
Depoe Bay
Yaquina Head
Newport
Albany
Seal Rock State Park
Waldport
Yachats State Park
Yachats
Eugene
Florence
0 50 km
0 25 miles

How to

When to go The razor clamming season north of Tillamook Head runs from October 1 to mid-July. South of Tillamook Head the clamming season is year-round. Crabbing is legal year-round in Oregon, but the best time is September through November. When tidepooling, plan to visit one to two hours before low tide.

Top tip Bait and tackle shops can rent clam guns and crab nets. In some locations these can be rented right on the pier or on the beach.

Clamming Oregon's coast is clamming country. There are several species, including Pacific razor clam, that burrow into the sand when startled. The highest concentration of razor clams is on an 18-mile stretch of **Clatsop beaches** near Astoria.

Softshell clams are a bit easier to catch as they remain stationary their entire life. Cameron Rauenhorst (aka Captain Clameron) offers clamming tours out of **Waldport**; he targets bay clams and mussels in Alsea Bay.

Crabbing There are a number of good crabbing locations. A good place to start is **Kelly's Brighton Marina** in Brighton, near Manzanita, where you can rent a boat and crabbing equipment, or cast a net off the dock. The marina operators will even cook the crabs you catch. Other spots include the Bay Street Pier in **Newport**, the public docks on the waterfront in **Florence**, and the crabbing pier in **Garibaldi**.

Tidepooling If you'd rather observe marine life than eat it,

you can look at sea creatures in tide pools, including **Haystack Rock** (Cannon Beach), **Yaquina Head** and **Yachats State Park**. At **Seal Rock State Park** volunteers offer guided tours of the pools.

Beachcombing Another fun coastal pastime is beachcombing. Start two hours after high tide to poke through the freshly exposed beach. Shells, driftwood, fossils and glass floats are all prized keepsakes. You may even spot debris from the 2011 tsunami in Japan. While you can collect items from public beaches, don't take things from protected areas such as Oregon State beaches, BLM land or areas marked 'marine gardens.'

Expert Clamming Tips

To locate a razor clam, just look in the sand for a marble-sized hole at low tide. You'll need to be quick, they are surprisingly fast and can burrow deeper if alarmed. You'll need a shovel and a clam gun, which can be rented at local bait shops, and a shellfish license (available at bait shops and supermarkets). The clam gun is actually a long tube that you twist into the sand to pull up your clam. Steamer and softshell clams are easier to catch and only require a gloved hand and regular shovel.

■ **Tips by Cameron Rauenhorst,** *guide for Oregon Outfitters*
captainclameron.com

Above Tidepooling, Seal Rock State Park

37 Astoria: Views & BREWS

HISTORY | BREWERIES | CULTURE

The oldest settlement west of the Mississippi, Astoria bears many hallmarks of its past, including a historic downtown and some splendid old Victorian homes. Fish packing was once big business in Astoria but most of these factories have closed and the city now thrives on tourism and breweries. Astoria also serves up some terrific seafood, or you can catch clams on nearby beaches.

Mash/Lauter Tun

IAN HOGG/ALAMY STOCK PHOTO ©

How to

Getting around Astoria is walkable, but for a fun twist, you can board the historic trolley ($1) that trundles along the Riverwalk, from the port to Pier 39. The conductor offers a little history lesson as you go.

When to go June to September has the mildest and driest weather of the year; pack a raincoat at other times. For foodies, the Crab & Seafood Festival is held during the last weekend in April. Beer lovers will enjoy the Festival of Dark Arts, a February celebration of stout beer.

GINA EASLEY/STOCKIMO/ALAMY STOCK PHOTO ©

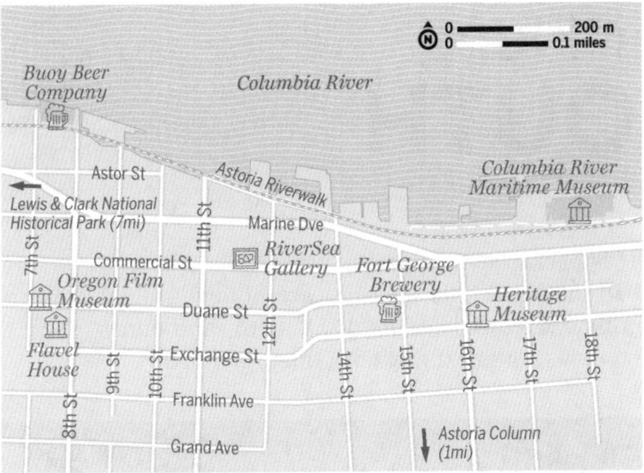
0 200 m
0 0.1 miles
Buoy Beer Company
Columbia River
Astor St
Astoria Riverwalk
Columbia River Maritime Museum
Lewis & Clark National Historical Park (7mi)
11th St
Marine Dve
7th St
Commercial St
RiverSea Gallery
Fort George Brewery
Oregon Film Museum
Heritage Museum
Duane St
12th St
Flavel House
9th St
10th St
Exchange St
14th St
15th St
16th St
17th St
18th St
8th St
Franklin Ave
Grand Ave
Astoria Column (1mi)

History, architecture & views Start your visit on the waterfront, anchored by the **Columbia River Maritime Museum**, which has an exceptional display of the town's connection to the ocean and its seafaring past.

To experience local architecture at its finest, visit the **Flavel House**. Set inside a gorgeous Queen Anne, it contains period decor and artwork. The **Heritage Museum** is also worth a visit for its historic artifacts and displays of the area's ethnic groups. **RiverSea Gallery** is great for contemporary art.

A more off-beat adventure is the 45-minute **Astoria Underground Tour** of the city's hidden tunnels.

For sweeping views of the area, climb the 164-step spiral staircase to the top of the historic **Astoria Column**. A local pastime is to launch a balsawood airplane from the top (sold in the gift shop for $1), then hunt for planes in the forest.

A good half-day trip is the **Lewis & Clark National Historical Park**, which holds **Fort Clatsop**, a reconstructed fort where volunteers dress up in period garb and describe the history of the Corps of Discovery.

Bites & beverages One of Oregon's best-known craft breweries, **Buoy Beer Company** occupies a renovated warehouse on the Riverwalk and serves up excellent beer, salmon, and oyster pies. You can get great views of the 4-mile-wide Columbia River from here and watch the giant cargo ships pass by. **Fort George Brewery** is another local favorite with a lively downtown location.

Far left top Buoy Beer Company **Far left bottom** Flavel House

☼ Local Life

Greet the morning with sunrise at the **jetty** to soak up the energy and the beauty of the Pacific Ocean (sunsets are great, too). Nearby, **Fort Stevens State Park** is a wonderful camping spot. It also has old bunkers from WWII where you may walk between pine trees and smell the ocean breeze in this wonderfully isolated place.

In Astoria proper, the **Oregon Film Museum** is always a fun stop whether or not you are a fan of *The Goonies* (the cult classic was filmed here in the 1980s). Come nightfall, visit one of Astoria's colorful dive bars. Triangle Tavern, Workers Tavern and Portway Tavern are all classic places for a pint.

■ **Recommended by Jeff Daly,** *retired TV cameraman, collector of history oldastoria.com*

38 Far-Flung SOUTH

DUNES | SEAFOOD | HIKES

Oregon's South Coast is packed with stunning coves and endless hiking trails. It's quieter than the North Coast, with peaceful towns and good opportunities for mountain-bike rides and sliding down giant sand dunes. The climate is more temperate too, with more sunny days than the north.

DANITA DELIMONT/SHUTTERSTOCK ©

Trip Notes

When to go October to April offers lighter crowds and lower prices, but fewer tours. May and September combine good weather and light crowds.

Hidden gems The cobra lily plants in **Darlingtonia State Natural Site** give it a Jurassic Park–like aura. Kids will love the life-sized dinosaurs hiding in the forest at **Prehistoric Gardens**.

For foodies The Wild Rivers Coast Food Trail (wrcfoodtrail.com) has a passport that allows you to visit the many businesses and collect prizes along the way.

Explore & Imbibe

Visit South Coast's wonderful state parks and dunes. Access the longest stretch of coastal dunes on the West Coast from many places, from Reedsport to Coos Bay. South Coast Breweries are awesome. Try Seven Devils in Coos Bay, Arch Rock in Gold Beach, and Chetco Brewery in Brookings.

■ **Dave Lacey,** *destination coordinator for South Coast Visitor's Association @south_coast_tours*

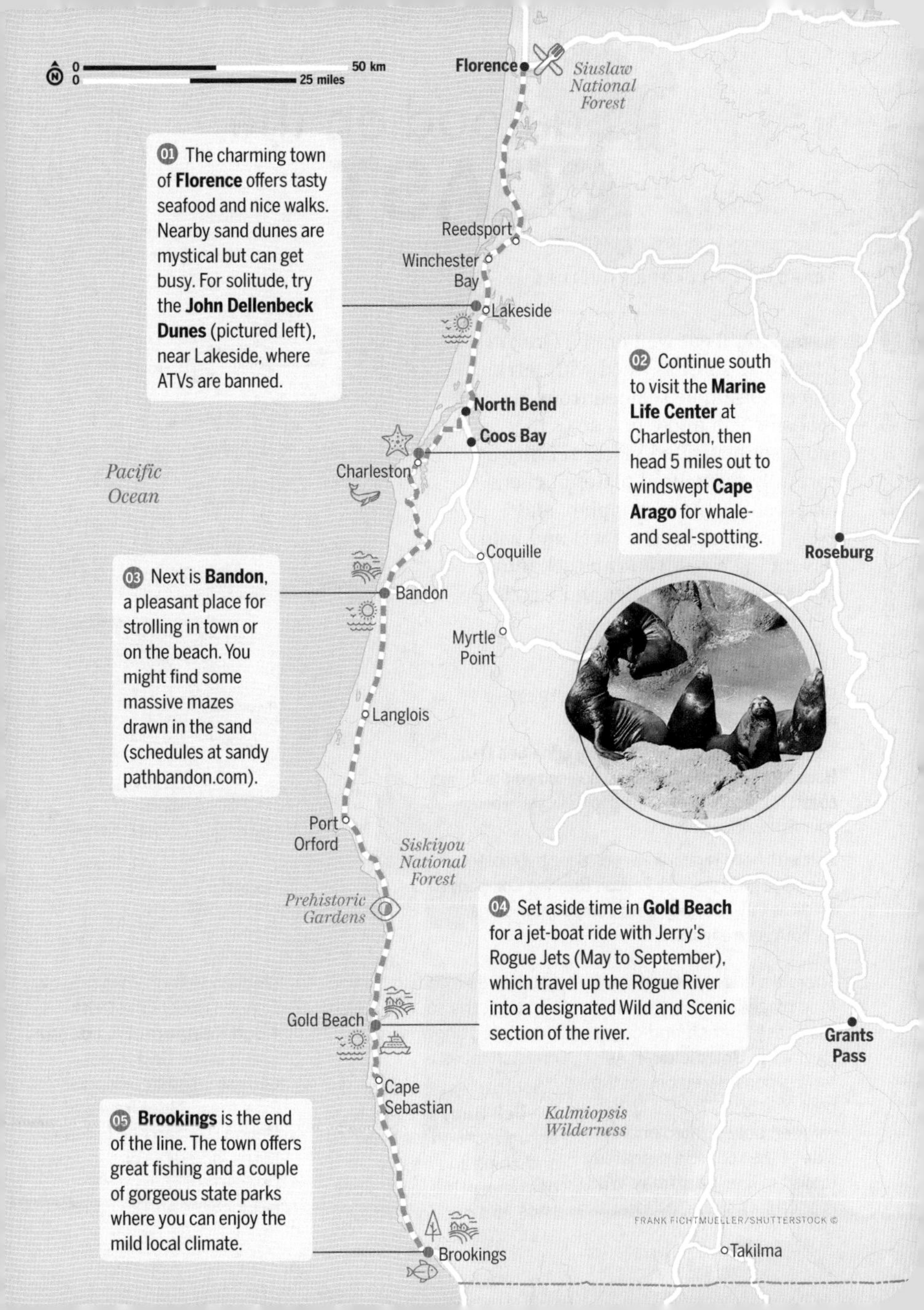

0 50 km
0 25 miles
Florence
Siuslaw National Forest
Reedsport
Winchester Bay
Lakeside
North Bend
Coos Bay
Charleston
Pacific Ocean
Coquille
Roseburg
Bandon
Myrtle Point
Langlois
Port Orford
Siskiyou National Forest
Prehistoric Gardens
Gold Beach
Grants Pass
Cape Sebastian
Kalmiopsis Wilderness
Brookings
Takilma

01 The charming town of **Florence** offers tasty seafood and nice walks. Nearby sand dunes are mystical but can get busy. For solitude, try the **John Dellenbeck Dunes** (pictured left), near Lakeside, where ATVs are banned.

02 Continue south to visit the **Marine Life Center** at Charleston, then head 5 miles out to windswept **Cape Arago** for whale- and seal-spotting.

03 Next is **Bandon**, a pleasant place for strolling in town or on the beach. You might find some massive mazes drawn in the sand (schedules at sandypathbandon.com).

04 Set aside time in **Gold Beach** for a jet-boat ride with Jerry's Rogue Jets (May to September), which travel up the Rogue River into a designated Wild and Scenic section of the river.

05 **Brookings** is the end of the line. The town offers great fishing and a couple of gorgeous state parks where you can enjoy the mild local climate.

39 Seafood on the COAST

SEAFOOD | VILLAGES | CULTURE

You'll eat well on the Oregon coast. The shore is lined with terrific places to sample seafood from roadside fish-and-chips dives to more sophisticated places serving up carefully manicured plates of clams and crab, bowls of cioppino, and pan-fried oysters. On a wet and wild day on the coast, you can tuck into a hearty bowl of chowder and watch the crashing surf.

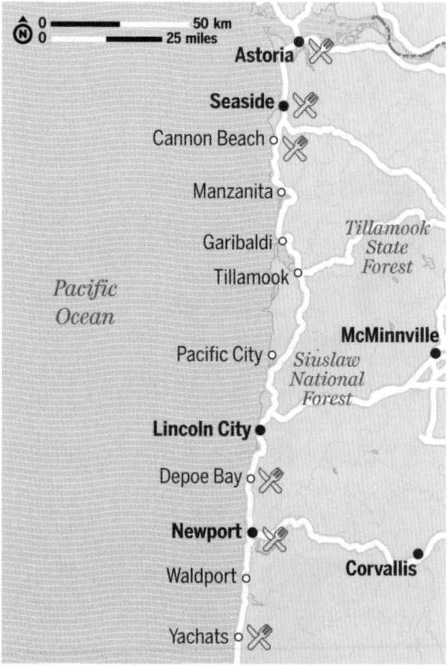
0 50 km
0 25 miles
Astoria
Seaside
Cannon Beach
Manzanita
Garibaldi
Tillamook
Tillamook State Forest
Pacific Ocean
McMinnville
Pacific City
Siuslaw National Forest
Lincoln City
Depoe Bay
Newport
Corvallis
Waldport
Yachats

How to

Costs An order of fish-and-chips from a simple roadside shack is $13 to $16.

Seafood treat Visit Yachats eatery **Luna Sea Fish House** for some of the freshest seafood on the coast. The whiteboard at the door tells you where your fish was caught.

Pair with beer Several breweries along the coast also serve good seafood. **Pelican Brewing Company** in Pacific City and **Buoy Beer Company** in Astoria are both good options.

There's a huge range of seafood places to sample along the coast. For fish-and-chips lovers, the **Bowpicker** in Astoria is considered one of the best. You order from a little wooden boat parked on the side of the road. Be prepared to wait in line. **Southbay Wild** is another Astoria favorite. It catches its own fish, so you can trust the source. It also does good chowder, calamari and fish tacos.

South of Astoria, stop at the **Bell Buoy** in Seaside, a casual location for fish-and-chips and fresh crab. It has been in business since 1946 and is renowned for its smoked salmon. In laid-back Cannon Beach, the **Driftwood Restaurant & Lounge** is one of the best, most consistent seafood spots for a meal. **Tidal Raves** at Depoe Bay can't be beaten for its incredible ocean views. Dungeness crab cakes, razor clams and cioppino

LIVE CRAB
OPEN
NATIONAL LEAGUE

(a seafood stew made with shellfish, tomatoes and wine) are some of the must-tries at this seaside eatery.

The **South Beach Fish Market** near Newport is unmistakable. It consists of a roadside shack, a 'CRAB' sign and a bunch of picnic tables along Hwy 101. It also makes some of the best fish-and-chips in the state. Travel along the coast and at some point you'll spot a **Mo's**, a chain famous for its chowder in a bread bowl. There are a few locations (Otter Rock, Cannon Beach); the original is in Newport.

Riches of the Sea

Astoria is a blue-collar town and our boats are still working hard to sustainably harvest the many forms of high-quality seafood that is so abundant off our coast. Crab, shrimp, albacore, sole and cod are just a few examples of the cornucopia of offerings delivered into Astoria daily to provide our local artisanal restaurants with high-quality protein from the sea as well as for export around the globe. Astoria is a small fishing town that feeds the world.

■ **By Rob Seitz,** *commercial fisher, restaurant owner and poet* *@southbaywildfishhouse*

Above South Beach Fish Market

Listings

BEST OF THE REST

Hit the Trail

Neahkahnie Mountain

One of the best hikes along the coast goes up Neahkahnie Mountain (5 miles) from Manzanita. The views toward the sea are well worth the walk.

Tillamook Head Trail

This moderate hike (6.3 miles one way or 12.6 miles return) extends from Tillamook Head to Indian Beach in Ecola State Park. You'll get a view of Terrible Tilly, a lonely lighthouse on a rocky island off the coast.

Cape Kiwanda

Near Pacific City, this is a fairly easy walk up a giant sand dune. Kids will enjoy it.

Cape Falcon Trailhead

A scenic out-and-back walk (4.6 miles) through old-growth forests to the coast. Located in Oswald West State Park near Cannon Beach. Very muddy during the rainy season.

Oregon Coast Trail

Serious hiking enthusiasts can walk the entire coast. It's 425 miles if walked in its entirety, or 380 miles if ferries are used to cross bays and river mouths. There is more information at oregoncoasttrail.org.

Outdoor Activities

Biking

Pineapple Express Adventure Rides in Port Orford on the South Coast rents fat-tire bikes for riding on the beach and coastal trails. Whisky Run near Bandon is one of the best mountain biking spots on the coast.

Horseback riding

C&M Stables located 8 miles north of Florence offers horse-riding trips on the beach.

Ocean Kayaking

Kayakers can paddle in the sea near Brookings and spot seals, sea lions, whales and pelicans. South Coast Tours organizes trips.

Fishing trips

Salmon and sturgeon fishing trips on the open ocean are organized by Lance Fisher Fishing in Astoria.

Scuba diving

Diving outfitters can be found in many towns along the coast. Shore dives are best between Newport and Florence. For a unique experience, the Oregon Coast Aquarium offers dives in its underwater exhibits.

Surfing

Beginner breaks include Indian Beach, Cannon Beach, Short Sand Beach and Pacific City Beach. Lincoln City and the South Florence Jetty are good spots for advanced surfers.

Surfer, Pacific City Beach

Local Flavors

Restaurant Beck $$$

Located in Depoe Bay, this restaurant has unbeatable ocean views. The food is sophisticated and perfectly plated. Wide-ranging menu, with seafood, vegetarian and meat dishes. Try the five-course tasting menu.

Tony's Crab Shack $

Seafood favorite in Bandon that sells fishing gear and catch of the day. Raw oysters are available, plus fish tacos and tasty chowder.

Drina Daisy $

This Bosnian restaurant in Astoria is a rare find in the Pacific Northwest. It serves excellent stuffed cabbage, beef stews and roasted lamb. Eastern European beer is available.

Grateful Bread $

Breakfast restaurant and bakery in Pacific City. Tasty eggs, omelets, soups and sandwiches. Delicious scones and baguettes. A coast highlight.

Osprey Café $

Don't miss this popular breakfast and lunch spot in Seaside. The varied menu includes fried razor clams, fish tacos, Saigon-style beef pho, Peruvian stir-fry and eggs Benedict.

Bedding Down

Tillicum Beach Campground $

Most of the 61 campsites have beachfront views. Flush toilets and drinking water but no showers. It's 4 miles north of Yachats.

Sea Ranch RV Park & Stables $

Private campground near Cannon Beach with a clean bathhouse and tent sites in a wooded area. Horses are available in summer.

GREAT
CHOWDER
oysters

MANUELA DURSON/SHUTTERSTOCK ©

Tony's Crab Shack

Jessie M Honeyman Memorial State Park Campground $

Well-maintained camp. There are dunes nearby, and a lake where you can fish and swim. Bathrooms have hot showers. Located near Florence.

Selina Commodore Astoria $$

Stylish hotel with a retro 1950s feel. Central locations and comfy beds but the walls are a tad thin.

Seaside Lodge & International Hostel $

Budget lodge with friendly staff and a pleasant setting on the inlet in Seaside. Dorms available. A fire pit is lit some evenings. Kayaks can be rented.

Waves $$

Cozy and comfortable beachside units in Cannon Beach, some with Jacuzzi and kitchenette. Rooms are large and have sea views.

Scan to find more things to do on the Oregon Coast online

CENTRAL OREGON & THE OREGON CASCADES

CRAFT BEER | HIGH DESERT | VOLCANIC SCENERY

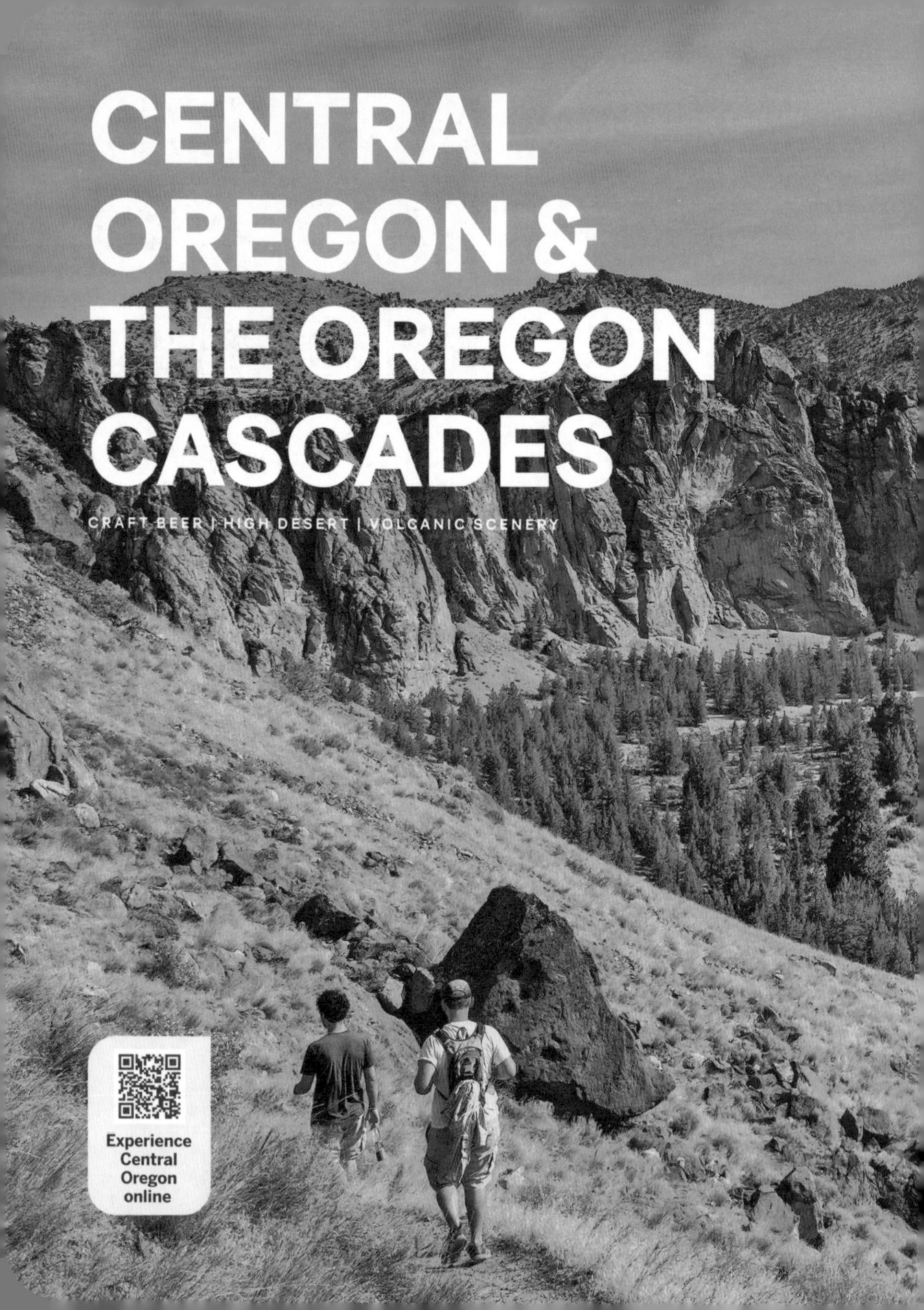

Experience Central Oregon online

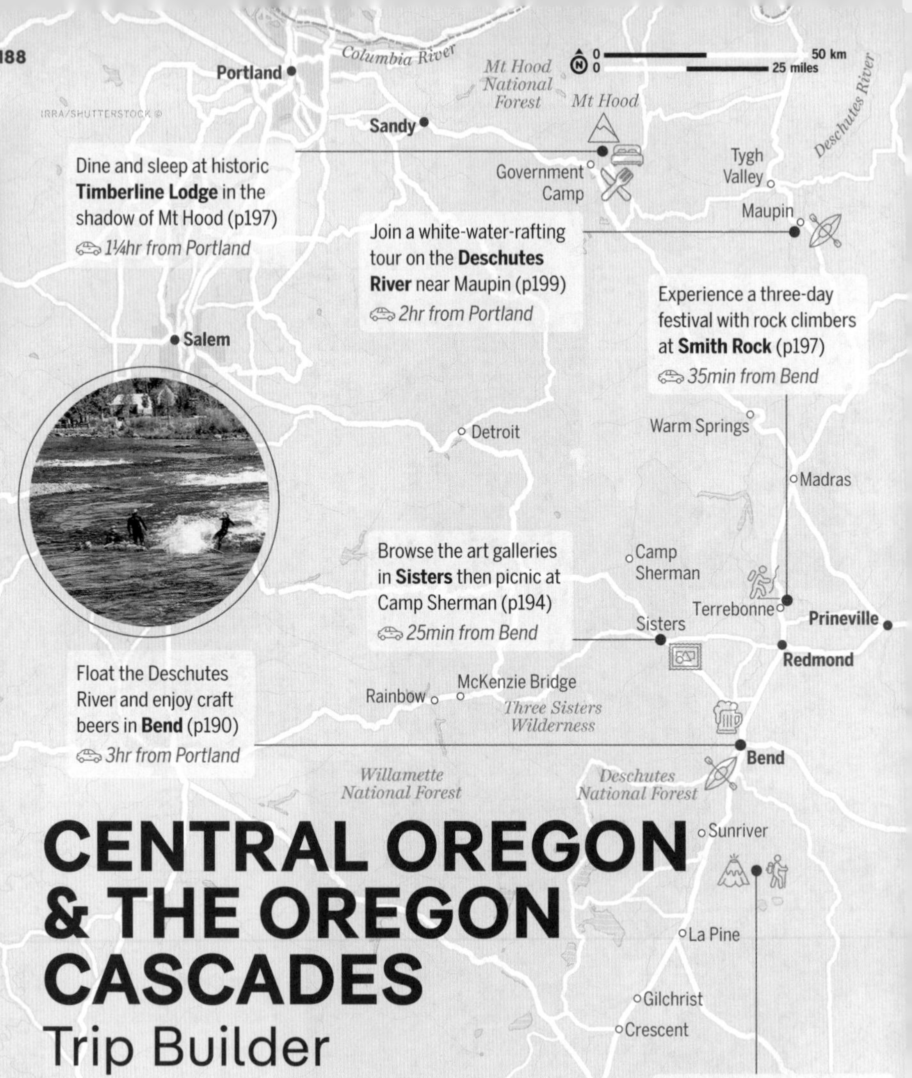
Portland
Columbia River
Mt Hood National Forest
Mt Hood
0 50 km
0 25 miles
Deschutes River
Sandy
Dine and sleep at historic **Timberline Lodge** in the shadow of Mt Hood (p197)
1¼hr from Portland
Government Camp
Tygh Valley
Maupin
Join a white-water-rafting tour on the **Deschutes River** near Maupin (p199)
2hr from Portland
Experience a three-day festival with rock climbers at **Smith Rock** (p197)
35min from Bend
Salem
Detroit
Warm Springs
Madras
Browse the art galleries in **Sisters** then picnic at Camp Sherman (p194)
25min from Bend
Camp Sherman
Terrebonne
Prineville
Sisters
Redmond
Float the Deschutes River and enjoy craft beers in **Bend** (p190)
3hr from Portland
Rainbow
McKenzie Bridge
Three Sisters Wilderness
Bend
Willamette National Forest
Deschutes National Forest
Sunriver
La Pine
Gilchrist
Crescent
Walk across volcanic fields at **Newberry National Volcanic Monument** (p192)
1¼hr from Bend

CENTRAL OREGON & THE OREGON CASCADES

Trip Builder

An adventure destination, Central Oregon lures visitors with promises of skiing, rafting, hiking and mountain biking by day, and a bevy of craft breweries to explore by night. Bend is the focal point, from here the High Desert sprawls across the landscape, punctuated by lava fields, canyons and alpine lakes.

Practicalities

ARRIVING

Redmond Municipal Airport Located 16 miles from Bend, this airport has connections to most West Coast cities. It's a 20-minute drive to Bend. Taxis and rideshares to Bend cost $30 to $50.

FIND YOUR WAY

Outdoor equipment shops in Bend sell maps and compasses. Visit Bend is a handy tour office.

MONEY

Hotel room rates soar in midsummer with average midrange rates at $250. The same room in winter can cost $100.

WHERE TO STAY

Location	Pro/Con
Westside, Bend	Quiet, good walking area. Closest area to Mt Bachelor.
Downtown, Bend	Good for shopping, eating and nightlife.
Old Mill, Bend	Great access to river. Close to shops and restaurants. Pricey.
Third St, Bend	Lower price options. Motels of varying quality.
Sisters	Atmospheric accommodations, but expensive (unless you camp).

GETTING AROUND

Bus Cascades East Transit offers a free, on-demand service anywhere in Bend on weekdays. CET runs buses from Bend to Mt Bachelor (in ski season) and Lava Butte (June 19 to September 6).

Bike Bike shops around town rent mountain bikes for around $45 a day. A good bike route also connects Bend and Sunriver.

EATING & DRINKING

Quick meals and beer on tap are available at food cart pods around Bend, especially around the Box Factory. Higher-end restaurants are downtown and in the Old Mill (pictured bottom). Galveston Ave is popular for budget restaurants. Local beer and cider are widespread – Bend is home to more than 20 breweries.

Best brewery
Crux Fermentation Project (p191; pictured top)

Must-try ramen
Miyagi (p200)

JUL–SEP
Peak season, summer concerts, hottest weather

OCT–DEC
Cooler temps, fall foliage, rafting season ends

JAN–MAR
Low season; short but sunny days, cold temps, good for winter sports

APR–JUN
Fewer crowds, good weather, rafting season starts

40 Mountain MALTS

BREWERIES | LOCAL | TOURS

Craving a fresh, locally made beer after an epic day adventuring in the mountains? Central Oregon has plenty of options to wet your palate. Bend and its surrounding towns boast more than 30 active breweries, some bottling nationally famous beers and others just brewing for the local crowd. If beer is not your thing, there are also delicious local ciders, wines and spirits.

crux
crux

JOSHUA RAINEY/ALAMY STOCK PHOTO ©

How to

Getting around Many breweries are within walking distance of downtown Bend. Use the Bend Ale Trail map to help you navigate.

Mecca Grade Estate malt Owner Seth Klann not only makes the beer, he also grows on his farm the grain, malt and other beer ingredients. It's located near Madras, about one hour north of Bend. There's a bunkhouse for guests if you want to stay the night.

DESCHUTES BREWERY
& PUBLIC HOUSE
DESCHUTES BREWERY

JOANNA KALAFATIS/ALAMY STOCK PHOTO ©

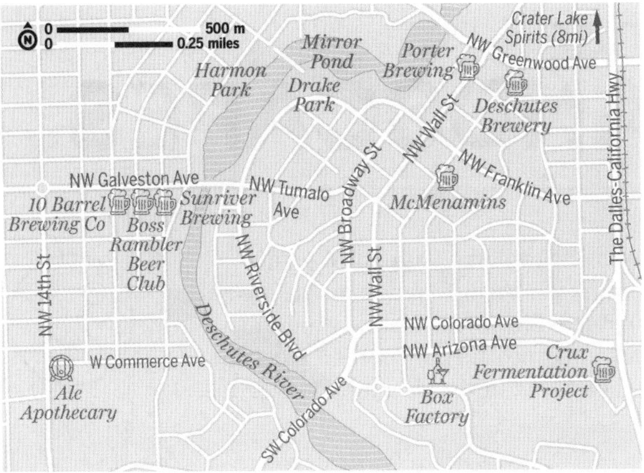
0 500 m
0 0.25 miles
Crater Lake Spirits (8mi)
Mirror Pond
Porter Brewing
NW Greenwood Ave
Harmon Park
Drake Park
Deschutes Brewery
NW Wall St
NW Broadway St
The Dalles-California Hwy
NW Franklin Ave
NW Galveston Ave
NW Tumalo Ave
McMenamins
10 Barrel Brewing Co
Sunriver Brewing
Boss Rambler Beer Club
NW Riverside Blvd
NW Wall St
NW 14th St
NW Colorado Ave
NW Arizona Ave
Crux Fermentation Project
W Commerce Ave
Ale Apothecary
Deschutes River
Box Factory
SW Colorado Ave

Far left top Crux Fermentation Project Far left bottom Deschutes Brewery

In 1988 **Deschutes Brewery** opened up the first brewpub in Bend. More than three decades later, Deschutes is one of the biggest craft-beer makers in the country. Enjoy a pint at its downtown pub, or for a unique experience, visit their bottling factory near Old Mill. You can take a tour of the facility, learn how beer is made, and get some samples. Next head downtown to **McMenamins**, an atmospheric place for beer set in a converted 1930s-era school. Ask your waiter for directions to the secret bar, located behind a false door.

If you've got kids in tow, try **Crux Fermentation Project**. There's a big lawn here to run around, and it's a great spot to down some beer and admire the mountain views. The nearby **Box Factory** is a hub of activity with a brewery and a few bars and some food-cart pods, but for something different try **Avid Cider Co**, which makes interesting, fruit-driven ciders. Galveston Ave in Bend's Westside has another cluster of breweries, including **10 Barrel Brewing Co**, **Boss Rambler Beer Club** and **Sunriver Brewing**. For an Old World experience, stop by the **Ale Apothecary**, where the beer is aged like wine, in barrels for months or even years. Drinkers of sprits can head out of town to **Crater Lake Spirits**, on the road to Sisters, where you can join a tour and sample booze in the tasting room.

Brews in Bend

For hazy or milkshake IPAs, I'd suggest **Boss Rambler Beer Club** or **Sunriver Brewing**. For British-style cask ales. I'd suggest **Porter Brewing**. For wild, wood-aged brew, I'd go with **Ale Apothecary**. But for overall quality of beer and variety of styles, I usually recommend starting with **Crux Fermentation Project**, and work out from there.

If you're looking for a meal with your beer, **Deschutes Brewery** and **Sunriver Brewing** both have a great kitchen. If atmosphere is essential, try **McMenamins Old St Francis School** – it's stylish and historic and is a terrific destination brewery and pub experience.

■ **Recommended by Jon Abernathy,** *craft-beer blogger and Bend local @brewsite*

41 Lunar LANDSCAPES

CRATERS | CAVES | HIKING

Drop into certain parts of Newberry National Volcanic Monument and you might think you've just landed on the moon. This lunar landscape is punctuated by forests, lakes, waterfalls and caves, one of which runs underneath Hwy 97. It's a day trip from Bend, and there's good camping in the area for a longer visit.

PERNELLE VOYAGE/SHUTTERSTOCK ©

How to

Getting here & around You'll need a car to get between sights. At Lava Lands Visitor Center, a shuttle bus ($3) can take you to the volcanic rim.

When to go The road to Newberry Crater (for Paulina and East Lakes) is closed from around mid-November to mid-May, depending on how much snow is on the ground. The Lava Lands Visitor Center and the Lava River Cave are open from May to September.

HRACH HOVHANNISYAN/SHUTTERSTOCK ©

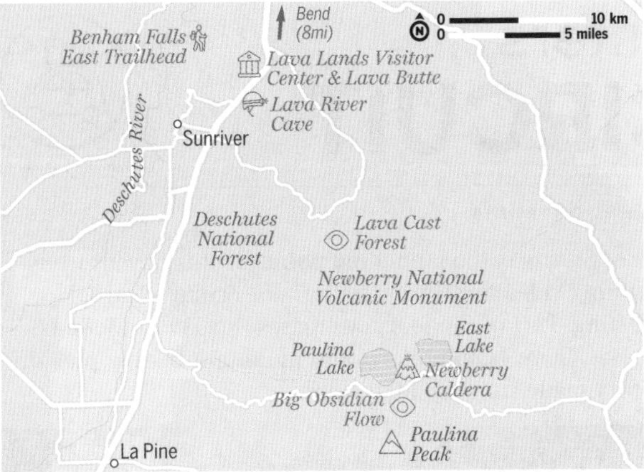
Bend
(8mi)
0 10 km
0 5 miles
Benham Falls
East Trailhead
Lava Lands Visitor
Center & Lava Butte
Lava River
Cave
Sunriver
Deschutes River
Deschutes
National
Forest
Lava Cast
Forest
Newberry National
Volcanic Monument
East
Lake
Paulina
Lake
Newberry
Caldera
Big Obsidian
Flow
Paulina
Peak
La Pine

Newberry Caldera Two impressively large twin lakes separated by a pumice cone lie at the heart of the crater. **Paulina Lake** is the first you'll encounter when driving in from the west. Continue along its south side to the **Big Obsidian Flow** and then **East Lake**, which has an attractive sandy beach and a small resort where you can have lunch and rent boats. Bring bait and tackle to catch your own meal. Nearby **Paulina Falls** is a double waterfall that plummets 80ft over volcanic cliffs; it makes for a good picnic spot.

Lava River Cave Created by lava flow, this mile-long, tube-like cave winds its way under Hwy 97. The opening is 50ft wide with a 60ft ceiling. The cave is not lit, but you can rent a flashlight for $5, or bring your own. To protect the local bat population from white-nose syndrome, don't wear clothes that have previously been worn in a cave.

Lava Lands Visitor Center & Lava Butte There's a small museum here that describes the geological history of the area. Trails behind the museum lead through a 7000-year-old lava field. You can take a bus to the top of the 500ft-high Lava Butte for awesome views of the Cascades. A 4-mile drive west of here is the **Benham Falls East Trailhead**, where you can hike along the Deschutes River.

Far left top View of Newberry National Volcanic Monument from Paulina Peak
Far left bottom Lava River Cave

Peak Sites at Newberry Crater

Paulina Peak (elevation 7989ft) sits atop the largest volcano in the Cascades. On a clear day, you can see the Cascade Range from Mt Shasta in California to Mt Adams in Washington. The **Lava Cast Forest** is a unique geological feature in the area: 7000 years ago tree molds formed when lava flowed into a forest and chilled around trees before they burned. **Big Obsidian Flow** is a thick rhyolite flow that formed on the floor of Newberry Crater 1300 years ago. An interpretive trail loops across the flow offering great views of many features in the caldera.

■ **Recommended by Bob Jensen,** *USGS volunteer and retired USFS geologist @volcanoguybob*

42 Sisters CIRCUIT

MOUNTAINS | WATERFALLS | HOT SPRINGS

The easygoing town of Sisters is the launching point for this adventurous road trip that includes stunning volcanic scenery, waterfalls, crystal clear lakes, hot springs and great fly fishing. Part of the journey crosses the 5325ft McKenzie Pass on the seasonal Hwy 242. There's good hiking and mountain biking, plus the chance to visit an observatory made from obsidian rock.

TYLER W. STIPP/SHUTTERSTOCK ©

Trip Notes

Getting around The 84-mile loop is drivable in one day, but it's best to bring a tent and complete it over several days. It also makes a good cycling route.

When to go Hwy 242 is closed mid-November to mid-June. Outside these months, Camp Sherman, Suttle Lake and Clear Lake are still accessible.

Top hike The Three Sisters – Obsidian Trailhead just off Hwy 242 is a spectacular 11.8-mile out-and-back hike of moderate difficulty. Permit required (recreation.gov).

Village Detour

Camp Sherman makes a great detour off Hwy 20. The tiny hamlet consists of a few resorts, a general store and some shady campsites by the river. In summer, locals float down the ice-cold Metolius River in tubes. The fishing here (pictured above) is also very good (only fly-fishing is allowed).

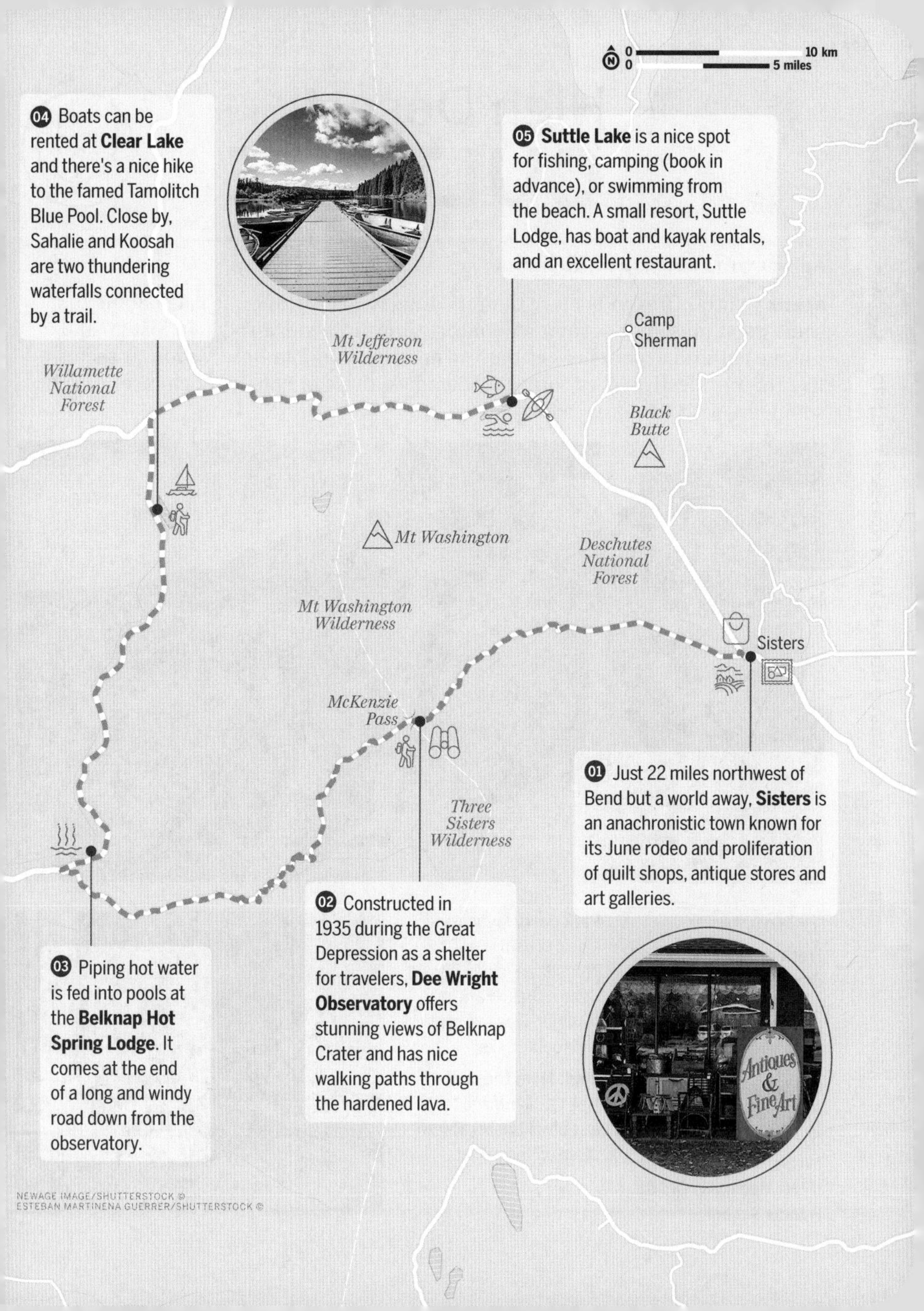
0 10 km
0 5 miles
Willamette National Forest
Mt Jefferson Wilderness
Camp Sherman
Black Butte
Mt Washington
Deschutes National Forest
Mt Washington Wilderness
Sisters
McKenzie Pass
Three Sisters Wilderness
Antiques & Fine Art

01 Just 22 miles northwest of Bend but a world away, **Sisters** is an anachronistic town known for its June rodeo and proliferation of quilt shops, antique stores and art galleries.

02 Constructed in 1935 during the Great Depression as a shelter for travelers, **Dee Wright Observatory** offers stunning views of Belknap Crater and has nice walking paths through the hardened lava.

03 Piping hot water is fed into pools at the **Belknap Hot Spring Lodge**. It comes at the end of a long and windy road down from the observatory.

04 Boats can be rented at **Clear Lake** and there's a nice hike to the famed Tamolitch Blue Pool. Close by, Sahalie and Koosah are two thundering waterfalls connected by a trail.

05 **Suttle Lake** is a nice spot for fishing, camping (book in advance), or swimming from the beach. A small resort, Suttle Lodge, has boat and kayak rentals, and an excellent restaurant.

43 High Desert CULTURE

HISTORY | TRADITIONS | MUSEUMS

Central Oregon is more than its dramatic landscapes. It's also home to some great museums, a summer concert series in Bend, a rodeo in Sisters and unique cultural experiences at the Warm Springs Indian Reservation. It seems like there's a festival every other weekend, so there are plenty of chances to rub shoulders with the local crowd.

How to

Fresh produce Northwest Crossing in Bend hosts a farmers market, with lots of arts and music, on Saturdays in summer.

Hidden gems Indie movies are released in the tiny **Tin Pan Theater**. For old and new classic films try **McMenamins Old St Francis School**.

Park party Munch and Music is held every Thursday evening in Bend's Drake Park in summer. Free live music and food trucks.

Blast from the past Make a pilgrimage to the last **Blockbuster video store** on the planet.

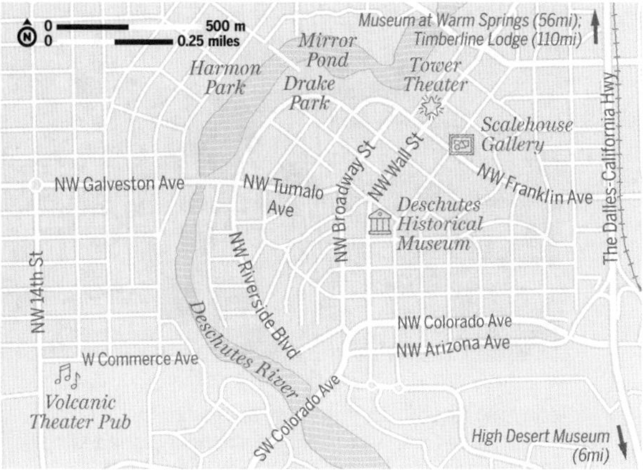
0 500 m
0 0.25 miles
Museum at Warm Springs (56mi); Timberline Lodge (110mi)
Mirror Pond
Harmon Park
Drake Park
Tower Theater
Scalehouse Gallery
NW Galveston Ave
NW Tumalo Ave
NW Broadway St
NW Wall St
NW Franklin Ave
The Dalles-California Hwy
Deschutes Historical Museum
NW 14th St
NW Riverside Blvd
Deschutes River
NW Colorado Ave
NW Arizona Ave
W Commerce Ave
Volcanic Theater Pub
SW Colorado Ave
High Desert Museum (6mi)

Bend is a cultural oasis in the High Desert. Start your experience at the **High Desert Museum**, a unique cross between a wildlife sanctuary and a cultural history experience. Pioneer history is on display and you'll gain an in-depth understanding of the Native American way of life. In downtown Bend, the **Deschutes Historical Museum** covers the town's development from its origins as a logging community. Nearby **Tower Theater**, built in 1940, is a classic theater experience to watch a play, concert or movie. For live music, **Volcanic Theater Pub** pulls in some great regional acts. **Scalehouse Gallery** is where Bend's alternative thinkers meet, display art and collaborate on creative projects.

North of Bend, the culture gets a little more rural. Stop at **Terrebonne Crescent Moon Ranch** to experience farm life on a locally owned alpaca farm. At nearby **Smith Rock State Park**, hundreds of rock climbers gather in early October for the **Craggin' Classic**. Next head north to visit the **Museum at Warm Springs**, where you can experience a rich trove of artifacts and photographs that document Native American history and culture. In downtown Warm Springs you can meet members of the Warm Springs tribe at the **Twisted Teepee** food cart or the local grocery store, which has a display of Native American artifacts in the back. Further north, high in the Cascades, you can get some mountain culture with a visit to **Timberline Lodge** on the slopes of Mt Hood. It's a classic overnight destination year-round or just a nice place to enjoy a meal in the lodge.

Far left top Smith Rock State Park
Far left bottom High Desert Museum

Arts & Culture

Growing up in Oregon, I've witnessed the region's arts and culture scene flourish. I visited the **High Desert Museum** as a child, and today it's still a highlight, sharing both historical and contemporary art and stories. The **Museum at Warm Springs** is a must-see for its wonderful permanent and temporary exhibitions about the Indigenous Plateau. There's also plenty of gallery hopping to experience in Central Oregon's towns – Sisters is an art hub, and **Scalehouse Gallery** features engaging rotating exhibitions and programs. **Art in Public Places** provides Bend with dynamic public artwork throughout the community, the **Tower Theatre** is always showcasing unique acts, and in the autumn the **BendFilm Festival** makes for a wonder-filled weekend.

■ **Tips by Dana Whitelaw,** *executive director of the High Desert Museum @highdesertmuseum*

CASCADE DRONE PHOTOGRAPHY/SHUTTERSTOCK ©

The Deschutes River

LIFEBLOOD OF THE HIGH DESERT

While the Cascades dominate Central Oregon's skyline, the Deschutes River is the area's beating heart. Its waters provided fish for Native Americans and later drew pioneers to settle in Bend and cultivate the land. Today it attracts a new kind of adventurer, one equipped with kayaks, rafts and even surfboards.

Left Mirror Pond, Bend **Middle** White-water rafters, Big Eddy rapid **Right** Wilderness campsite, Deschutes River

Today the Deschutes River may appear an idyllic place to cast a line for trout or float on a flamingo-shaped inflatable tube. But during its 20 million years of geological history, the Deschutes was at times a place of extreme danger, with molten lava flowing over its banks and hot ash filling up its water. The present course of the Deschutes River begins its journey high in the Cascades, above Little Lava Lake, and ends 252 miles downstream where it joins the Columbia River. In between, there are dams that supply power to the region, world-class rapids, steep canyonlands, and even a surf park with a wave that can be manipulated with an iPad.

Native Americans were the first people attracted to the Deschutes and its fish-filled waters. Pictographs on rock walls are proof of their presence in the area. They were followed by white entrepreneurs and loggers lured by the thick stands of ponderosa. A sawmill was erected on the Deschutes at the 'Farewell Bend' of the river, and a community soon grew into a town along its banks. The loggers were followed by ranchers and farmers, enticed by newly built canals that siphoned water from the Deschutes into the High Desert. The river was dammed in places too. One of those dams created Mirror Pond in Bend and supplied the city with electricity in its early years. Another series of dams formed Lake Billy Chinook and generated enough electricity to power 150,000 homes.

But the dams and canals that are celebrated because they helped settle Central Oregon have come at an environmental cost. From a geological standpoint, the river is highly stable: its porous lava bed acts like a sponge, holding the river flows consistent throughout the year. For

BOB POOL/SHUTTERSTOCK ©

JOSHUA RAINEY PHOTOGRAPHY/SHUTTERSTOCK ©

millions of years this stability provided an excellent habitat for the Oregon spotted frog and other aquatic species. Dams changed that by holding water back in winter and letting it fly full force in summer for irrigation. Sensitive frog egg masses are easily washed away when the water rises and falls between seasons. The species is now considered threatened. Fish populations (sockeye salmon, bull trout, and steelhead) were similarly devastated by the dams, which blocked access to spawning areas in the Upper Deschutes.

> During its 20 million years of geological history, the Deschutes was at times a place of extreme danger, with molten lava flowing over its banks and hot ash filling up its water.

Conservation efforts are now underway to try and reverse some of the damage and bring back the threatened wildlife. One way this is being done is through the conversion of the canals to modern pipes. It's estimated that half the water that goes into the canals seeps into the porous rock before it even reaches farming areas. Farmers are also being incentivized to upgrade from wasteful flood irrigation to more efficient sprinklers. More water conservation translates to more water in the river for wildlife, as well as human users who plummet down the rapids in kayaks and rafts. The current winter flows in the Deschutes are around 100 cubic feet per second near Wickiup Reservoir, by 2028 the conservation work is expected to triple the river's flow to 300 cubic feet per second.

Floating Fun

There are lots of ways to enjoy the Deschutes River around Bend. A good place to start is **Riverbend Park**, near the Old Mill, where locals put plastic tubes in the river and float downstream to the Whitewater Park. The park has a series of rapids in one section and a larger standing wave for kayakers and surfers. From here it's possible to float down to Drake Park where a bus brings floaters back to the Old Mill area. For a more raucous adventure, tour operators offer **white-water rafting** on the upper Deschutes near Bend and the lower Deschutes near Maupin.

Listings

BEST OF THE REST

Local Flavors

Miyagi $

Compact ramen bar that feels like a slice of Tokyo dropped into downtown Bend. The tonkatsu ramen is a favorite and it also offers tasty steamed-bun appetizers.

The Lot $

This was the original food-cart lot in Bend. This one has roll-down drapes for cold weather days. Sushi, burgers and salads are among the options and the bar has 16 taps.

Jackson's Corner $$

Formerly a corner grocery store (drink coolers still take up one wall), this friendly place in Bend is great for wood-fired pizza, sandwiches and freshly baked bread.

McKay Cottage $$

On Bend's north end, this is justifiably considered one of the city's best spots for breakfast favorites like eggs Benedict and pancakes. It's a popular place so be prepared for a wait.

Sno-Cap Drive-In $

At the end of the main drag in Sisters, this little burger and ice-cream joint has a 1950s feel, with a walk-up window and picnic tables outside.

Joolz $$

Middle Eastern cuisine in downtown Bend serving excellent hummus, kebabs and shawarma plates. Good vegan options too.

Terrebonne Depot $$

This converted train station in Terrebonne is an atmospheric spot with an eclectic menu that ranges from burgers and steaks to Vietnamese sandwiches and pulled-pork nachos.

El Sancho $

Hip spot on Galveston in Bend with streetside picnic tables where you can enjoy tasty boutique tacos, tequila and margaritas. Good veggie options and large portions. Don't miss the fried plantains.

Podski $

Grab a taco, a pierogi or a plate of Pad Thai at this cozy food-cart pod next to Bend's Box Factory. The adjacent bar has six beers on tap, plus ciders, kombucha and occasional live music.

Bedding Down

Mill Inn B&B $$

Start your day with a perfectly prepared frittata or Belgian waffle in this tiny boutique hotel. Rooms are classically designed, each sporting a different theme. It's within walking distance of downtown Bend and the Old Mill District.

Pine Ridge Inn $$$

A boutique hotel on Bend's westside; most rooms have hot tubs and gas fireplaces. Some have sweeping views of the Deschutes River.

OCEAN KAYAK

Elk Lake

McMenamins Old St Francis School $$

This nearly 100-year-old schoolhouse in Bend has been converted into a hotel. Rooms are cozy and there's a tiled saltwater Turkish bath for soaking. Non-guests can use the baths for $5.

Camping $

Central Oregon offers some great camping locations, including Tumalo State Park, just 5 miles northwest of Bend, where you can tent camp or stay in a yurt. Great camping spots can also be found at Camp Sherman, Suttle Lake, East Lake and La Pine State Park. Book well in advance to secure a spot (recreation.gov).

Outdoor Thrills

Rock Climbing

Located 25 miles north of Bend, Smith Rock State Park has world-class rock climbing and some challenging hikes in a varied landscape that looks more like Utah than Oregon. Chockstone Climbing Guides offers professional climbing tours and classes.

Caving Adventures

There are a number of caves and lava tubes around Bend, including Boyd Cave off China Hat Rd. Wanderlust Tours in Bend offers a good tour of the area's caves.

Mountain Biking

Bend offers some of the best mountain-biking trails in the state. The Phil's Trail area has lots of singletrack and is a great place to start. You can ride there from downtown. Bike rental is widely available in town.

Skiing

Mt Bachelor, a 25-minute drive from Bend, is one of the largest ski areas in the country. Hoodoo Ski Resort is about an hour away, and smaller, but lift tickets are more affordable. Good cross-country skiing is a short drive from Bend in the Deschutes National Forest.

THYE-WEE GN/SHUTTERSTOCK ©

Tumalo Falls

Boating

Kayaks, stand-up paddleboards, and boats can be rented at many lakes across Central Oregon. Popular spots include Elk Lake and Paulina Lake.

Hit the Trail

Smith Rock State Park

Smith Rock offers a number of excellent hikes through steep canyons and under sheer cliffs. Misery Ridge is one recommended hike for awesome views of the otherworldly scenery and famed Monkey Face rock.

Green Lakes Trail

A 9.1-mile out-and-back hike of moderate difficulty that offers great views of South Sister and several lakes in the Cascades. In summer, this hike requires a Central Cascade Wilderness permit, available online.

Tumalo Falls

A 6.5-mile out-and-back hike with great views and moderate elevation gain. The 97ft Tumalo Falls is close to the start of the trail, from here the hike ascends to some smaller falls.

Scan to find more things to do in Central Oregon online

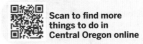

VANCOUVER

COASTAL | URBAN | NATURE

W Broadway
EXCEPT BUSES
W 8th Ave

Experience Vancouver online

W Broadway
W 8th Ave
EXCEPT BUSES

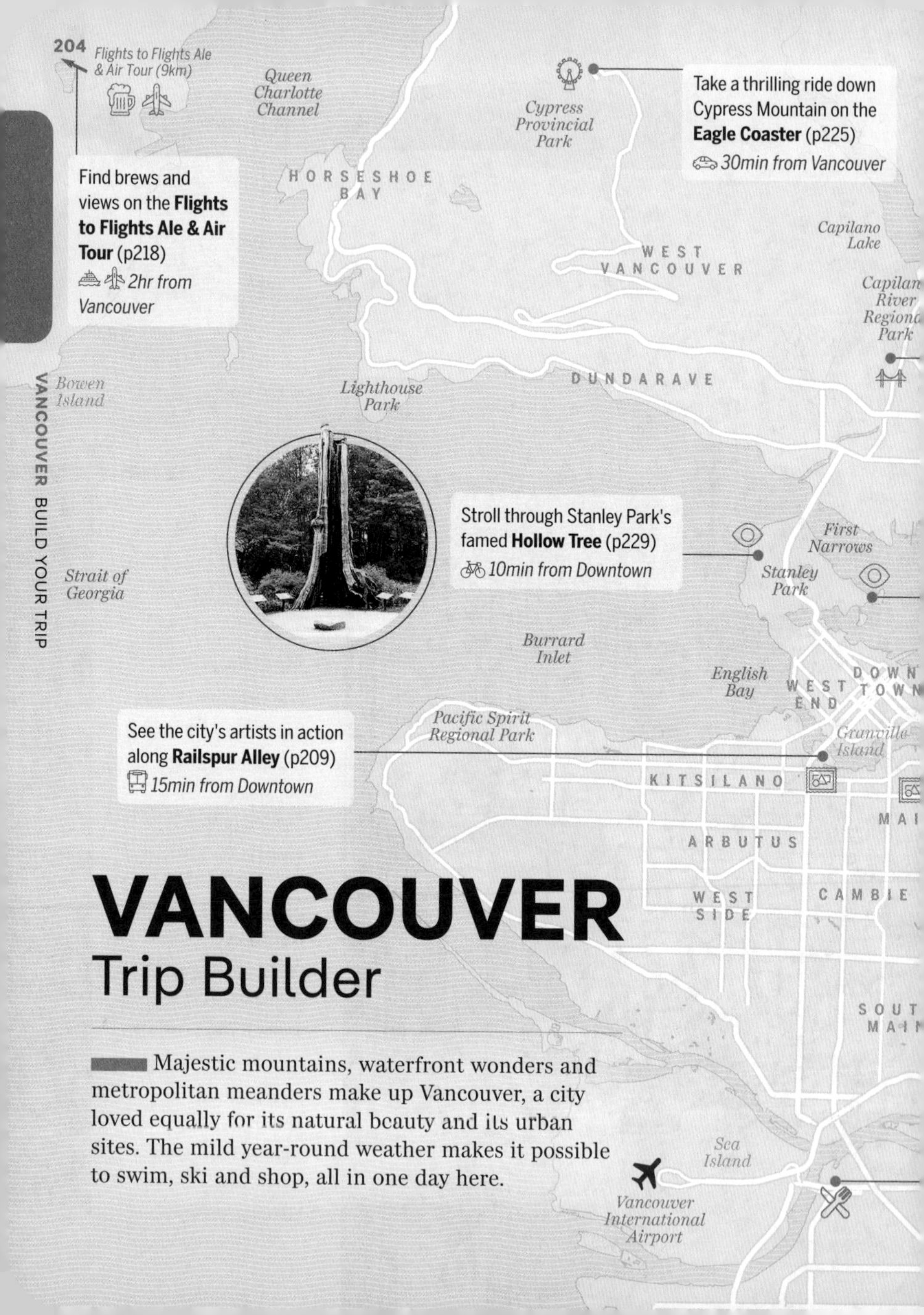
Flights to Flights Ale & Air Tour (9km)
Find brews and views on the **Flights to Flights Ale & Air Tour** (p218)
2hr from Vancouver
Take a thrilling ride down Cypress Mountain on the **Eagle Coaster** (p225)
30min from Vancouver
Stroll through Stanley Park's famed **Hollow Tree** (p229)
10min from Downtown
See the city's artists in action along **Railspur Alley** (p209)
15min from Downtown
Queen Charlotte Channel
Cypress Provincial Park
HORSESHOE BAY
WEST VANCOUVER
Capilano Lake
Bowen Island
Lighthouse Park
DUNDARAVE
First Narrows
Stanley Park
Strait of Georgia
Burrard Inlet
English Bay
WEST END
Pacific Spirit Regional Park
Granville Island
KITSILANO
ARBUTUS
WEST SIDE
CAMBIE
Sea Island
Vancouver International Airport

VANCOUVER
Trip Builder

Majestic mountains, waterfront wonders and metropolitan meanders make up Vancouver, a city loved equally for its natural beauty and its urban sites. The mild year-round weather makes it possible to swim, ski and shop, all in one day here.

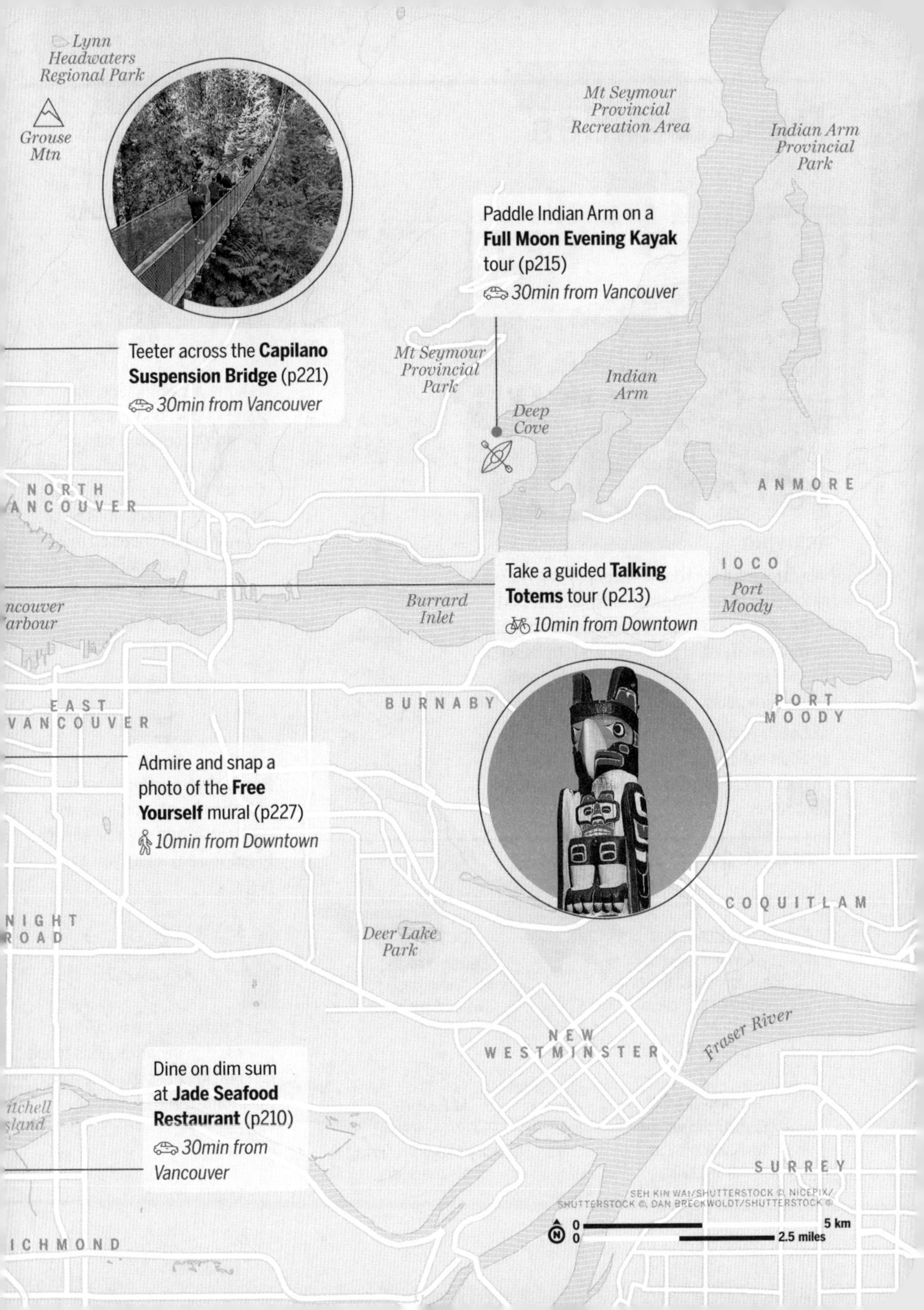

Lynn Headwaters Regional Park
Grouse Mtn
Mt Seymour Provincial Recreation Area
Indian Arm Provincial Park
Paddle Indian Arm on a **Full Moon Evening Kayak** tour (p215)
30min from Vancouver
Teeter across the **Capilano Suspension Bridge** (p221)
30min from Vancouver
Mt Seymour Provincial Park
Indian Arm
Deep Cove
NORTH VANCOUVER
ANMORE
IOCO
Port Moody
Take a guided **Talking Totems** tour (p213)
10min from Downtown
Burrard Inlet
BURNABY
EAST VANCOUVER
PORT MOODY
Admire and snap a photo of the **Free Yourself** mural (p227)
10min from Downtown
COQUITLAM
Deer Lake Park
NEW WESTMINSTER
Fraser River
Dine on dim sum at **Jade Seafood Restaurant** (p210)
30min from Vancouver
SURREY
SEH KIN WAI/SHUTTERSTOCK ©, NICEPIX/ SHUTTERSTOCK ©, DAN BRECKWOLDT/SHUTTERSTOCK ©
0
5 km
0
2.5 miles

Practicalities

DAVID BUZZARD/SHUTTERSTOCK ©

ARRIVING

Vancouver International Airport (YVR) Rated among the best in North America, this airport is the best way to arrive from an international destination. Taxis, shuttles or public transportation will take you into the city in approximately 30 to 45 minutes.

Abbotsford Airport A smaller international and domestic airport located in Abbotsford, an hour by car or hired service from downtown Vancouver.

HOW MUCH FOR A...

2hr kayak rental
$45

craft-beer pint
$7

plate of poutine
$10

WHEN TO GO

JUL–SEP
Warmest weather; ideal for hikes, boating and beach days

OCT–DEC
Fewer crowds; your home base for winter sports

JAN–MAR
Cooler temps call for snow play and spring skiing

APR–JUN
Rising temps set the city in bloom, luring locals outdoors

GETTING AROUND

Walking & cycling Scenic Stanley Park and the compact downtown core are easily accessed by foot. Vancouver's mild climate makes it easy to access attractions and activities by bike too, with rental shops on most streets and bike paths, dedicated bike lanes, and trails weaving throughout the city.

Bus & skytrain Public transportation is safe and easy, with regular bus and skytrain services to get you anywhere you want to go.

Car Parking can be pricy downtown, but many attractions found just outside the city come with the promise of free parking.

EATING & DRINKING

Vancouver's culinary scene is deliciously diverse. Get a taste of the Sunshine Coast while enjoying craft brews and sky-high views on the Flights to Flights Ale & Air Tour (p218) or enjoy fresh-off-the-boat fish (alongside bottomless fries) at Pajo's on the Wharf (p231; pictured top). Break bannock and dine on bison pot roast with authentic Indigenous dining at Salmon n' Bannock (p213; pictured bottom) or cool down with a Passive Aggressive pale ale from Brassneck Brewery (p226).

Best tour
Richmond's Dumpling Trail tour (p210)

Must-try snack
Honey Doughnuts & Goodies (p215)

WHERE TO STAY

Although pricey during peak season, with more than 25,000 guest rooms in the region, there are accommodations for almost any price point.

Neighborhood	Pro/Con
Gastown	Industrial-chic loft rentals. Oldest shopping district in the city. Gritty vibe, lively atmosphere.
Yaletown	Boutique hotels, trendy restaurants, and chic shops. Best for celebrity-spotting. Pricey.
West End	Quieter downtown, near beach and Stanley Park. More residential.
Coal Harbour	Waterfront, close to cafes, shopping and seawall strolls. Pricey.
Richmond	Affordable, filled with markets, and the best Asian food spots. Outside the city.
North Vancouver	Bustling waterfront community. Easy access to outdoor adventures. Outside the city.

CONNECT & FIND YOUR WAY

Wi-fi Over 550 locations in downtown Vancouver and surrounding areas offer free public wi-fi access for both residents and visitors.

Navigation While Vancouver's street system is simple to navigate, the Visit Vancouver app launched by Tourism Vancouver is a great tool to help you get around, and it's easily accessible while offline, too.

FAMILY ATTRACTIONS PASS

Book multiple family attractions, including Science World, FlyOver Canada and the Vancouver Aquarium, and save on your admission fees. See vancouverattractions.com/family-fun-pass.

MONEY

Credit and debit cards are widely accepted. Purchases are subject to added provincial and federal taxes. The loonie ($1) and toonie ($2) coins are part of the Canadian currency.

44 Isle of THE ARTS

ART | ENTERTAINMENT | KIDS

Once an industrial wasteland, Granville Island has evolved into a cultural wonderland, packed with creative curiosities for art enthusiasts. A gallivant through Granville Island reveals talented buskers, hidden studios, hands-on workshops, world-class cuisine and unique keepsakes, all presented against a breathtaking waterfront backdrop, only minutes from downtown Vancouver.

STUART DEE/GETTY IMAGES ©

How to

Getting here Go car-free with a mini ferry from downtown by Aquabus (theaquabus.com) or False Creek Ferries (granvilleislandferries.ca). A scenic bike path leads to the island, where a free bike valet awaits.

When to go Granville Island is open year-round. June to August is bustling with festivals and live outdoor events, while September to April promises smaller crowds.

Top tip Plan ahead and book a show at one of the island's live-performance venues.

DEYMOSHR/SHUTTERSTOCK ©

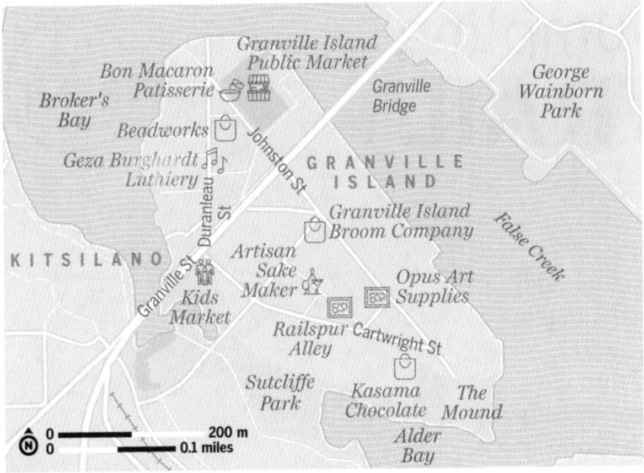
Granville Island
Public Market
Bon Macaron
Patisserie
Broker's
Bay
Beadworks
Geza Burghardt
Luthiery
Granville
Bridge
George
Wainborn
Park
Johnston St
GRANVILLE
ISLAND
Duranleau
St
Granville Island
Broom Company
False Creek
KITSILANO
Granville St
Artisan
Sake
Maker
Opus Art
Supplies
Kids
Market
Railspur
Alley
Cartwright St
Sutcliffe
Park
Kasama
Chocolate
The
Mound
Alder
Bay
0
200 m
0
0.1 miles

Far left top Handmade brooms, Granville Island Broom Company **Far left bottom** Deli stall, Granville Island Public Market

Artists in action Stroll through **Railspur Alley** and watch artists create masterpieces before your eyes. See jewelers, glassblowers, potters, painters, blacksmiths and carvers craft beautiful pieces live in-studio and listen as they share the inspiration behind their work. Head to the **Granville Island Broom Company** and watch two sisters handcraft Shaker-style woven brooms in their whimsical storefront, and visit the **Geza Burghardt Luthiery**, where you can watch as a Hungarian luthier builds, repairs and restores guitars, violins, cellos and other string instruments.

Get hands-on At **Beadworks**, you can shop through an expansive collection of beads – from Swarovski crystals to bone beads – before creating your own original piece of jewelry to take home. Satisfy your sweet tooth while mastering the art of macaron-making with a private class at **Bon Macaron Patisserie**, or sign up for an in-store painting class at **Opus Art Supplies**, a spacious store that has become a staple of the Vancouver art community.

Sip & sample Visit the **Artisan Sake Maker** – the first boutique premium sake winery of its kind in North America – and sip on unique, small-batch sake made on-site. For a sweet treat, head to **Kasama Chocolate** for bean-to-bar chocolate made using unique ingredients like durian, a pungent tropical fruit. Satisfy your cravings with a stroll through **Granville Island Public Market**, where you can sample from a slew of bakeries, butchers and specialty food shops offering food and drink sourced fresh from the ocean, the oven or the field.

Just for Kids

Granville Island is home to the largest free outdoor water park in North America, and **Kids Market**, a three-story kid-centric mall that features handcrafted toys, multi-level play spaces, and interactive arcades for kids of all ages. **Pirate Adventures** offers an interactive pirate cruise adventure for kids, and the **Vancouver International Children's Festival** – the longest-running professional performing-arts festival for young audiences and the first of its kind in North America – is a must for imaginative kids during the summer season. After strolling through the studios and shops, little ones can stretch their legs with a play on one of the three outdoor playgrounds.

45 Dumpling TRAIL

FOOD | CULTURE | TOURS

Slurp on steaming wonton soup, nibble on crunchy, deep-fried dumplings, or gobble up pork-stuffed pouches. On this dumpling trail tour through Richmond – home to the largest Chinese population in the world (beyond Asia) – top-notch tastes are elevated by textures. Richmond is renowned for its authentic Asian cuisine, and here we highlight the best spots.

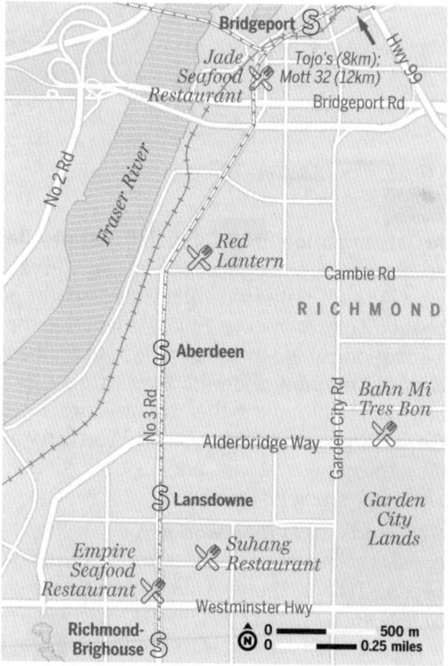
Bridgeport
Jade Seafood Restaurant
Tojo's (8km); Mott 32 (12km)
Hwy 99
Bridgeport Rd
No 2 Rd
Fraser River
Red Lantern
Cambie Rd
RICHMOND
Aberdeen
No 3 Rd
Garden City Rd
Bahn Mi Tres Bon
Alderbridge Way
Lansdowne
Garden City Lands
Empire Seafood Restaurant
Suhang Restaurant
Westminster Hwy
Richmond-Brighouse
0 500 m
0 0.25 miles

How to

Getting here Richmond is only 30 minutes from downtown Vancouver by car, and public bus and Skytrain services make it easy to get around once you're here.

When to go The Dumpling Trail can be enjoyed year-round; however, to avoid crowds aim for weekdays. For dim sum, plan your visit between 10am and 2pm.

Where to start Begin with dim sum, a traditional Chinese brunch that is usually served late morning.

Plan your route Visit the Dumpling Trail website (visit richmondbc.com), where suggested itineraries help set the scene. With over 20 eateries on this self-guided tour, it can be challenging to choose your course.

Do dim sum This quintessential Chinese brunch is the best way to consume Cantonese cuisine, where dumplings are served in small portions and enjoyed family-style, traditionally paired with hot jasmine tea. Standout dim sum spots include **Jade Seafood Restaurant**, offering traditional dishes with Western-inspired fusion fare, and **Empire Seafood Restaurant**, an elegant eatery that's among the oldest in Richmond.

Savor the process Juicy *xiao long bao* (soup dumplings) are a treat from Shanghai, and the process by which you consume these piping hot pouches is part of the fun. **Suhang Restaurant** does them best, with quality meat and dumplings that are

EDA HO/GETTY IMAGES ©

Signature Experiences

Find elevated dim sum dishes and Peking duck sliced and served tableside at **Mott 32**, where innovative Chinese fare is perfectly paired with a surprising mix of craft cocktails. At **Tojo's**, a seasonal *omakase* (chef's selection) takes fine dining to a new level, combining traditional Japanese ingredients with a modern 'Tojo twist' inspired by the Pacific Northwest. Experience it all with a custom-designed private dinner tour by **Dine Like a Critic** (dinelikeacritic.com), led by an esteemed food critic and well-connected culinary expert who guides guests through the best Asian dining spots found in and around Vancouver – from classic Cantonese cuisine to new wave Chinese culinary creations.

perfectly pinched. These are best eaten when the tip of the wrapper is carefully nibbled off, and the soupy insides are slurped out. Top the rest with vinegar, pop it in your mouth and enjoy!

Best bites Decor and delivery impress at **Bahn Mi Tres Bon**, where Vietnamese *bahn bot loc* (shrimp and pork tapioca dumplings) come topped with fish sauce, crispy shallots and fresh green onion. The *shui jiao* (water boiled, meat-stuffed dumplings) at **Red Lantern** are the perfect comfort food, and if you're lucky, you'll catch them being handmade before your eyes.

Above Steamed *xiao long bao*

46 Indigenous STORIES

LOCAL | CULTURE | ART

Located on the traditional, ancestral and unceded territory of the Coast Salish peoples of the Squamish, Musqueam and Tsleil-Waututh Nations, Vancouver's rich history shines through the stories and experiences shared by those who first called the land home. Immerse yourself in Indigenous tales and traditions, kept alive through the art, dining and guided experiences offered throughout the city.

MICHAEL WHEATLEY PHOTOGRAPHY/ALAMY STOCK PHOTO ©

How to

Getting around These experiences are all found in downtown Vancouver, accessible by public transit, bike or foot.

When to go All are open year-round. Summer weather is best for outdoor tours, but smaller crowds are a draw during the cooler months.

Top tip Ask questions. These businesses are all Indigenous-owned and operated, and the stories and knowledge shared are as unique and diverse as the 200+ Indigenous communities found throughout BC.

URBAN NAPFLIN/SHUTTERSTOCK ©

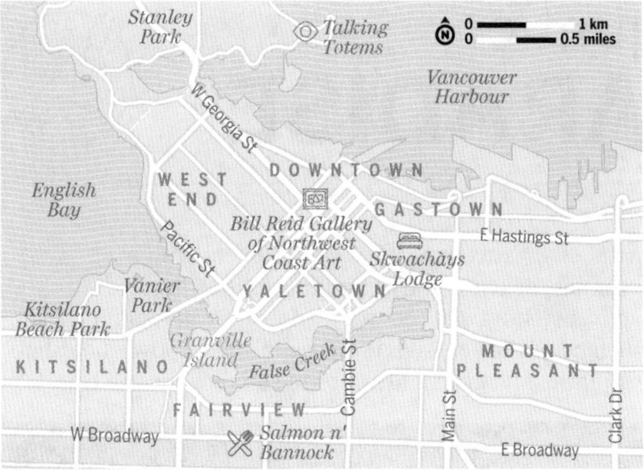
Stanley Park
Talking Totems
0 1 km
0 0.5 miles
Vancouver Harbour
W Georgia St
DOWNTOWN
WEST END
English Bay
GASTOWN
Bill Reid Gallery of Northwest Coast Art
E Hastings St
Pacific St
Skwachàys Lodge
Vanier Park
YALETOWN
Kitsilano Beach Park
Granville Island
False Creek
Cambie St
MOUNT PLEASANT
KITSILANO
FAIRVIEW
Main St
Clark Dr
W Broadway
Salmon n' Bannock
E Broadway

Indigenous dining The only Indigenous-owned restaurant in Vancouver, **Salmon n' Bannock** serves modern dishes made using traditional indigenous ingredients. But the dining experience is more than a meal. The space is filled with Aboriginal artwork, stories are shared, and traditional music is played as you dine on delectable dishes, such as the must-try mushrooms on toasted bannock, and the bison pot roast, a melt-in-your-mouth meat dish that simmers for 24 hours before serving.

Fine art The **Bill Reid Gallery of Northwest Coast Art** is Canada's only public gallery dedicated to contemporary indigenous art of the Northwest Coast. Find original works by the famed Haida artist, Bill Reid, who carved some of the most prominent sculptures found throughout the city, such as the *Jade Canoe,* a carving on display at Vancouver International Airport.

Immersive experience Offered by Talaysay Tours, the **Talking Totems** tour takes guests on an eye-opening journey through the towering totem poles that have stood erect in Stanley Park since 1920. Led by an indigenous guide, you will be awed by the art of the gateways and totems that make the site a must-see.

Cultural stay Art takes the spotlight at **Skwachàys Lodge**, Canada's first indigenous arts hotel. On-site, you'll find a gallery filled with indigenous art and guest suites with original local artwork on display. The property features immersive cultural activities, including sweat lodge ceremonies, traditional smudge ceremonies, and in-studio visits with artists-in-residence.

Far left top Bill Reid Gallery of Northwest Coast Art **Far left bottom** Skwachàys Lodge

Cultural Keepsakes

The Thunderbird Dark French Roast or Eagle Medium Roast coffees from **Spirit Bear Coffee Company** are my personal favorites. Its coffee is certified organic and fair trade, and it supports social initiatives like the Ocean Alliance and the Raincoast Conservation Foundation. **Sḵwálwen Botanicals** is a great Indigenous, plant-based beauty brand that celebrates ancestral Sḵwxwú7mesh (Squamish) plant knowledge. I love its lip balm and rose facial oil. **Totem Design House** has beautiful silver jewelry and stylish cotton organic shirts. **Sisters Sage** makes wonderful wellness products, I love its soaps, which are poured, cut and packaged by hand using the traditional cold-process method.

Tips by Candace Campo, *ancestral name Xets'emits'a, Shishalh Nation, Talaysay Tours @talaysay_tours*

47 Aquatic PARADISE

COASTAL | OUTDOORS | BOATING

As a captivating coastal city, Vancouver lures water lovers with a wide selection of sea-view venues, beaches, parks and attractions, but for a particularly unique perspective, visitors can see the west-coast waters and explore the city from the surface of the sea, too. From paddling to powerboating to picnicking at sea, these aquatic adventures are sure to steady your sea legs.

STEPHANIE BRACONNIER/SHUTTERSTOCK ©

How to

Getting around The waterways are easily accessible, with direct access to the ocean by bus, car, bike or foot, depending on your destination.

When to go Sunseekers will prefer adventures by water during the summer months, but with Vancouver's mild climate (and the right rain gear), most of these activities can be enjoyed year-round.

Day trip These aquatic activities can all be found near charming communities, with boutiques and cafes only steps from the water. Choose one destination and make a day of it!

JOE'S BBQ BOAT
JOE'S BBQ

MICHAEL WHEATLEY PHOTOGRAPHY/ ALAMY STOCK PHOTO ©

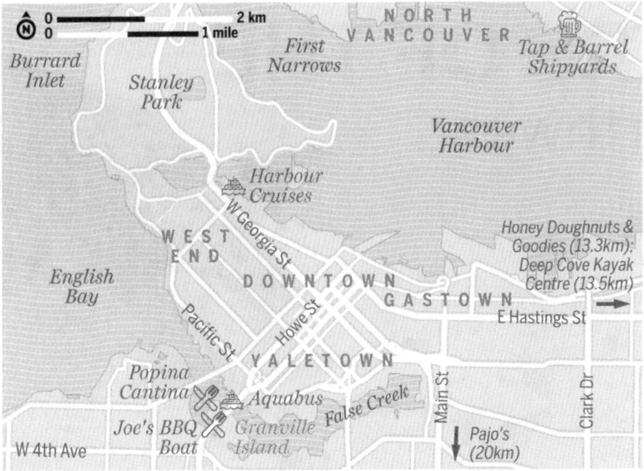
0 2 km
0 1 mile
N
NORTH VANCOUVER
Burrard Inlet
First Narrows
Tap & Barrel Shipyards
Stanley Park
Vancouver Harbour
Harbour Cruises
W Georgia St
WEST END
Honey Doughnuts & Goodies (13.3km); Deep Cove Kayak Centre (13.5km)
English Bay
DOWNTOWN
GASTOWN
E Hastings St
Pacific St
Howe St
YALETOWN
Popina Cantina
Aquabus
False Creek
Main St
Clark Dr
Joe's BBQ Boat
Granville Island
Pajo's (20km)
W 4th Ave

Deep Cove Head to the far eastern edge of North Vancouver, where aquatic adventures await in Deep Cove. The **Deep Cove Kayak Centre** is Vancouver's premium paddling site for kayaking, stand-up paddleboarding, and surfskiing, with one of the largest fleets of human-powered watercraft rentals in Canada. Pick your craft and paddle along Indian Arm – North America's southernmost fjord. Experience the thrill of a night-time paddle on a **Full Moon Evening Kayak** guided tour, or simply learn how to paddleboard or surfski in the calm bay.

Granville Island Visit the Granville Island wharf and take to the water on a grill-equipped boat for a picnic at sea! **Joe's BBQ Boat** is one of the only BBQ boat businesses in the world to offer electric-powered vessels, and you get to be the captain (no boat license required) as you cruise the coast while cooking your meal and taking in city views from the water. If you'd prefer someone else to do the driving, hop on the iconic rainbow-colored **Aquabus** and take a tour of the city by sea – you can even bring a bike!

Coal Harbour If a romantic dinner aboard a luxury yacht is more your speed, consider a sunset dinner cruise with **Harbour Cruises**, where live music and West Coast cuisine can be enjoyed as you take in Vancouver's best views from the water and watch the sun set over the city.

Far left top Kayakers, Deep Cove **Far left bottom** Joe's BBQ Boat

Seaside Snack Spots

On Granville Island, head to **Popina Cantina**, a great spot to enjoy tacos while people-watching from the waterfront patio, found only steps from the dock. **Honey Doughnuts & Goodies** is a must-visit snack stop in Deep Cove, where you can pick up a fresh honey dip to-go, and enjoy it outdoors at the nearby Panorama Park. Also found in North Vancouver, **Tap & Barrel Shipyards** has a great (and spacious) patio. Its PB&J Burger pairs perfectly with a cold brew – its local craft-beer selection is extensive. **Pajo's** on the wharf in Steveston Village is known for its world-famous fish-and-chips – also a must here.

■ **Recommended by Dennis Pang,** *local foodie, @dennispang, @pangcouver*

CRITTERS OF THE
Pacific Northwest

01

04

02

05

03

06

01 Banana slug
Ranging in colour from bright (banana) yellow to green to brown, these native forest-dwelling detritivores can grow up to 10in long.

02 American pika
These cute herbivorous mammals – related to rabbits and hares – live in alpine areas. Listen for their squeaky vocalisations on Mt Rainier.

03 Tufted puffin
If there's anything cuter than a puffin, it's a tufted puffin, found on Cannon Beach's iconic Haystack Rock.

04 Orca
The undisputed spirit animal of the Pacific Northwest waters, orcas live in social family groups (pods) led by dominant females.

05 Roosevelt elk
With full-grown males weighing up to 1100lb and carrying 5ft racks of antlers, elk are certainly a signature PNW creature.

06 Sage grouse
Inhabiting sagebrush grassland, these chest-puffing birds put on quite the elaborate show during their spring mating season.

07

08

10

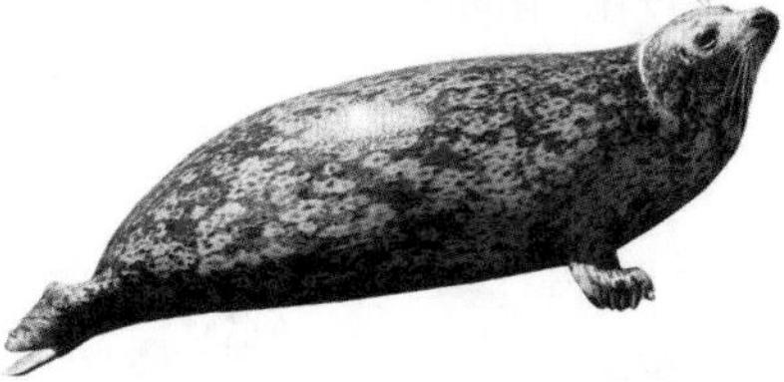

11

12

09

07 Gray whale

A major reason for visiting the Pacific Northwest coast, these magnificent creatures, along with their humpback cousins, make the longest migrations of any mammals in the world.

08 Beaver

Meet North America's largest rodent! After late-18th-century fur trading decimated their populations, beavers are now rarely seen.

09 Salmon

Iconic, and under threat. Read more on p46.

10 Harbor seal

Spot these small seals draped over rocky headlands or, from April to July, their pups waiting on beaches for their mothers to return.

11 Bald eagle

The Pacific Northwest is a stronghold for bald eagles, who feast on the annual salmon runs and nest in old-growth forests.

12 Pronghorn

Running at up to 60mph, these deer-like mammals are the second-fastest land animals in the world.

48 Flights to Flights: ALE & AIR

DAY TRIP | FLIGHTSEEING | COASTAL

Enjoy crafted brews and sky-high views on this exciting day trip from the city, where you can soar over Sechelt Inlet on the Sunshine Coast, then embark on a guided tasting tour of the local Sechelt breweries and distilleries. Part of the BC Ale Trail, this exclusive tour is a great way to get a taste of the region.

WWW.BRICKERSCIDER.COM ©

How to

Getting here A 45-minute ferry from Horseshoe Bay to Langdale by BC Ferries will take you to your pickup spot, where a 15-passenger van will meet you for your tour.

When to go Offered year-round, but for the best views, May to August is recommended.

What to bring Wear comfortable footwear, and bring a camera!

Tour length Seven hours, with lunch and snacks included, as well as a complimentary flight of beer.

TAMASV/SHUTTERSTOCK ©

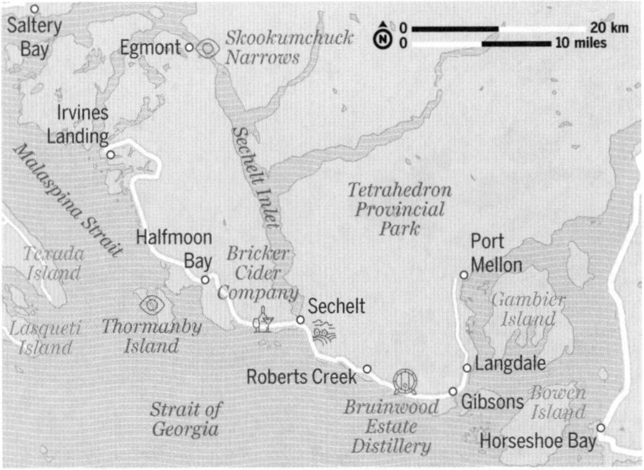
Saltery Bay
Egmont
Skookumchuck Narrows
0 20 km
0 10 miles
Irvines Landing
Sechelt Inlet
Malaspina Strait
Tetrahedron Provincial Park
Halfmoon Bay
Bricker Cider Company
Port Mellon
Texada Island
Sechelt
Gambier Island
Lasqueti Island
Thormanby Island
Langdale
Roberts Creek
Gibsons
Bowen Island
Strait of Georgia
Bruinwood Estate Distillery
Horseshoe Bay

Far left top Bricker Cider Company
Far left bottom Sunshine Coast Air seaplane

Gateway to the Sunshine Coast On the **Flights to Flights Ale & Air Tour**, offered by Sunshine Coast Art Tours (sunshinecoastarttours.com) and Sunshine Coast Air, you'll discover the culinary and coastal highlights of Sechelt – the gateway to the Sunshine Coast. Through engaging stories, you'll learn about the origins of the Coast Salish people who first called the land home, and discover the diverse community of artists and makers that thrive in this small town, home to over 1000 art studios and nearly a dozen high-end craft breweries and boutique distilleries.

Secret spots From the backroad beauty of **Bruinwood Estate Distillery**, where you can sample creative concoctions of spirits inspired by international flavors while marveling at the modern West Coast structure in which the tasting room is housed, to **Bricker Cider Company**, a family-run farmstead surrounded by apple trees, each stop is a tucked-away treasure best discovered with a local guide behind the wheel.

Soar over Sechelt The tour includes a 25-minute flightseeing tour with **Sunshine Coast Air**, which takes you above the Sunshine Coast aboard a vintage, six-seater De Havilland Beaver floatplane. Spot the powerful rapids of the Skookumchuck Narrows, and take in the tropical-like coastline of Thormanby Island from a bird's-eye view while the pilot shares tales of Sechelt Inlet while showing off the area's most beautiful features from the air.

Superb Sips

The Earl Grey Gin at **Bruinwood Estate Distillery** blends flavors of bergamot and juniper to create a tasty tea-flavored tipple, and the Pechuga, a savory Mexican liqueur made of chicken, mango, rice, corn, garlic and spices is like a meal in a glass. They are also the only producers in Canada of Advocaat – a custard-like traditional Dutch treat.

At **Batch 44**, a small-batch brewery that sits snug in the center of downtown Sechelt, the Halfmoon Pale Ale makes the perfect summer sipper.

Bricker Cider makes elderberry-and-lavender cider on-site using freshly grown ingredients – one you'll want to take home to sip and savor later.

49 Treetop TREKS

NATURE | WILDLIFE | FAMILY

Surrounded by lush temperate rainforest, Vancouver has become a favored destination for treelined treks and, more specifically, the stress-relieving activity of forest bathing, with several forested sites found within city limits. For a squirrel's eye view, try these treetop adventures.

PETER ADAMS/GETTY IMAGES ©

How to

Getting around Most attractions can be accessed by transit from downtown Vancouver. For the sites found further afield, rent a car and cruise the picturesque Sea-to-Sky Hwy to Squamish or Whistler.

When to go All of these destinations are enjoyable year-round, just be sure to dress for the weather!

What to bring Pack essentials in a hands-free backpack so you can steady yourself on the bridges and platforms. Wear comfortable shoes.

Sky Pilot Suspension Bridge (34km);
Train Wreck Hike (88km);
Ziptrek Ecotours (95km)
Capilano Lake
Grouse Mountain
Capilano Suspension Bridge
Lynn Canyon Suspension Bridge
Burrard Inlet
Stanley Park
Vancouver Harbour
Pacific Spirit Regional Park
VANCOUVER
Strait of Georgia
Fraser River
George C Reifel Migratory Bird Sanctuary
0
10 km
0
5 miles

Suspension bridges Suspended 230ft high above the Capilano River and stretching 450ft long, a teeter along the **Capilano Suspension Bridge** has been an epic experience enjoyed by visitors to Vancouver since the bridge was first built in 1883. And once you cross the bridge, the adventures aren't over! On the other side, Treetops Adventures offers a series of seven small suspension bridges connecting trekkers to several viewing platforms that sit perched above old-growth Douglas fir trees, some as old as 1300 years.

Also found on Vancouver's North Shore, the **Lynn Canyon Suspension Bridge** is a lesser-known spot, where a stroll across the 160ft-high bridge reveals views of rushing rapids and winding waterfalls, and leads to a series of scenic hiking trails. Best of all, it doesn't cost anything to cross the bridge.

A riveting ride up the Sea to Sky Gondola in Squamish leads to the **Sky Pilot Suspension Bridge**, where 360-degree views span from alpine peaks to the waters of Howe Sound below.

Left Forest bathing
Above left Capilano Suspension Bridge

Illuminated nights From November to January, the Capilano Suspension Bridge lights up the night with **Canyon Lights**, where the bridges and platforms are all aglow against the dark night sky, decorated with a dazzling multi-color light-changing display made up of over 50,000 lights and illuminated decorations.

Sky-high thrills For an added thrill, stroll along the **Cliffwalk**, also found at Capilano Suspension Bridge Park. It's a narrow series of cantilevered walkways and platforms that weave along a jagged granite cliff, dangling high above Capilano Canyon.

For a real adrenaline rush, a zipline in Whistler will carry you on a high-flying adventure above the trees. **ZipTrek Ecotours** offers a variety of tours for all levels that take you through a series of ziplines accessed by suspended treetop bridges. During the summer

Wildlife Viewings

Home to 250 bird species, the **George C Reifel Migratory Bird Sanctuary** is one of Canada's top birdwatching sites. Road trip along the 'Pacific Flyway' on the **BC Bird Trail**, a series of self-guided birdwatching tours, and seek out feathered friends year-round.

For closer interaction with Vancouver's resident birds and bears, take the gondola up to Grouse Mountain and check out the **Birds in Motion** experience. Stop by and meet 'Grinder' and 'Coola,' Grouse's rescued orphan grizzly bears.

Head out onto the Salish Sea on a marine adventure and seek out orcas, otters and other marine life in their natural habitat.

Tips by Jami Savage, *family travel writer*
@adventureawaits.ca

Majestic Maple

The maple leaf is a symbol of Canada, and for good reason! The bigleaf maple tree is the largest in BC, can be spotted throughout the country, and is Vancouver's most common tree, accounting for around 25% of the trees found in the city. During fall, the maple leaves transform into an explosion of colors – a truly stunning sight.

SMILEATDAYS2COME/SHUTTERSTOCK ©

months, the Sasquatch zipline opens to visitors – a heart-pumping zipline that is the longest in Canada and the USA, with visitors zooming over 2km while dangling more than 600ft above the ground!

Train wreck in the trees Step onto the trailhead of the **Train Wreck Hike**, which can be found along the Sea-to-Sky Hwy just before Whistler. A short stroll will take you through the coastal rainforest, across a bridge that dangles suspended over rushing river rapids, and into a clearing where you will be awed by a series of rainbow-colored boxcars that sit scattered among the trees. The train remains are the result of a derailment that occurred in 1956. Since then, the site has become an ever-changing public art display of graffiti, and an outdoor playground for curious climbers, who teeter along the top of each train car while taking in forest views from above.

JOHN CRUX/SHUTTERSTOCK ©

Left Wood duck, George C Reifel Migratory Bird Sanctuary **Above top** Maple leaves **Above** Abandoned train, Train Wreck Hike

50 Peak PURSUITS

MOUNTAINS | ADVENTURE | FAMILY

Vancouver is framed by a trifecta of local ski hills: Cypress Mountain, Mt Seymour and Grouse Mountain, all accessible in under an hour. While this means visitors can swim in the ocean, shop in the city and ski the slopes all in one day, alpine adventures aren't limited to seasonal snow play. There's fun to be had in these mountains all year long.

JAU-CHENG LIOU/SHUTTERSTOCK ©

How to

Getting here All three mountains can be reached by car in less than an hour. They are also easily accessible by direct shuttle bus from downtown Vancouver.

When to go For slopeside snow play, November to March is the best time to visit. For off-season fun beyond the slopes, activities can be enjoyed year-round.

Top tip Be sure to book in advance as these adventures can fill up very quickly.

SKYRIDE

JUSTEK16/SHUTTERSTOCK ©

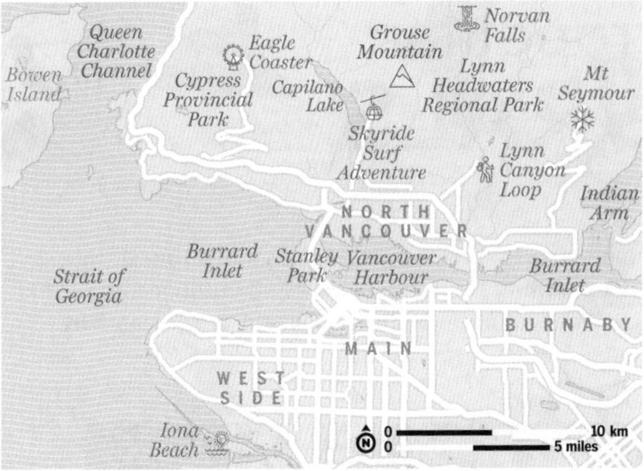
Queen Charlotte Channel
Bowen Island
Eagle Coaster
Cypress Provincial Park
Capilano Lake
Grouse Mountain
Norvan Falls
Lynn Headwaters Regional Park
Mt Seymour
Skyride Surf Adventure
Lynn Canyon Loop
Indian Arm
NORTH VANCOUVER
Burrard Inlet
Stanley Park
Vancouver Harbour
Burrard Inlet
Strait of Georgia
BURNABY
MAIN
WEST SIDE
Iona Beach
0 10 km
0 5 miles

Ride a mountain coaster Canada's longest mountain coaster, the **Eagle Coaster** on Cypress Mountain is an exhilarating, open-air rollercoaster that travels over 1.7km down the mountainside, winding along a track that takes you through forested vistas. The coaster reaches speeds of up to 25mph, but don't worry, hesitant riders can control the speed.

Surf a gondola Why ride in a gondola when you can feel the wind on your face while riding on its rooftop! The Grouse Mountain **Skyride Surf Adventure**, available only during the summer months, ascends 2800ft up Grouse Mountain, offering unparalleled views of the sparkling Pacific Ocean, the dazzling Douglas fir trees and the snow-capped mountains that surround you. This special viewing platform is only available to a select few, so be sure to book before you go.

Snowshoe with fondue One of the top resorts for snowshoeing in North America, Mt Seymour offers a slew of snowshoe tours for every experience level. From first-timers to nature lovers, to advanced athletes, everyone will enjoy views of old-growth forests, scenic lakes and city views from the mountain. For a particularly unique experience, take a snowshoe trek through the trails at night on the **Fondue Snowshoe Tour**, which ends with delicious chocolate fondue, enjoyed against a dark night sky.

Far left top Snowshoeing, Mt Seymour
Far left bottom Grouse Mountain Skyride

Best Hikes for Beginners

Iona Beach (Richmond) A great place for bird-watching, bringing kids to watch planes land and take off, and enjoying the beach views.

Norvan Falls (North Vancouver) A good hike in early spring and summer. On a hot day, the trees shield you from the sun and the waterfall has a great swimming hole to cool off in once you arrive.

Lynn Canyon Loop (North Vancouver) A good hike for families, with lots of water access to cool off or just enjoy the outdoors while enjoying more room to roam.

Tips by Judith Kasiama, *CEO of Colour the Trails*
@colourthetrails

51 Metropolitan MURALS

ART | CITY | FESTIVALS

Explore the city through an artistic lens with a self-guided tour of the Vancouver Mural Festival – a stunning showcase of over 300 outdoor murals and public art displays found in 11 neighborhoods throughout the city, created by local and international artists.

Love all Your Neighbours

MURAL FESTIVAL ©

Trip Notes

Getting around Take public transit, then stroll the streets to take it all in.

When to go Check the site for seasonal festivals featuring live events, demos and workshops. Public art and murals, such as Jocelyn Wong's *Love all Your Neighbours* (pictured above), are on display year-round.

Where to start Visit vanmuralfest.ca or download the app to choose your adventure based on neighborhood or artistic style (the indigenous art mural map is a great place to start).

Best Brews

33 Acres: Sunshine Pair this unfiltered wheat ale with nearby murals like Alexia Tryfon's wolfish *Argos*.

Brassneck Brewery: Passive Aggressive Sip this pale ale, then view *Eagle Opens Up*, a collab between Indigenous artists.

Faculty Brewing: Minzeveizen This peppermint-tinged beer complements Olivia Di Liberto's *Cosmic Breeze*.

■ **Lucas Aykroyd,** *BC Ale Trail writer lucasaykroyd.com.*

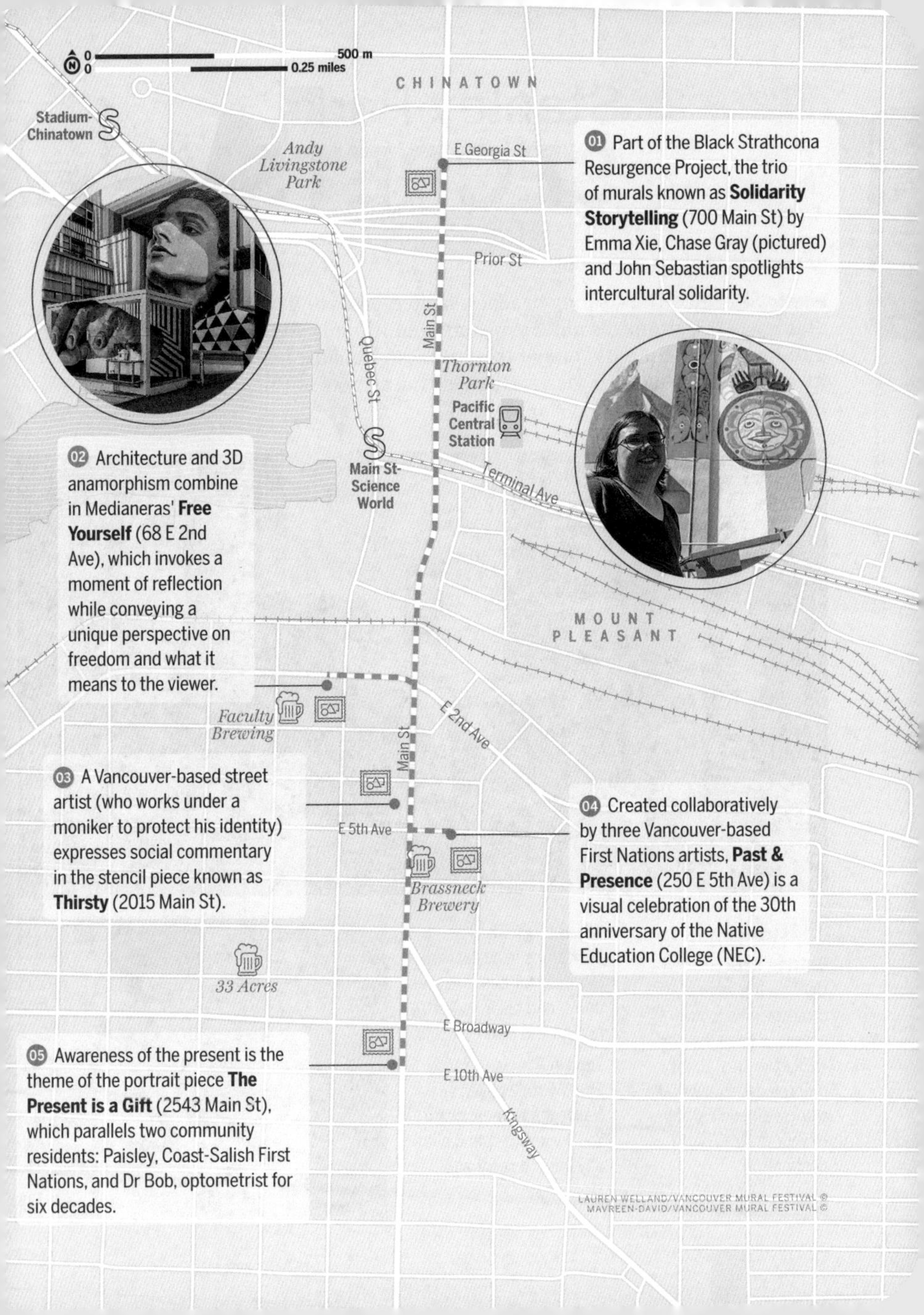

0 500 m
0 0.25 miles
CHINATOWN
Stadium-Chinatown
Andy Livingstone Park
E Georgia St
Prior St
Main St
Quebec St
Thornton Park
Pacific Central Station
Main St-Science World
Terminal Ave
MOUNT PLEASANT
Faculty Brewing
E 2nd Ave
E 5th Ave
Brassneck Brewery
33 Acres
E Broadway
E 10th Ave
Kingsway

01 Part of the Black Strathcona Resurgence Project, the trio of murals known as **Solidarity Storytelling** (700 Main St) by Emma Xie, Chase Gray (pictured) and John Sebastian spotlights intercultural solidarity.

02 Architecture and 3D anamorphism combine in Medianeras' **Free Yourself** (68 E 2nd Ave), which invokes a moment of reflection while conveying a unique perspective on freedom and what it means to the viewer.

03 A Vancouver-based street artist (who works under a moniker to protect his identity) expresses social commentary in the stencil piece known as **Thirsty** (2015 Main St).

04 Created collaboratively by three Vancouver-based First Nations artists, **Past & Presence** (250 E 5th Ave) is a visual celebration of the 30th anniversary of the Native Education College (NEC).

05 Awareness of the present is the theme of the portrait piece **The Present is a Gift** (2543 Main St), which parallels two community residents: Paisley, Coast-Salish First Nations, and Dr Bob, optometrist for six decades.

52 Stanley Park SECRETS

PARKS | HISTORY | BEACHES

Seawall strolls, sandy beaches, heated pools and woodland trails – Stanley Park epitomizes natural beauty, and it's only steps from the city. But the 400-hectare urban park, one of the largest in Canada, has more to offer than its green spaces and sea views. Discover the secrets of this world-famous site through these lesser-known spots.

REGIEN PAASSEN/SHUTTERSTOCK ©

How to

Getting here Located right on the edge of downtown Vancouver, access is easy. You can walk, bike, bus, scoot, rollerblade, drive or take a horse-drawn carriage to your desired park destination.

When to go Stanley Park stuns in all seasons. Summer for beaches and pools, and fall for colorful foliage and fewer crowds.

Top tip Plan your route. The 5½-mile paved seawall leads to most sites. You'll want to spend a full day here to see it all.

RONNIE CHUA/SHUTTERSTOCK ©

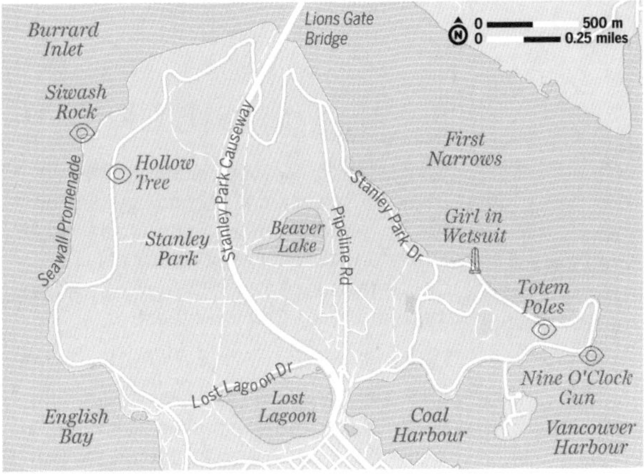
Burrard Inlet
Lions Gate Bridge
0 500 m
0 0.25 miles
Siwash Rock
Hollow Tree
Stanley Park Causeway
First Narrows
Seawall Promenade
Stanley Park Dr
Stanley Park
Beaver Lake
Pipeline Rd
Girl in Wetsuit
Totem Poles
Lost Lagoon Dr
Nine O'Clock Gun
Lost Lagoon
English Bay
Coal Harbour
Vancouver Harbour

Totem poles Stanley Park shines with cultural pride, showcasing the history of the area through the totem poles that stand tall at the park's edge. Located on the traditional, unceded territories of the Musqueam, Squamish and Tsleil-Waututh peoples, the totem poles tell the story of the park's roots through the creative methods and people behind the works of art, which have stood just steps from the city since 1920.

Nine O'Clock Gun Every night at 9pm, a cannon is fired from Brockton Point in Stanley Park, its blast heard from across the city. The Nine O'Clock Gun fires nightly, a Vancouver tradition that has been seen and heard for over a century. Originally located at the Brockton Point Lighthouse and fired manually each night for people to set their timepieces, the tradition remains, now managed by the Parks Board. You can view the blast from its site, just be sure to wear ear plugs for the big boom!

Hollow Tree An old western red cedar tree in Stanley Park is one of the most visited sites in Vancouver, thanks to its huge hollow stump, which has become a photo op for tourists. Known simply as the Hollow Tree, the remains of the nearly 1000-year-old tree features an interior opening with a circumference of about 60ft.

Far left top Totem poles, Stanley Park
Far left bottom *Girl in Wetsuit* statue

Seawall Landmarks

As you bike, stroll and rollerblade along the scenic Stanley Park seawall, be sure to look out for the **Girl in Wetsuit** statue that sits on a rock in the water just off the north side of the park. The statue – which is often mistaken for a mermaid – was a gift from sculptor Elek Imredy in 1972, to represent Vancouver's dependence on the sea. **Siwash Rock** is another landmark to look out for, a famous rock with a tree on its tip. Over thousands of years, the water has separated the rock from the park, and it now sits on its own in the sea.

Listings

BEST OF THE REST

Beachfront Brews & Bites

Cactus Club Cafe – English Bay $$

Grab lunch and libations with a view at this Cactus Club location that overlooks English Bay Beach. A popular Canadian-owned chain, Cactus Club offers affordable, modern West Coast cuisine and cocktails.

Ancora Waterfront Dining and Patio $$$

Peruvian and Japanese cuisine combine with a touch of West Coast flair to create a unique blend of flavors at Ancora, with two locations to serve you, both featuring waterfront, picturesque patios.

Tap & Barrel – Olympic Village $$

Craft brews and sprawling sea views are the draw, with a diverse menu that combines classic comfort foods with fresh, seasonal fare.

Mahony Tavern – False Creek $$

Located right on the False Creek seawall, this locally owned Irish pub offers casual comfort food and craft beers with majestic marina views.

The Boathouse – Kits Beach $$$

Located on the edge of sandy Kitsilano Beach, you'll find sustainable seafood, premium steaks and a varietal wine menu here, as well as unparalleled water views.

Family Attractions

Vancouver Aquarium

Stroll through Canada's largest aquarium, home to 65,000 creatures and over 30 unique exhibits. While you're here, be sure to check out the 4D Experience, which brings learning to life.

Science World

Step inside Vancouver's iconic geodesic dome for science-and-technology-based fun for the whole family, featuring hands-on indoor and outdoor exhibits and galleries, live performances, and film viewings in the state-of-the-art Omnimax theatre.

FlyOver Canada

Soar over Canada without ever leaving your seat! Get up close with the most stunning sights in the country using state-of-the-art technology that gives you a true feeling of flight.

Kids Market

Explore this two-story shopping mall on Granville Island, a dreamy destination for kids of all ages, filled with toy stores, play spaces, interactive games and activities, and kid-friendly snacks and treats!

Playland

From June to September Playland is the place to be. BC's most famous amusement park is packed with riveting rides, attractions and shows.

Science World

Superb Seafood

Tojo's Restaurant $$$

Head to the city's epicenter for celebrities and famed chefs, where Chef Tojo – inventor of the California roll – combines traditional Japanese cuisine with seasonal ingredients from the Pacific Northwest to create a special *omakase*.

Miku Restaurant $$

This restaurant introduced Japanese Aburi-style cuisine to Vancouver, incorporating Ocean Wise seafood options and waterfront views to showcase the best of Vancouver. The traditional kaiseki menu is a must-try.

Coast $$

Seafood towers full of fresh fish and succulent shellfish impress at this modern restaurant focused on West Coast cuisine. For landlubbers, meat and pasta dishes are available too.

Pajo's on the Wharf $

Enjoy world-famous fish-and-chips right off the dock at Pajo's on the Wharf in Steveston (Richmond), where wharfside picnic tables invite casual diners to nosh on freshly caught cod and bottomless fries.

Culinary Tours

Surrey Spice Trail

Sample the best South Asian and multicultural cuisine in the city on this self-guided food tour (discoversurreybc.com), where over 30 restaurants offer the best flavors from India, Afghanistan, Jamaica, Nepal and more.

Dine Like a Critic

Exclusive culinary experiences (dinelikeacritic.com) guided by one of Canada's top food experts. From a fine-dining walking tour to a dim sum tasting tour, you can sample the best cuisine the city has to offer.

LAWRENCE WORCESTER/LONELY PLANET ©

Tojo's Restaurant

Gastronomic Gastown Tour (Vancouver Foodie Tours)

Quirky pubs and distinguished dining rooms impress on this walking food tour (foodietours.ca) along the cobblestone streets of Vancouver's historic restaurant district, where savory and sweet dishes are paired with beer, wine and cocktails.

Arts & Culture

Museum of Anthropology at UBC

Global artifacts and First Nations art are showcased in this museum, prompting awareness of the past and present cultural communities that make up the province of British Columbia.

Museum of Vancouver

The largest civic museum in Canada and the oldest museum in Vancouver, the Museum of Vancouver showcases the stories, objects and shared experiences of the city and its people.

Vancouver Art Gallery

An innovative institution recognized as the largest public art museum in Western Canada. Housed in an iconic building downtown, the groundbreaking exhibits, engaging events and public programming appease all art lovers.

Chinatown Storytelling Centre

The Chinese Canadian community is celebrated and honored through cultural stories, interactive elements and protected artifacts at this storytelling center found in Vancouver's historic Chinatown.

Takaya Tours

Immerse yourself in the culture, traditions and history of the Tsleil-Waututh First Nation on guided paddling cultural tours through the calm waters of Indian Arm on Vancouver's North Shore.

City Spas

Willow Stream Spa

Perched on the 5th floor of the Fairmont Pacific Rim, the Willow Stream Spa is an oasis in the city, boasting mountain and sea views from an outdoor terrace, and energy-restoring treatments.

CHI, The Spa at Shangri-La

Enjoy a wellness journey in a calming setting with eastern influences at CHI, The Spa at Shangri-La, where relaxing services focus on finding personal peace, enchantment and wellbeing.

Vida Spa

Ayurvedic treatments rejuvenate the body and mind at this spa in the Westin Bayshore, which is located in the heart of downtown, but feels like a remote escape.

Spa Utopia (Pan Pacific Hotel)

This is a one-stop shop for salon and spa services, with 11,500 sq ft of treatment rooms, relaxation lounges, essential oil-infused steam rooms, a dry sauna and luxe private treatment suites.

Parks & Beaches

Stanley Park

Known as the Central Park of Vancouver (but bigger), Stanley Park is home to a lagoon, an outdoor pool, an aquarium, sandy beaches and a paved seawall that stretches for miles.

Queen Elizabeth Park

A hub for horticulture, this park is home to the Bloedel Conservatory, an indoor tropical garden, a landscaped quarry garden and the upscale Seasons in the Park restaurant.

Kitsilano Beach Park

Home to the city's largest fully accessible playground, an outdoor saltwater pool found steps from the ocean, sandy beaches and large green spaces, this the ideal place to play in summer.

John Hendry (Trout Lake) Park

Home to Trout Lake, the best farmers market in the city, and grassy fields that invite picnic lunches and frisbee play, Trout Lake at John Hendry Park is a summer drawcard.

Ambleside Park

This picturesque West Vancouver park has a seawall walkway that weaves along the coast and leads to green spaces and sandy beaches.

Trout Lake, John Hendry Park

Wildlife Encounters

BC Bird Trail

British Columbia is home to some of the best birdwatching in North America, and the Fraser Valley stop on the BC Bird Trail houses a diverse range of bird species along its waterways and marshlands.

Lost Lagoon

Picturesque trails of Stanley Park's Lost Lagoon lead to a slew of wildlife, steps from downtown. Look for ducks, geese, herons and swans, and spot eagles soaring overhead as they search for prey.

Strait of Georgia

The Strait of Georgia off the Salish Sea offers endless opportunities to spot sea life via whale-watching boat tours, kayaking trips and scuba diving.

Grizzly Bear Habitat

Head up Grouse Mountain and meet the resident grizzly bears, Grinder and Coola, once orphaned and now living in a protected habitat that is part of the Grouse Mountain Refuge for Endangered Wildlife.

Day Trips

Shipyards District

Located on Vancouver's North Shore, this waterfront community is bursting with restaurants, bars, breweries, galleries, activities and stunning skyline views – easily accessed by a short passenger seabus from downtown.

Grizzly Bear Habitat, Grouse Mountain

Harrison Hot Springs

Find lakeside fun in the town of Harrison Hot Springs, located only an hour by car from the city. Bumper boats, jet skis and a massive floating waterpark are a highlight in summer.

Bowen Island

A short 20-minute ferry ride will take you to this quiet oasis in Howe Sound. The natural surroundings are the draw, where you can enjoy hiking, kayaking or yoga in the woods.

Whistler

Hit the slopes at the largest ski resort in North America, or visit year-round for the thriving arts and cultural offerings, the Nordic-style spa, or the West Coast–inspired culinary scene.

Gibsons

A 40-minute sail with BC Ferries will take you to the picturesque town of Gibsons, where marina views and quaint streets lined with cafes and boutiques provide a true taste of life on the coast.

Scan to find more things to do in Vancouver online

53 Weekend in WHISTLER

NATURE | OUTDOORS | ADVENTURE

Whistler is the largest ski resort in North America and was home to the 2010 Olympic and Paralympic Winter Games. Snowsports slay here, but beyond the slopes, Whistler wows with alpine adventures that can be enjoyed all year long.

STOCKSTUDIOX/GETTY IMAGES ©

How to

Getting here A scenic two-hour drive north of Vancouver, you can access Whistler by rental car, bus or shuttle. Seasonal seaplane options will also get you here in 35 minutes.

Getting around Once in Whistler, a public bus service and seasonal free shuttles will get you around. Whistler is also very walkable.

When to go Winter and spring are best for slopeside fun, but Whistler is a year-round destination with lots to do every season.

CAROLYNE PARENT/SHUTTERSTOCK ©

RIC JACYNO/SHUTTERSTOCK ©

Cultural immersion Cycle or stroll along the Cultural Connector – a scenic, tree-lined pathway that links you to a series of significant cultural sites. Whistler has become a hub for arts and culture, featuring galleries that house some of the country's top works of art. The **Audain Art Museum**, for example, has acquired an Emily Carr masterpiece from 1912. For an immersive Indigenous cultural experience, visit the **Squamish Lil'wat Cultural Centre**. It showcases, through historical stories and cultural works, the traditional territories of Squamish and Lil'wat Nations, which overlap in the Whistler region. This self-guided tour takes you to six spots, all marked for easy discovery.

Nordic spa In a destination that is celebrated for its outdoor exploits, downtime remains a necessity. At **Scandinave Spa** you can

Alpine Cocktails

At **Sidecut Steakhouse**, the 'Spirit of the Mountains' multi-sensory cocktail offerings take you on a taste journey through the alpine regions of the world. Mixing gastronomy with geography, award-winning bartender Lauren Mote turns creative cocktails into works of art, like the Golden Bridge Sour, served in a glass powdered with passion fruit.

Left Squamish Lil'wat Cultural Centre **Top left** Skier, Whistler **Top right** Audain Art Museum

enjoy the benefits of traditional Nordic-style hydrotherapy with steams and soaks set in a West Coast wilderness setting. Silence is mandatory at this spa, where a cycle of hot-cold-rest-repeat takes you through a series of eucalyptus steam rooms, outdoor hot baths, chilly Nordic waterfalls and cold plunge pools, and fireside resting spots and solariums. Wrap up your visit with a restorative, deep tissue, or Swedish relaxation massage and you'll leave feeling totally refreshed.

Illuminated night walk When the sun sets, some alpine adventures are just beginning. Step into the darkness of dimly lit trails and enter a wilderness wonderland filled with songs, stories and incredible sights. The **Vallea Lumina** multimedia night walk, which can be found on Cougar Mountain (just outside Whistler), is part of a multi-city series created by Montreal-based Moment Factory. As you stroll along the trails, you'll follow the journey of a father-daughter duo – the legend

Best Après-Ski

Found at the base of Whistler, the **Garibaldi Lift Co Bar & Grill** is a great place to enjoy a drink next to an outside fireplace and watch people ski down the mountain. On the village stroll, **Basalt** offers charcuterie and cocktails. If you're hankering for a burger and fries, try **Splitz Grill**. For sit-down dinner spots, **Caramba** has the best calamari in town and huge caesars. **Sushi Village** has a fun atmosphere and tasty sushi. You can't go wrong with the **Red Door** – but book ahead, it's that good! Its chuck flats and bouillabaisse are something else.

■ **Tips by Mercedes Nicoll,** *snowboarder, Winter Olympian and podcast host @mercedesnicoll*

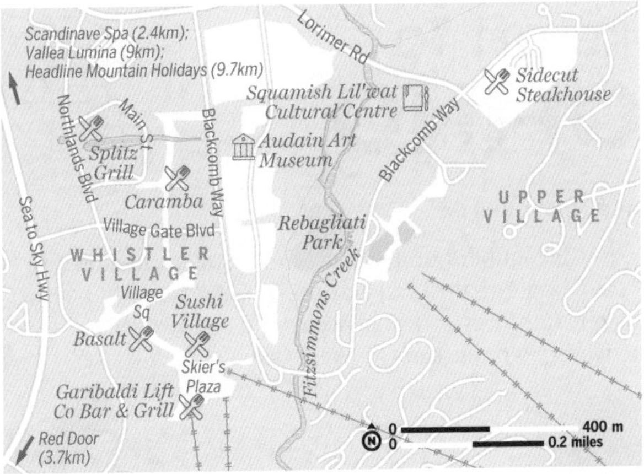
Scandinave Spa (2.4km);
Vallea Lumina (9km);
Headline Mountain Holidays (9.7km)
Lorimer Rd
Squamish Lil'wat Cultural Centre
Sidecut Steakhouse
Northlands Blvd
Main St
Blackcomb Way
Splitz Grill
Audain Art Museum
Blackcomb Way
Caramba
Sea to Sky Hwy
Village Gate Blvd
Rebagliati Park
UPPER VILLAGE
WHISTLER VILLAGE
Village Sq
Sushi Village
Basalt
Fitzsimmons Creek
Skier's Plaza
Garibaldi Lift Co Bar & Grill
Red Door (3.7km)
0
400 m
0
0.2 miles

Far left Scandinave Spa Below Ice cave, Blackcomb Peak

of two long-ago hikers – and see what they discover in the depths of the forest. Through stunning visuals, soothing songs and curious clues, you'll uncover the mysteries that surround you on an illuminated night journey like no other.

Helicopter & ice cave tour For an unforgettable, ultra-luxe escape, fly over Canada's southernmost ice fields on an A-class helicopter and then explore a series of incredible ice caves by snowmobile, snow bike or snow buggy once you arrive at the top. The fully guided, five-hour **Heli Sled & Ice Caves Tour** offered by Headline Mountain Holidays will take your breath away as you navigate through a labyrinth of aqua blue ice caves while learning about the geological features of the grottos. Then sit in awe and enjoy a mountaintop artisan lunch while taking it all in. This tour allows you to explore an evolving landscape of ice flows, volcanic peaks and wildlife that can only be accessed by air.

54 Take off to TOFINO

SURFING | WILDLIFE | REMOTE TRANQUILITY

Situated in the heart of Clayoquot Sound, a Unesco Biosphere Region and the traditional territory of the Tla-o-qui-aht First Nation, Tofino (pictured below) lures nature lovers with ancient rainforests, ocean swells and sandy beaches – ideal for playing among the watery wonders of the West Coast.

EB ADVENTURE PHOTOGRAPHY/SHUTTERSTOCK ©

Trip Notes

Getting here Fly from Vancouver to Tofino in as little as 45 minutes, or sail with BC Ferries to Nanaimo, followed by a scenic three-hour drive.

When to go Find endless adventures year-round. June to August for warmer temperatures, but prepare for peak-period prices. November to February is more tranquil and best for storm watching.

Need to know Check for updates on Hwy 4 (drivebc.ca), the only road into town.

Taco the Town

From slinging tacos from a truck to becoming an iconic West Coast brand, **Tacofino** is now a staple, serving up the best tacos in town. Get a taste at a Vancouver location, or hit the original orange truck, which still stands in a parking lot in Tofino – just be prepared to wait in line!

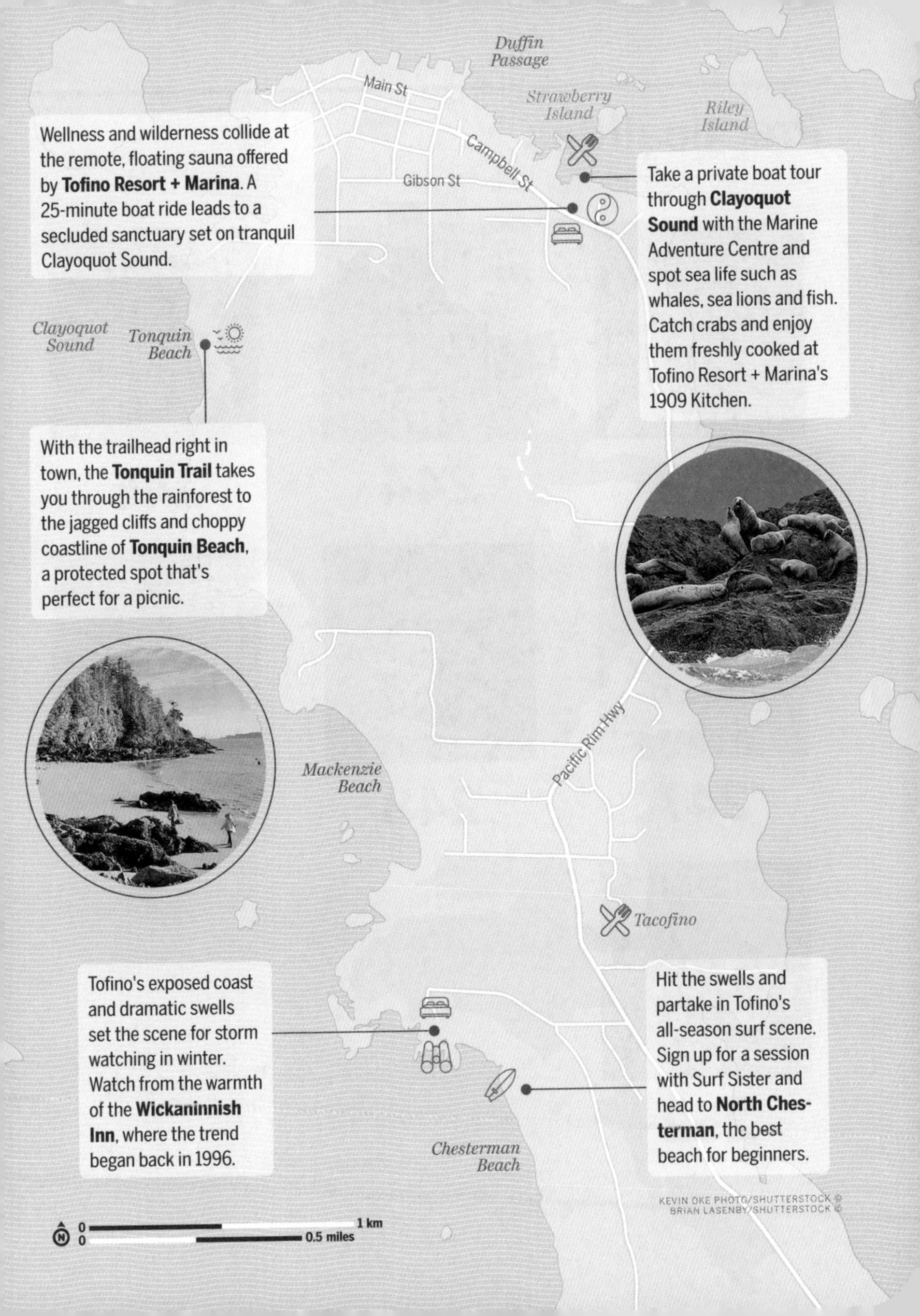

Duffin Passage
Main St
Strawberry Island
Riley Island
Campbell St
Gibson St
Clayoquot Sound
Tonquin Beach
Mackenzie Beach
Pacific Rim Hwy
Tacofino
Chesterman Beach
0
1 km
0
0.5 miles

Wellness and wilderness collide at the remote, floating sauna offered by **Tofino Resort + Marina**. A 25-minute boat ride leads to a secluded sanctuary set on tranquil Clayoquot Sound.

Take a private boat tour through **Clayoquot Sound** with the Marine Adventure Centre and spot sea life such as whales, sea lions and fish. Catch crabs and enjoy them freshly cooked at Tofino Resort + Marina's 1909 Kitchen.

With the trailhead right in town, the **Tonquin Trail** takes you through the rainforest to the jagged cliffs and choppy coastline of **Tonquin Beach**, a protected spot that's perfect for a picnic.

Tofino's exposed coast and dramatic swells set the scene for storm watching in winter. Watch from the warmth of the **Wickaninnish Inn**, where the trend began back in 1996.

Hit the swells and partake in Tofino's all-season surf scene. Sign up for a session with Surf Sister and head to **North Chesterman**, the best beach for beginners.

KEVIN OKE PHOTO/SHUTTERSTOCK ©
BRIAN LASENBY/SHUTTERSTOCK ©

Practicalities

Right Lions Gate Bridge, Stanley Park (p228), Vancouver

EASY STEPS FROM THE AIRPORT TO THE CITY CENTRE

The Pacific Northwest is home to three large international airports: Seattle-Tacoma (SEA), Portland (PDX) and Vancouver (YVR). Seattle is central of the three and has the most US connections. Regional flights can also connect to smaller airports, including Redmond (RDM), which serves Bend, and Spokane (GEG).

AT THE AIRPORT

N13

BILL ROQUE/SHUTTERSTOCK ©

SIM CARDS
Available at airport electronics shops, but plans can be pricey. If you can wait, use wi-fi until you can reach an authorised phone-carrier shop or big-box store in the city. An unlocked GSM phone offers the best compatibility.

CURRENCY EXCHANGE
Available at all three airports, but you'll get a better rate outside the airports in the cities. Bring enough dollars from your home country for a day or two. Your Visa debit card will also work in stores upon arrival.

FREE WI-FI Available in all three major airports. Coverage may not extend to rideshare pickup points.

ATMS Machines linked to large banks include US Bank at Portland and Seattle airports. Vancouver has an RBC Royal Bank ATM.

CHARGING STATIONS Can be found in both international and regional airports. Wall outlets can accommodate standard US two-prong or three-prong plugs.

CUSTOMS REGULATIONS

Duty-free Limits per incoming passenger include 1L of alcohol and 200 cigarettes. The person carrying the alcohol must be 21 years or older, and it must be for personal use and not for sale.

Restricted items Fruits, vegetables, plants, seeds, meat products and some cultural artifacts are restricted and admitted only under special circumstances.

GETTING TO THE CITY CENTRE

SEATTLE-TACOMA Sound Travel Train runs from the airport to downtown Seattle (about 40 minutes). King County Metro buses also connect to the airport. Most rideshare services will wait in the rideshare zone of the 3rd floor of the parking garage.

PORTLAND INTERNATIONAL MAX light rail runs from the airport to downtown (about 40 minutes). For Bend, you can take the Central Oregon Breeze bus (cobreeze.com). Rideshare pickups are on the lower level in the center of island 2.

VANCOUVER Vancouver Airport Sky-train runs from the airport to downtown (26 minutes). The N10 bus connects to downtown during the late-night and early-morning hours. The rideshare pickup zone is located on the arrivals level; follow the signs to the Ground Transportation Pickup Area.

HOW MUCH FOR A TRIP DOWNTOWN...

Seattle
$3

Portland
$2.50

Vancouver
$9

TAXI

Pickup areas are outside the arrivals concourse at all three airports.

PLAN YOUR JOURNEY

Downloadable transport apps for the region include PDX Bus (Portland) and Transit GO Ticket (Seattle).

ORCA CARD Purchase at transit points. You can use this card on the ferry, light rail, bus and other forms of transportation in Seattle. The card works like cash, and there is no extra fee if you have to link between services (within two hours of your first ride). Monthly passes are available.

OVERNIGHTING NEAR THE AIRPORT

If you are transiting in one of the region's big three airports (Seattle-Tacoma, Portland and Vancouver), or have an early morning flight, it's a good idea to spend the night close to the airport. All three have clusters of hotels near the airport, one advantage being that these hotels offer free shuttle services to/from the airport. Most hotels near these airports are budget or midrange, with the occasional higher-end place also available. Call the hotel prior to flying to get shuttle pickup points.

If you don't mind roughing it, sleeping in the airport is possible. At the Portland and Vancouver airports, you can find comfortable overnight lounge seating or benches. In Seattle, lying down is more difficult due to armrests. All three airports also have luggage storage where you can keep your bags while making a trip into the city. Food and shopping are available in all these airports, with Vancouver having more late-night options available. Vancouver is the most appealing of the three, with lots of art, aquariums and waterfalls. Comfortable TV lounges are available, as well as pay showers.

TRANSPORT TIPS TO HELP YOU GET AROUND

The Pacific Northwest is best explored with your own vehicle. Both cars and RVs can be rented across the region. Bicycles are a good way to save on gas and lower your carbon footprint. The region is a fine long-distance cycling destination, with a good mix of coastal highways, mountain passes, wine country and high desert.

CAR, RV & TRAILER RENTAL

Car hire is available in major towns; rates are similar across the big international firms. Picking up a car and dropping it off in a different city can increase costs. Renting an RV or trailer is possible in many mid-sized cities.

AUTOMOBILE ASSOCIATIONS

AAA (aaa.com) offers roadside assistance, insurance and discounts to members at hotels and attractions. Its offices are stocked with maps and brochures. Breakdown service is available to many affiliated overseas auto associations (bring your membership card).

CAR RENTAL PER DAY

from $70

Gasoline approx $4.00/gallon

RV rental per day from $150

RV PARKS RV holiday parks are plentiful in the Northwest. You'll get a warm welcome at these spots and there is usually lots of room for kids to run around. State parks and national parks are also great places to bring an RV or trailer. Avoid taking your RV or trailer into a large city, as parking will be a challenge. Park outside and then drive a car in to explore metro areas.

ROAD CONDITIONS Winter storms can wash out roads, create sinkholes and cause flooding. Mountain roads in winter can get icy and blanketed in snow (bring chains). State transportation departments in Oregon (tripcheck.com), Washington (wsdot.com) and British Columbia (drivebc.ca) post road conditions online.

INSURANCE Rental-car companies typically offer insurance on top of the rental fee. Check with your own insurance company on your personal car as it often extends coverage to rental cars. Make sure the insurance is comprehensive, which covers theft, vandalism, hail, and damage caused by hitting an animal.

DRIVING ESSENTIALS

Drive on the right; the steering wheel is on the left.

65 — The speed limit is 65mph on most freeways.

The legal driving age is 16.

SPEED LIMIT 20 — In school zones slow down to 20mph.

0.08 — The blood-alcohol limit is 0.08%.

BUS Bus services connect towns and cities in the Northwest, but frequency of travel can be limited, and services may not cover places of interest in rural areas. Once you arrive at your destination, you may still need a tour to reach sights and attractions. Greyhound buses are reliable for long-distance journeys and Flix Bus (flixbus.com) is another good service between the region's main cities.

PLANE Air travel around the region is quick but not always cheap, especially if you book last minute or during the summer high season. Alaska Airlines is the main carrier in the Northwest, but there are others, including some discount airlines.

TRAIN Amtrak (USA) and VIA Rail (Canada) offer comfortable travel between main cities. Amtrak's Cascades train offers connections via Thruway buses (a regional bus line) to smaller cities. Main routes head from Seattle east to Spokane, and from Portland south to Eugene.

KNOW YOUR CARBON FOOTPRINT From Portland to Seattle by plane would emit 97.5lb of carbon dioxide per passenger, by SUV vehicle 88lb of carbon dioxide, and by train 22lb of carbon dioxide. There are a number of carbon calculators online. Try calculator.carbonfootprint.com.

ROAD DISTANCE CHART (MILES)

	Bend, OR	Eugene, OR	Portland, OR	Astoria, OR	Seaview, WA	Seattle, WA	Anacortes, WA	Vancouver, BC	Whistler, BC
Eugene, OR	129								
Portland, OR	175	109							
Astoria, OR	251	198	98						
Seaview, WA	269	213	110	18					
Seattle, WA	328	282	174	181	170				
Anacortes, WA	408	363	254	261	250	81			
Vancouver, BC	470	425	316	323	312	143	94		
Whistler, BC	544	499	391	398	386	217	168	121	
Tofino, BC	643	598	489	433	426	316	267	283	372

SAFE TRAVEL

Travel in the Pacific Northwest is relatively safe, although downtown areas of Portland, Seattle and Vancouver saw an uptick in crime during the pandemic. The biggest dangers are the winter snowstorms and the rough seas off the coast.

SNOW & STORMS

Be prepared for winter travel conditions from late October through March, especially when heading over mountain passes.

SNEAKER WAVES

Never turn your back on the ocean while beachcombing or tide-pooling, and don't let small children wade into the waves alone.

WILD FIRES

Humans cause most of the fires; always douse flames when camping. If there's smoke pollution from fire, get an N95 mask from a hardware store.

Pharmacies Walgreens and Rite-Aid are two of the biggest pharmacy chains in Oregon and Washington. Look for London Drugs and Shoppers Drug Mart in Vancouver. Most large grocery chains also have pharmacies.

WESLEY FOULDS/SHUTTERSTOCK ©

JORDAN SIEMENS/GETTY IMAGES ©

Hiking Leave a travel plan with a friend or relative, and let your hotel know where you are headed. Check the forecast and pack protective clothing in case the weather turns. Take a map, compass and GPS.

INSURANCE

Walking into a hospital for any ailment can result in a high medical bill. Before departing home, ask your health insurer whether overseas services are covered.

ROAD SAFETY

For real-time travel data and road conditions in Oregon, check tripcheck.com; in Washington, wsdot.com; and in British Columbia, drivebc.ca. Road cameras on these sites are good for checking snow conditions.

QUICK TIPS TO HELP YOU MANAGE YOUR MONEY

CREDIT CARDS Widely accepted for almost any purchase, and pretty much essential for plane tickets, car hire and booking hotel rooms. It does help to have a small amount of cash on hand, for tipping or small purchases. Visa and MasterCard are the most common, while American Express and Diner's Club are not accepted everywhere.

CHANGING MONEY
Large banks such as Bank of America will exchange foreign currency. Exchange kiosks are also located at major airports.

PAYING THE BILL
At sit-down restaurants, your server will bring the bill to your table. Pay at the register at places with counter service.

CURRENCY
US $/Canadian $

HOW MUCH FOR A...

cappuccino
$5

craft beer
$7

dinner for two
$40

TIPPING

Restaurants For decent service, 20% of the pretax bill.

Taxi & Uber Tip 10% to 15% of the metered fare.

Gas stations In Oregon an attendant pumps your gas; a $1 to $2 tip is appreciated, but not essential.

Bars Leave $1 to $2 per drink or 20% of the bill.

DISCOUNTS Most sights, activities and public transport offer reduced rates to seniors, kids under 12, and families. Some museums in the region offer discounted or free entry once a month.

BANKS & ATMS
Banks with ATMs are found in every town in the Northwest. Out-of-network ATMs charge between $1 and $5 to withdraw cash. Asking for cash back when you go to a store is a way to avoid ATM fees.

USING CASH
Donut shops, bagel shops, or other places dealing in small amounts may not accept plastic or will charge you a fee for using a card. Gas stations will also charge about 10 cents per gallon more when you use a card instead of cash.

ON A BUDGET The Pacific Northwest is a pricey destination, with hotels, car rentals and restaurants the biggest budget busters. Fortunately, the region has plenty of outdoor activities that are free or low cost, including visits to state and national parks, waterfalls, beaches and hiking trails. A camping trip helps to lower costs, with tent sites costing $25 to $50, and if you have cooking equipment, you can make your own meals.

POSITIVE-IMPACT TRAVEL

Tips to leave a lighter footprint, support local and have a positive impact on local communities.

ON THE ROAD

Cut your carbon emissions Rent an electric vehicle. Hertz rents Tesla vehicles and charging stations are now widespread.

Cycle or scoot Explore cities and towns by bike or scooter. Rent Lime (li.me) in Portland or Seattle. Mobi Bike (mobibikes.ca) stations are available in Vancouver.

Public transport Another way to cut your carbon emissions. Ideal day trips on buses include the Columbia River Gorge on the Columbia Gorge Express (ridecat gorge.org) from Portland.

Farmers markets These support local growers, and the food is usually fresher than store-bought. Since products don't travel far to market, less fuel is used in delivery.

Caves White-nose syndrome can devastate bat colonies and can be transferred via clothing even if you wash it. Don't wear the same set of clothes in different caves.

Calculate your carbon There are a number of online calculators. Try the UN-affiliated calculator (offset.climateneutralnow.org/ footprintcalc).

GUNTER MARX/SW/ALAMY STOCK PHOTO ©

GIVE BACK

Volunteer Beach clean-up days are possible through a number of organizations. These include Solve (solveoregon.org) in Oregon, Washington Coast Savers (coastsavers.org) near Seattle, and the City of Vancouver (cityofvancouver.us).

Donate Northwest Center (nwcenter.org) is a Seattle-based non-profit that supports people with disabilities. Clothing and financial contributions are accepted.

Trail building Pacific Northwest Trail Association (pnt.org) accepts volunteers to build and maintain trails.

Camping etiquette When you depart your campsite, leave it better than you found it, picking up trash that's not your own.

Saving orcas Contact the Orca Conservancy (orcaconservancy.org) to donate to this organization or ask about volunteer opportunities.

Helping wild salmon The organization Save Our Wild Salmon (wild salmon.org) helps restore salmon populations. They accept donations.

DOS & DON'TS

Don't walk off designated trails as this can lead to erosion.

Do be mindful of Native American culture and customs.

Don't feed wild or domestic animals, unless given permission.

Do buy local seafood; it will be from a sustainable source.

Don't ride your bike on the sidewalk; use the road.

LEAVE A SMALL FOOTPRINT

Build your own base camp Pick a specific region and hunker down, exploring the area by bike or on foot. Eat and shop locally.

When booking tours Manage your carbon footprint by selecting tours that involve activities such as cycling, horseback riding, hiking, skiing or kayaking, rather than tours that use ATVs or other motorized vehicles.

On camping trips Avoid single-use cups, plates, packaging and cutlery. Use your own cooking utensils and wash after each use.

MARKET HOURS
10-2
Buy local Eat local Be local
Shop Your Farmers Market

DANITA DELIMONT/ALAMY STOCK PHOTO ©

SUPPORT LOCAL

Support local businesses Book accommodation and tours run by locals, and buy products and handicrafts made in the area.

Eat locally Support locally owned restaurants and ask servers what products are locally produced.

Visit farmers markets They're full of locally produced food, handicrafts and other products.

CLIMATE CHANGE & TRAVEL

It's impossible to ignore the impact we have when traveling, and the importance of making changes where we can. Lonely Planet urges all travelers to engage with their travel carbon footprint. There are many carbon calculators online that allow travelers to estimate the carbon emissions generated by their journey; try resurgence.org/resources/carbon-calculator.html. Many airlines and booking sites offer travelers the option of offsetting the impact of greenhouse gas emissions by contributing to climate-friendly initiatives around the world. We continue to offset the carbon footprint of all Lonely Planet staff travel, while recognising this is a mitigation more than a solution.

RESOURCES

traveloregon.com
pnwmicroadventures.com
vancitygreenvision.weebly.com
thecentralcascades.com
sustainabletravel.org

UNIQUE AND LOCAL WAYS TO STAY

There is a huge range of accommodations in the Northwest, from farmstays and yurts to beachside cottages and B&Bs. You'll have an almost endless selection of locally run, high-quality places to stay. In metro areas, you may need to pay extra for parking. You can get great deals on hotels if you are prepared to travel in the off-season.

HOW MUCH FOR A...

yurt
$60

B&B
$185

standard hotel
$180

RIGUCCI/SHUTTERSTOCK ©

FARMSTAYS

A number of working farms in the Northwest have placed accommodation on their properties, allowing travelers to experience rural America up close. These make for a great family destination as kids will enjoy petting animals, inspecting gardens and wandering through fields. A highlight is cooking your dinner with veggies plucked from the property. Accommodation can vary on farms, from cottages and bunkhouses to yurts, tents and RV sites. Some farms have specialty activities such as horseback riding, cheesemaking and fishing.

LODGES

Wonderful at any time of year, lodges are particularly atmospheric in winter when rooftops are covered with snow and fireplaces are roaring. Some offer activities such as horseback riding and golf, and a ski resort is usually not too far away. The most famous one in the Northwest is probably Timberline Lodge (pictured above left) on Mt Hood.

CAVAN IMAGES/ALAMY STOCK PHOTO ©

RESORTS

There's a wide range of resorts, from simple places with cabins by a lake to upscale retreats with swimming pools and other amenities. Popular upscale resorts include Brasada Ranch (OR) and Skamania Lodge (WA). Low-key options include Metolius River Resort (OR; pictured left) and Snug Harbor Resort (WA).

AGAVE PHOTO STUDIO/SHUTTERSTOCK ©

CAMPGROUNDS

Campgrounds are the lifeblood of the Pacific Northwest. Plentiful and affordable, you can hop between them across the region, as long as you're properly equipped and don't mind roughing it a bit. Camp managers are usually great sources of info on local attractions. Book well in advance, as places fill up fast, especially in summer.

Kampgrounds of America (KOA) A network of privately operated campgrounds found throughout the region.

State parks & national forests Tent sites in state parks and private campgrounds will have access to a spigot for water and toilet facilities. You can also camp anywhere in a national forest for free, but practice leave-no-trace principles.

Yurts Popular at state parks and various campgrounds. They're warm and furnished, allowing you to 'camp' without actually having a tent and gear. You'll still need warm clothes for night trips to the bathroom. Some have a little porch for outdoor eating, and many are ADA accessible.

Cabins In state parks cabins are rustic but affordable, going for around $80 a night in summer, with off-season discounts. Bed linen and blankets probably won't be provided.

BOOKING

The best way to find and book accommodation is online through specific hotel or campground websites, or through a third-party booking service.

Prices rise steeply during holidays and when places are close to full. High-season dates include the week between Christmas and New Year's Eve, then in summer when school is out – June to early September. Book as early as possible if you plan to travel during high season.

State park campgrounds Full listing of Oregon (stateparks.oregon.gov) and Washington (parks.wa.gov) state park campgrounds, with booking portal.

Oregon Bed & Breakfast Guild (obbg.org) Listings and a booking engine.

Campsite booking (recreation.gov) Allows you to book campsites in state parks, national forests, and national parks.

Washington INNSiders (wainnsiders.com) Washington's B&B offerings.

B&B Canada (bbcanada.com/british_columbia) Listings and reviews of B&Bs in British Columbia.

GOOD FOR KIDS

When traveling with kids, look for places with a good, heated swimming pool, a kitchenette and a playground. Youth hostels and B&Bs may be less kid-welcoming and may not accept children under a certain age.

ESSENTIAL NUTS-AND-BOLTS

HYDROPOWER

Hydropower accounts for around half of the energy production in the PNW, but dams have fallen out of favor because they have decimated fish populations.

BREASTFEEDING

Women breastfeed in public, but may cover themselves and their baby with a thin cloth or shawl.

SMOKING

Smoking is prohibited throughout the region in public places, including outdoor spaces such as city parks and state parks.

FAST FACTS

Time Zone
GMT-8

Country Code
+1

Electricity
120V/60Hz

GOOD TO KNOW

The legal age for buying, possessing and using cannabis is 21 in Oregon and Washington, and 19 in British Columbia.

Hiking permits are needed for some trails in the Enchantments in Washington and the Central Oregon Cascades.

The legal drinking age is 21 in Oregon and Washington, and 19 in BC.

The border between the US and Canada is open 24/7.

Pumping your own gas is illegal in Oregon; an attendant must fill your tank.

ACCESSIBLE TRAVEL

The Americans with Disabilities Act (ADA) requires all public buildings – including most hotels, restaurants and museums – to be wheelchair accessible.

Transport Lift-equipped buses are normal in the Pacific Northwest. Many taxi companies will have wheelchair-accessible cabs.

Service animals Certified service dogs are allowed on virtually all forms of transport, as well as in shops and restaurants.

Hotels & campsites Larger hotels with more than 150 rooms are required to have at least six accessible rooms, and a growing number of campsites in the Pacific Northwest are ADA accessible.

Apps Wheelmate helps travelers with disabilities locate the nearest wheelchair-friendly bathroom and parking space. Be My Eyes is an app that connects blind or low-sighted people with sighted volunteers and companies.

DINNER INVITE
If invited to a friend's house for a meal, bring a bottle of wine or an appetizer.

SALES TAX
Oregon has no sales tax on goods and services, which makes shopping there cheaper than Washington.

DRIVER'S LICENSE
If issued in English, foreign driver's licenses are recognized in the US and Canada.

PROFESSIONAL SPORTS
Several pro sports clubs are based in the Pacific Northwest, including the Seattle Mariners (baseball), Seattle Seahawks (football), Vancouver Canucks and Seattle Kraken (hockey) and the Portland Trailblazers (basketball).

FAMILY TRAVEL

Restaurants & cafes Kids' menus and high chairs are usually available. Many places can cater to the needs of picky eaters. Crab and fish shacks on the coast are good for finger food.

Sights & attractions Kids aged five and under are usually admitted free at museums and attractions. Discounts available for older kids. Some attractions have strollers for little ones.

Transport Rental-car agencies can provide a car seat upon request, but you may need to pay for it.

RELIGION
Nearly 50% of people polled in Oregon, Washington and British Columbia say they aren't affiliated with any religion. The other half is almost entirely Christian. There are small percentages of Jews, Sikhs, Buddhists and Muslims. Adherents of traditional Native American spirituality make up less than 1% of the population.

DIEGO G DIAZ/SHUTTERSTOCK ©

LGBTIQ+ TRAVELERS

Pacific Northwest Large cities have vibrant gay cultures. Attitudes may be more conservative in small, rural areas.

Portland Among the gayest cities in the US. Don't miss the legendary Darcelle XV drag show. In 2020 it was placed on the National Register of Historic Places.

Seattle The center of Seattle's gay community is the Capitol Hill neighborhood, along a section of Pike St.

Vancouver Davie Village is this city's gay enclave. Commercial Dr in east Vancouver is popular with the city's lesbian community.

Index

N

O

P

R

S

000 Map pages

T

V

W

Z

'Camping along the coast near the Oregon Dunes was an awesome experience. We woke up early, climbed the dunes to the beach, dug for critters in the sand and watched a massive gray whale slowly swim past.'

MICHAEL KOHN

'Doing dim sum for breakfast was a first for me while dining along Richmond's Dumpling Trail, and now I'm hooked. I daydream about those deep-fried, pork-stuffed pouches!'

BIANCA BUJAN

'Watching otters scurry up the beach at Discovery Park is a life highlight – and a reminder that nature is never far from reach in Seattle.'

MEGAN HILL

'Touring San Juan Island is magical. I walked through the aromatic lavender fields and at dusk I hiked out to the John S McMillin Memorial Mausoleum and saw a black fox trotting through a meadow.'

LARA DUNNING

BOB POOL/SHUTTERSTOCK ©, J. M. GATES/SHUTTERSTOCK ©

THIS BOOK

Design development Lauren Egan, Tina García, Fergal Condon

Content development Anne Mason

Cartography development Wayne Murphy, Katerina Pavkova

Production development Mario D'Arco, Dan Moore, Sandie Kestell, Virginia Moreno, Juan Winata

Series development leadership Liz Heynes, Darren O'Connell, Piers Pickard, Chris Zeiher

Commissioning editor Daniel Bolger

Product editor Saralinda Turner

Coordinating editor Simon Williamson

Cartographer Corey Hutchison

Book designers Hannah Blackie, Clara Monitto

Assisting editors James Appleton, Mani Ramaswamy, Gabrielle Stefanos

Cover researcher Lauren Egan

Thanks Jessica Boland, Gwen Cotter, Amy Lynch, John Taufa